DEAD-END

Drugs and viole
city shadows

Daniel Briggs and
Rubén Monge Gamero

First published in Great Britain in 2017 by

Policy Press
University of Bristol
1-9 Old Park Hill
Bristol
BS2 8BB
UK
t: +44 (0)117 954 5940
pp-info@bristol.ac.uk
www.policypress.co.uk

North America office:
Policy Press
c/o The University of Chicago Press
1427 East 60th Street
Chicago, IL 60637, USA
t: +1 773 702 7700
f: +1 773-702-9756
sales@press.uchicago.edu
www.press.uchicago.edu

British Library Cataloguing in Publication Data
A catalogue record for this book is available from the British Library

Library of Congress Cataloging-in-Publication Data
A catalog record for this book has been requested

ISBN 978-1-4473-4169-7 paperback
ISBN 978-1-4473-4168-0 hardcover
ISBN 978-1-4473-4171-0 ePub
ISBN 978-1-4473-4172-7 Mobi
ISBN 978-1-4473-4170-3 ePdf

Cover design by Liron Gillenberg
Front cover image kindly supplied by the authors:
Printed and bound in Great Britain CMP, Poole
Policy Press uses environmentally responsible print partners

"This is what criminology should be about!"

Leah Moyle, Griffith Criminology Institute, Australia

"An exceptional study and a fascinating read. Briggs and Monge Gamero have the rare capacity to both inform and excite their readers at the same time. This is ethnography at its best; the small-scale cultural contours of problematic drug use in one of Europe's most marginalised and impoverished districts are set firmly here in their respective historical and socio-economic contexts. The authors skilfully throw light on a hidden population in this text, and their efforts should be commended. This is as close to a European *Righteous Dopefiend* as anyone has yet come. All scholars, practitioners and policy-makers with a stake in the drugs field should read this book."

Steve Wakeman, Liverpool John Moores University, UK

"Just the type of research and critique Spain so desperately needs."

Jorge Ramiro Pérez Suárez, University of Huddersfield, UK, and the European University of Madrid, Spain

Dead-end Lives offers a vision of life at the new margins of Europe's cities today. An unflinching, yet ultimately compassionate rendering of human vulnerability, Briggs and Monge Gamero examine social frailty amidst the ruins of unifying national projects and dilapidated utopian housing estates. For those concerned with our contemporary social condition, and perhaps even more so for those who are not, *Dead-end Lives* is a work of great importance."

Rowland Atkinson, Sheffield University, UK

This book is dedicated
to Julia as well as to the
very people who are at
the centre of the research:
those who visit and live in
Valdemingómez and have
to survive, day in, day out,
on its violent front line.

Contents

List of photos, figures and tables

Photos

Figures

Table

About the authors

Dr Daniel Briggs is a Consultant to the British Foreign Office who works part time at the Universidad Europea in Madrid, Spain. As a researcher, writer and interdisciplinary academic who studies social problems, he has undertaken ethnographic research into social issues from street drug users to terminally ill patients; from refugees to prostitutes; and from gypsies to gangs and deviant youth behaviours. He also lectures across the social sciences and has published widely.

Rubén Monge Gamero has a first-class undergraduate degree in Criminology from Universidad Europea and his final-year project was based on participant observation of Valdemingómez. He recently concluded a Masters in Intelligence Analysis and hopes to be a police officer.

Acknowledgements

We firstly thank all the drug users who knowingly or unknowingly participated in our work. Their assistance in this work has been integral, and we are grateful that they took time out from daily chores, often waking up feeling sick, and delayed drug taking to be able to talk to us. We are ever indebted to the harm reduction team, in particular Roberto, who spent many hours and days with us, not only in the area, but in his personal time, helping us clarify our findings and shape our concepts. Having got to know him, we can see why he is one of the central characters to the *poblado*, who is dearly loved by the people he helps: he truly is an underappreciated worker who has a major impact personally on the people of Valdemingómez. Diego and Nacho, from the Local Police in Madrid, have also given us detailed and valuable insights into how Valdemingómez works, often describing in disturbing detail the reality of the situation.

Several people have also helped in shaping the vision for research and this resulting book. In particular, we thank Inma Ruiz Finicias, a worker we have come to know dedicated to drug prevention work and generally helping vulnerable people. Cristina Alonso gave us access to people in recovery in the Basida programme, just south of Madrid, where they do wonderful work with people who are often dying of drug-related illnesses. Some expert academics have kindly volunteered to review and comment on our work: they are Professor Philippe Bourgois, Professor Dick Hobbs, Professor Rowland Atkinson, Professor Simon Winlow, Professor Steve Hall, Dr Steve Wakeman, Dr Marina Mattera and Dr Leah Moyle. Their feedback has been important in moulding the correct theoretical and structural parts of the book, and they also did it in a very short space of time, on top of their busy schedules. Thanks to our publishers, Policy Press, in particular

Victoria Pittman and Rebecca Tomlinson, for taking forward our project and believing in its social significance. Lastly, we think a new form of humble appreciation is required of what it means to research social miseries, and that it shouldn't turn into a circus of institutional back patting. We did this work ourselves to give voice to those in the book, so thank no one else – no government body, no funder, no political entity – because none of them had any hand or interest in our endeavours to highlight what is happening in Valdemingómez. We thank, last and least, our family and friends: this goes without saying.

Personal acknowledgements

Daniel would like to personally thank Rubén for his skill and enthusiasm in helping with the work. It is rare that such a student shows such interest, determination and the dedication to put themselves in risky situations in the name of research. He would also like to thank colleagues at Criminología y Justicia, who form part of a new critical criminological movement that is entirely necessary in Spain if the discipline is to advance itself from the dry terrain of its current status quo. Thank you, Jorge Ramiro Pérez Suárez and Antonio Silva.

Rubén would like to personally thank Diego, his contact and now friend in the Local Police in Madrid, who helped him orient his dissertation that formed the basis for the study. Diego is someone, who, in the face of the challenging environment of Valdemingómez, has always tried to improve it for the people, and for this reason he is a person of great character. Rubén also thanks Daniel for having been able to learn about research under his direction, about developing a careful sensitivity when studying vulnerable groups, and also valuable life lessons.

Preface

When we first heard about Valdemingómez, it was difficult to believe that a place with such multifaceted social problems had only received piecemeal academic interest: a sign, perhaps, that the methods we used to do this study are becoming defunct in the neoliberal era, and that our discipline is disappearing into the internal ideological politics of satisfying our seniors by getting shit loads of money for university coffers and publishing in high-impact journals to gratify our own sense of importance. Or maybe not. There is an alternative, and in this book we show that if really we want to get to the heart of a social problem, we simply need to get out of our offices and abandon standardised ways of researching, moulding ourselves to some degree to the realities under investigation.

This is what we have done in this book, which is based on two years of self-funded ethnographic research in Spain's principal drug market, Valdemingómez, on the outskirts of Madrid. We tried to play the research funding game but were rejected three times from formal state research mechanisms on the grounds that our methods were too risky. Nevertheless, we did the research, and this resulting book is about how various forms of structural violence produce mass degradation across swathes of the urban populace; it is about how these very processes crush the cultural outlook and everyday lives of drug users in the urban peripheries of Madrid. It shows how global processes, coupled with market economics, have hollowed out these people's livelihoods, to the point that many invert and internalise their own suffering into a fatalistic form of drug use that only makes them visible as a threat to the urban dream, thus making them easy fodder for criminal justice institutions. Having developed an almost irreversible drug dependency, as a consequence, many simply end up between prison, the street and Valdemingómez, a place politically imagined where they will not poison the aesthetics of the city, and just die quietly among the rubbish and the waste.

Foreword

Long before urban ethnography came of age with the Chicago School, Henry Mayhew had trawled London's streets for narratives of the poor, dispossessed and excluded. For all of their rightly celebrated qualities, the sociologists of the Chicago School seldom provided the kind of vivid detail that is central to Mayhew's journalism for the *Morning Chronicle*. He was particularly concerned with men and women for whom transgression was an inevitable consequence of the material conditions in which they found themselves. Seamstresses squeezed by the punitive pressures of piecework turned to prostitution to feed their families, street traders who relied on their own invented language and transgressive leisure pursuits to resist harassment by the new social control agencies, and some of the poor reduced to collecting dog shit from Albertoian pavements before delivering their fetid buckets to the capital's leather tanneries. For Mayhew, crime/deviance/transgression was a social product, and very much part of the relentless unforgiving meat grinder of life in the city.

However, the Chicagoans' establishment of urban ethnography as a central and enduring prop of social scientific endeavour did open the door to the city's dirty secrets, and through this door have passed many thousands of scholars intent on bringing to the fore issues that most urban dwellers seek to scrape from the soles of their shoes. Most, but not all, of Chicago-influenced ethnography was based on an urban template created as an explanatory model of industrialism. The industrial city was essentially zonal, and when drilling down into these zones, deviant behaviour – predominantly, but not exclusively, youthful delinquency – could be unwrapped, analysed and, crucially, rehabilitated. While later proponents of urban ethnography sometimes withdrew from engagement with rehabilitative policy engagement, its replacement was often a romanticised misfit sociology that valorised both the deviant and the intrepid researcher who would then shamelessly trade on this brief brush with outlaw status for the remainder of an academic career.

The post-industrial city, where the now superfluous poor of the industrial project have been supplanted by previously unfamiliar forces of economic apartheid, offers few of the assured inevitabilities of industrialism. The shape and form of urban existence has changed, and as a consequence, the trajectories of existence in the alcoves where working-class lives are lived are now dominated by population churn, by fragmentation and by a vernacular cosmopolitanism based on informal modes of survival that have little connection with institutions of governance.

Valdemingómez is one such alcove, and in describing life, death and commerce in this area on the edges of Madrid, we are introduced to a world that is uncomfortably close to Mayhew's London. Thankfully, Daniel Briggs and Rubén Monge Gamero are as sensitive to the multiple complex forces that created Valdemingómez as they are to the harrowing conditions of survival of its population, where addiction and the servicing of addiction dominate social life. Cities churn, global populations shift and with capitalism in a state of permanent crisis, the flotsam and jetsam of 'Europe's largest ghetto' compete and co-exist within a range of informal economies, in particular, the drug trade. Briggs and Monge Gamero explore this world of poverty, profit, hope and addiction with enormous skill. For this is the future, the ghetto at the edge of the city, life at the periphery largely abandoned by the state, occasionally subjected to police operations, but not often enough to impact on the illegal economies that are the poisonous lifeblood of Valdemingómez, where 'the Wild West meets the third world'.

The authors do not valorise deviance, but do describe and explain a world where destructive social and personal practices are the norm. Indeed, the descriptive passages, which constitute this book's strength, are among the most vivid and insightful to be found in contemporary ethnography. Highlighted are the impacts of often ignored causal factors such as the withdrawal of the state, and the consequences not only for the addicted and their families, but also for the poor bloody infantry of police and drug agencies that seek to make an impact on this blighted domain. The limits of intervention, particularly during an era of austerity, along with the predatory culture of many of Valdemingómez's residents, are emphasised by harrowing description and interviews. This is a deeply upsetting book about an alcove of the global economy where death and degradation are embedded into every pore. Enhanced by photography, this excellent and innovative ethnography stands as a powerful and unnerving document of contemporary and probable future urban life.

Yet, as with Henry Mayhew's seminal work, written in a long distant era of exploitation, deprivation and squalor, it is the heart-rending stories of the poor that leave the most indelible impact on the reader. The utter impossibility of their plight is genuinely disturbing, and the term 'social exclusion' has seldom been more appropriate, its causation more complex, or its reality more distressing.

Professor Dick Hobbs, Emeritus Professor at the University of Essex, and Professor of Sociology at the University of Western Sydney, Australia

Glossary of terms

Before you dive into this book, please familiarise yourself with these terms to make it easier for your reading (although we describe them along the way as well, so don't worry)…

barrio	neighbourhood
chabola	shack or shanty improvised constructions
chatarra	scrap metal/goods
chuta	from the verb *chutar*, meaning to 'shoot up' or 'to inject'
cunda	illegal taxi that transports drug users
cundero	the driver of the illegal taxis that transport drug users
fumadero	drug dealing/using location, predominantly for smoking heroin/cocaine
gitanos	gypsies
machaca	person working for the gitanos, deriving from the verb *machacar*, which means 'to mash, crush, batter or be pounded'
mono	withdrawal symptoms from heroin and/or cocaine use
pipa	pipe from which to smoke heroin/cocaine
plata	foil on which to smoke heroin/cocaine
plaza	square in a public space
poblado	*gitano* settlements/camps
puta	colloquial term for a 'bitch' or 'whore'

1

Introduction: Welcome to Valdemingómez

This book is about a population of drug-dependent people locked out of society who survive in the dark corners at the edge of the city of Madrid in Spain. We spent two years with these people, studying how the space in which they occupy came to be, how they had come to find themselves in this area, and what daily life was all about for them. Without giving the story away, from the outset we can say that their desolate misery is related to having fallen foul of various social, political and economic processes which, over time, have been internalised and reproduced in a destructive form of drug use that compromises their own health and wellbeing. In this area, Valdemingómez, they work/live side by side with the gypsies (*gitanos*[1] hereafter), seen as another socially defunct group, that habitually inflict suffering and violence on them. They are also regulated by corrupt police forces, and are assisted on a daily basis by the limited intervention of the Agencia Antidroga (Anti-Drugs Agency) ('harm reduction team' hereafter). Without further ado, we introduce you to these people and their dilemmas. Welcome to their world. Welcome to Valdemingómez.

Meet Juan and Julia

As we speak with Juan, Julia nervously comes out of the tent with a loaded heroin syringe wedged behind her ear; she stands next to us, furiously biting her nails and looking into the distance, as if her mind is elsewhere on the horizon. To us, it seems obvious now. Suddenly, Juan changes the subject and recalls how last summer the police raided four houses on the same day in the main street of Valdemingómez (Photo 1), and in the process, arrested an entire *gitano* family for drug trafficking charges. There is then a silence as he sits down and starts to rub his face and scratch his wiry hair. He looks around as if he is to break the secret of the meaning of life, pauses, looks up at us, and tells us that Julia is between three to four months pregnant. That's his estimate anyway.

Photo 1: View overlooking Valdemingómez, Sector 6 of the Cañada Real Galiana

Later that day

When we finally return to the main square (*plaza* hereafter), the harm reduction team bus has almost packed up and the last few drug addicts race towards it, collecting what they can before it goes – food, drug paraphernalia, perhaps a cigarette. *"Last chance to give the urine sample in,"* says Daniel (author), but Julia is unmoved by his persuasion. Soon the support will disappear for 15 hours or so as it does every night of the week and each month of the year. When there is no support, the risks amplify, for, as the bus drives off, a man laments his missed opportunity to collect syringes from them, and starts to search around on the ground before picking up a used one; all the while he talks to himself, curses himself, and occasionally hits himself. As the sun starts to set over Valdemingómez, we stand around and return to the dilemma of Julia's pregnancy while she stands there smoking in a state that seems to resemble something between relief and absolute frustration; another day has passed and she has avoided contact with the services regarding her pregnancy. Daniel puts his hand on her stomach and makes a guess that the baby is far more mature than four months as he feels the baby's head.

Two weeks later

It is an unseasonably wet afternoon in early May 2016 when we approach the entrance to Valdemingómez in the Cañada Real Galiana; this time, in the back seat we have Inma, a worker we have come to know who works in drug prevention. As we pass the illegal businesses on the left-hand side of the settlement, there is a short delay as we let the large lorries pass by before we start to navigate the vast potholes in the road filled with muddy water. Reliable as ever at the side of the road, the drug-addicted workers known as *machacas* make business as best they can for the *gitanos*, and beckon us over to make drug purchases from the *kiosks* (drug sales venues) and *fumaderos* (drug sales and drug-taking venues) where they are employed.

As it starts to spit with rain, we take a right into a small alley where there is a line of other *kiosks*, and we pass *gitanos* talking in the street who look cautiously at us as we pass. Even though our faces are familiar, having spent almost 18 months here, most people are untrusted in Valdemingómez. We then take a left and come into the *plaza* before driving across it to the main road, heading up to the bridge. On the right and left, as we pass for the first 400m, there are numerous parked cars full of men and women who have come to smoke and inject heroin and cocaine in the new *fumaderos* that have opened up over the last six months or so.

Having passed through the predominantly *gitano* communities and the quieter Arab area, we reach the bridge, pulling over so that we can get out and walk for a while as a vomit/shit smell drifts over. Returning on the same road back towards the *plaza*, a car passes us, and in the front seat we see two children no older than 11 or 12 driving it. Outside the houses and *kiosks* the *gitana* women sit around in small groups, and make swift moves towards our car as we pass, waving us down to make drug purchases as we near the *plaza*. One *gitana* woman in her late 30s manages to persuade us to stop and we wind down the window; she is tireless in her persuasion to buy drugs from her so she can feed her children. As she leans into the car, her son peeps over the window on Daniel's side; his dirty face smiles at him as he asks him if it is his car. Somehow we manage to decline the continual offer of a free cocaine hit and drive on towards the *plaza*.

More introductions

We pull up opposite the church in the *plaza*, practically outside Juan and Julia's tent, and brief Inma on the dynamics of their relationship. They have been together for the last year or so – Juan is in his late 40s and Julia in her early 30s – and have exhausted practically all contact with their families, lost their homes, and now live in Valdemingómez. Over the years, and for various reasons that we will explore in this book, both have become dependent on heroin and cocaine. We step out among the rubbish and discarded drug paraphernalia; the wind is warm as we amble over to their ripped tent that flaps around in the breeze. We call out to them but there is no answer, and so we decide to look for them. As we turn the corner behind the church, we see Juan administering a heroin and cocaine injection as he sits on the church steps;

blood trickles down his arm and drips intermittently on to the concrete floor. He then proceeds to lick the bloody wound on his arm from where he has just injected. Around him there are more fresh blood stains up the wall, on the floor and others that have long scarred the ground over the seasons. As he looks up at us and clutches his bloody arm with his dirty hand, we introduce him to Inma.

We walk back together to the main *plaza*, practically outside the two largest and busiest *fumaderos* in the area, and talk to Juan. Julia, it seems, is working for one of the *gitano* families in one of the more recently established *fumaderos* so we can't see her. As always, in his animated way, he describes the dilemma and how he has tried to do everything to help her get the pregnancy tests so they can move out of Valdemingómez and care for their soon-to-arrive child. He says she is *"mad"* and has a *"mental problem"* when he describes Julia's mood swings, which he says are intensified by paranoia deriving from continual doses of cocaine. As a consequence, he says that she *"invents problems"* and unleashes *"unpredictable jealousy"* when she sees him with other women, insulting them both in the process. Inma stands there with folded arms, listening to all this without judgement, and suggests an alternative housing option if Julia is prepared to start to engage with the formalised process of undergoing pregnancy tests, while Juan continues to gesticulate erratically in the middle of the *plaza*. All the while, illegal taxis (hereafter *cundas*) full of groups of drug users arrive in their droves around us.

Juan tells us he will try and persuade Julia to take a break from her work in the *fumadero* and speak to Inma, and potters off past its secure gate into the building to talk to her. Since Juan told us two weeks ago about her pregnancy, we have been trying to persuade Julia to walk a matter of metres to the harm reduction team bus that comes each day to Valdemingómez and to undertake a test. Rather than waiting in the open area, we head towards the bus, passing a half-naked unshaven man holding his stomach in pain as he searches through the rubbish. We greet the harm reduction team who stand resolutely in their positions behind the table where drug users can collect food, clothes and clean drug paraphernalia. The hours can be long and it is quiet after lunch, so in their boredom, some flirt with each other while others fiddle with their mobiles phones and smoke.

Sometime later, Juan returns with news, *"Julia says she will come out"*. We saunter back towards the *fumadero* and wait around for a while. After half an hour, the only people who come and go are the clients buying drugs. After another 15 minutes, it becomes obvious that she isn't coming out, and Juan goes back inside, patting the *machaca* on the arm as he passes the secure steel door. Some minutes later, he returns, shaking his head in dismay, saying how she *"searches for any excuse"* to avoid the tests and just attempts to keep herself busy, hoping that the impending certainty of her pregnancy is not happening. Such is the frustration inside Daniel, and knowing that the harm reduction team has done everything they have to convince her to take the tests, he suggests we go into the *fumadero* to talk to her.

Abre! *(Open!)*

While we have been into some of the *fumaderos* in Valdemingómez, we have not just walked into one without knowing the *gitano* owners. During these times, we have always been with trusted people like Juan, or in some cases, with the police. However, we are about to enter somewhere unfamiliar to us with someone (Inma) who the *gitanos* don't know. The *fumaderos* normally compose of high walls, a steel or iron door that opens into an inside patio area, which is next to a principal dealing location inside a house. As we approach it, the *machaca* timidly gets up from a perching position on his broken stool. There is almost no time for him to question us as we walk past his wooden shack where he lives, which looks distinctly more grand than he does in his rags. Juan yells *"abre!"* ("open!") to the man behind the steel door as we follow him, and a large clank is heard as the tall, metal door is unlocked and in we walk, passing the alarmed face of the other *machaca* who hides behind the door. Inside the courtyard, there are a few boulders laying around under the pine trees, a water supply in the middle and a sort of washing line draping from one side to the other. In the far corner is the dealing house where inside we see Julia briskly sweeping up after she has just had a quick hit of cocaine. Several characters emerge whom we have come to know in the area, including Raul and a thin woman with scars and scabs all over her face.

Julia sweeps away frantically as we approach her in the dealing house, her eyes as wide as discs as she is high as a kite. Yet when she sees us, she starts yelling at Juan, *"Estoy trabajando, no puedo salir!"* ("I'm working, I can't leave!"). She insults Juan and stares at him as if she is about to kill him while we sort of stand around next to them. As Julia and Juan shout at each other, Daniel intervenes before Inma asks for five minutes of Julia's time and takes her aside, near the far wall. Daniel and Rubén take Juan aside and try to calm him down under a pine tree in the courtyard. As we talk in our respective corners of the *fumadero*, like coaches may do at a boxing match before the final round, Juan complains about her calling him *"cabezona"* ("stubborn"). Periodic glances from the *gitano* family inside dealing drugs from behind solid bars don't seem to aid the situation as clients come and go from the *fumadero*. We look over as Inma asks Julia to lift up her baggy jumper that she wears to hide her pregnant stomach; it seems obvious that she is more than three months pregnant. Feeling under pressure from her employers for potentially slacking on the job, Julia tells Inma she will come out in 15 minutes and meet us outside before doing the pregnancy test. She tells us to wait by the harm reduction team bus.

We amble out, past the speechless *machaca* who still has his mouth open from when we entered, and stand in the adjacent part of the *plaza*. All around us are cars parked up, full with people smoking and injecting heroin and cocaine. As we wait, a man in his early 50s steps out of his *cunda* and vomits a brown/red lumpy mixture on the floor. Soon after, in another corner, a woman screams to herself as she washes her hair from the church tap that is the only public source of fresh, cold water in Valdemingómez. She seems to be shrieking and shouting at someone as the other drug users around her sprawl out and can only gaze up in their sleepy states from the rotten mattresses. It turns out that she is talking to herself. Then another *machaca* who works in another *fumadero* emerges; she marches over and shouts at the woman talking to herself, calling her *"puta"* ("whore") in a semi-serious tone as she smiles to herself, revealing her two teeth. They then play out a scenario as they position themselves seductively against the church, as if offering sexual services.

The minutes pass and as we wait, more cars pull up and more leave, something we have come to view as normal given that thousands come to buy drugs here every day. Juan then starts to get impatient and goes off with Rubén to buy some cocaine from another *fumadero* while Inma and Daniel wait for Julia. About 10 minutes later, she appears and marches over to us, cursing us, saying how she *"has to work"* and how we have upset her bosses by coming into the *fumadero* because we didn't make a drug purchase. Even though Juan had explained we were not *chapas* (secret police), the *gitanos* cannot understand the notion of social research. In entering the *fumadero*, we had jeopardised our own trust with Juan and Julia, generating tension between her and her employers, and for this reason she is angry. Inma once again pulls her aside and offers to accompany her to do the pregnancy test, but she declines and scuffs her feet back to the *fumadero*.

When Juan returns with Rubén, he disappears back to his tent, and all three of us walk slowly back to the car, feeling dejected, passing, as we trundle, a veteran drug injector administering a shot in someone else's arm. As Inma had said, they had underestimated the pregnancy, and Juan's three-to-four-month approximation was, in her view, more like five to six months. Inma tells us she had tried to convince Julia that her consumption could massively impact on the baby, and she ran the risk of killing herself if her baby died inside her. We stop and talk about the passive approach of the harm reduction team, and how their engagement methods relate more to a person summoning personal will to engage with them than anything more proactive. Of course, it is not their remit to go into the *fumaderos* to intervene in these situations, but nor should it be their job to just let it happen – half the team know Julia is pregnant and she has not yet done any tests, has missed essential scans, and has no idea about the health of the baby. Neither is it our role as researchers. Juan and Julia do not have HIV but they do have hepatitis C, and their daily methadone and cocaine consumption is problematic. But they have previously failed rehab and are homeless, without any support network. We return to Juan who sits in the entrance of his broken tent having smoked some cocaine. He looks stressed. We wish him well, get in the car and drive off, passing more cars and *cundas* that arrive as we leave.

Welcome to Europe's largest ghetto

Julia and Juan currently live in Valdemingómez, or the sixth of six sectors of the Cañada Real Galiana, a site that stretches 14km in length and is only 12km from the centre of Madrid. The most recent official census estimates that the six sectors house 9,228 people with 2,516 buildings, all illegally constructed (ACCEM and Fundación Secretariado Gitano, 2010). However, since the publication of these data, the area has continued to expand, largely because the 2008 economic crisis froze thousands of people out of the labour market, which meant that many lost their homes, in particular, poor families of mostly Arab, *gitano* or Romanian origin, who then relocated to the area. There they stay, predominantly with other family and friends as a way to survive; some pay no electricity, gas or water bills as these utilities are hijacked from mains sources, and they are able to take advantage of social security benefits for their children and qualify for further support due to their status as a 'vulnerable ethnic minority'. For this reason, and as we write in 2017, we would estimate that the residents of the Cañada Real Galiana – including Juan and Julia, and perhaps their son or daughter – to be in the region of between 11,500 and 12,500.

Juan and Julia, however, have very little contact with people who live in the other five sectors, not only because their daily lives revolve around problematic drug use and the acquisition of money and other exchangeable items, but also because of the spatial distribution of the other zones. Valdemingómez is practically a closed community. Although one road (that varies in condition) connects Sectors 1 to 5, it is essentially blocked by the A3 – one of the six main roads out of Madrid – thus cutting

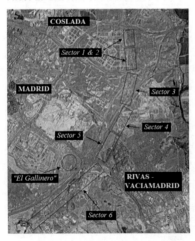

Photo 2: Ariel view of the six sectors

off Valdemingómez. There are also vast differences in the population demography; Sectors 1 and 2, for example, are heavily populated by working-class Spanish families and industrial businesses respectively. Here, the local government of Coslada has all but incorporated these sectors into their management, which is why the houses and buildings in these areas are decent. There are public services, electricity, water and a good quality road, even though this area was illegally populated in the 1960s and 1970s by rural migrant workers moving to the city in search of labour opportunities (see Chapter 3).

Sectors 2 and 3 are divided by a small road between Coslada and Rivas Vaciamadrid (hereafter Rivas; interestingly, *vaciamadrid* literally translated means 'empty Madrid'), where there are mostly *gitanos*. Here in Sector 3 these people get by selling used domestic goods such as fridges, freezers, washing machines, toilets and baths, while others rob and sell copper and industrial cables. Between the sectors, there are also some

Photo 3: Sector 3 sign pointing to Valdemingómez; 'Peligro' means 'Danger'

cafes and restaurants. However, the largest business without doubt is dedicated to selling scrap metal, or *chatarra*. This sector marks a notable change in the quality of the housing in that it is more improvised. There are some derelict sites and in one area, someone has managed to mount a caravan on top of a house. The roads are more difficult to navigate in the absence of asphalt, and lining them are large cables that illegally connect the large pylons to the houses and businesses.

Sector 4 comes under the spatial and social management of the Rivas local government, but the conditions of the roads and houses are distinctly poor. The area's community is a blend of northern African and Arab families and *gitanos*, and while there is almost no sign of drug dealing, there are some illegal vehicle workshops and small tool workshops, and from here on, the electricity, gas and water are also illegally acquired. Small vegetable gardens can be found from time to time, and random vehicles passing up and down selling the very same produce to other members of the community.

However, in Sector 5, the setting starts to change as well as the ambiance (see Photo 4). In this sector, which lies right next to Rivas town centre, similar forms of business take place among a predominantly Arab population, although there are also some *gitano* families. Perhaps the main differences between this sector and those before it are that a significant number of the children in the area attend a nearby school, and there is an active community association seeking to defend the rights of its habitants. This has mostly been set up as a consequence of the increased police raids and house demolitions (see Chapter 7), because drugs are sold on a small scale, and this has attracted more crime to the area in the form of robbery and car theft. However, over the two years of our fieldwork, radicalised jihadis have also been detained in the area.

Photo 4: Barbed wire and broken bottles indicate precaution is needed in Sector 5

As we have indicated, however, much of this is alien to Julia and Juan, since their contact with these other sectors is limited. Around them in Valdemingómez in Sector 6 – far more in abundance than in the other sectors – are also numerous illegal companies dedicated to construction, (bus) transport, furniture and car workshops. Their sector is also similarly diverse. Their most immediate neighbours are the *gitanos* who construct, occupy and manage the *kiosks* and *fumaderos* around them, and lead in the organised distribution of drugs. Further up, towards the edge of the sector, is an Arab community that has a small grocery, general stores and workshops. Additionally, alongside them in the sector also live a Romanian community that tends to survive by selling *chatarra* and buying and selling various miscellaneous goods robbed by the sector's active drug-using population who live and visit the area – the numbers of whom vary from the 140 *machacas* who live permanently in the area to the 5,000 clients who come here each day to purchase and/or use drugs.

So Juan and Julia are not only well immersed in this environment of drug use and crime, but also within other informal economies operating in tandem with it. Every day they are among the *machacas* who recruit potential clients and work in the *kiosks* and *fumaderos* and are well familiar with the thriving theft and sale of national identity cards, mobile phones, clothes, and in the afterhours of the harm reduction team bus, the exchange of syringes and other drug paraphernalia. They witness women living in the area, as well as those who travel from Madrid's prostitution hotspot, the Polígono Marconi, sell sexual services for a couple of Euros or just enough for a hit of heroin or cocaine. They observe the violence exercised by the *gitanos* in the management of the drug business and the arms trade that takes place alongside Spain's principal drug market.

Why here, why now?

The drug market in Valdemingómez in the Cañada Real Galiana is a relatively recent development since drug sales evolved around the turn of the 21st century. However, its growth, as we will see, has been, on the one hand, as a consequence of the dismantling of other *gitano* drug-dealing settlements known as *poblados* in and around Madrid, leading to its consolidation in one drug hypermarket on the outskirts. It has also come as a consequence of inept social reintegration policies that have consistently failed and ostracised the *gitanos*.

Perhaps the most significant population growth in Valdemingómez occurred between 2004 and 2006, when a nearby *poblado* called Las Barranquillas was demolished over a short period of time in an effort to generate support for what was to be another failed Olympic bid (see Chapter 10), essentially transferring what were major parts of Madrid's drug market to Valdemingómez. This transfer was also significant in that it displaced a large number of people who had come to own properties in Sector 6, giving way for the availability of more estates that could be used for the distribution of drugs; in some cases, they were threatened and physically forced from their homes if they didn't surrender the space to the *gitano* families. Although in a minority, those unable to sell because they could afford no other place in Madrid can still be seen trying to live a normal life in the midst of the incessant sale of heroin and cocaine.

The real boom years for Valdemingómez were then between 2007 and 2008, when it became famous as Spain's drug hypermarket, known nationwide as the place to buy good-quality drugs at cheaper prices than in the local neighbourhood, or *barrio*, as we refer to it hereafter. By then, new young users and dealers had started to visit the area in the absence of political alternatives as law enforcement interventions started to engage in phases of raids and demolitions. Yet Valdemingómez's location was also geographically advantageous for drug distribution as it was well connected by main roads and motorways in and around Madrid, in particular the M50, which pretty much circumnavigates the capital, as well as the A3, which connects the city centre to the coastal city of Valencia, making it easy for new dealing routes to evolve.

Of course, there are other processes that we will also acknowledge in this book that explain how Valdemingómez's growth also relates to Spain's exposure to globalising drug markets, the shifts in both the political and economic scenery, combined with its cultural adaption to a consumer society. But within these processes, we want to tell the story of the people who live and visit there, so the insight into Juan and Julia's situation is one of the many that take place there on a daily basis. Although the 2008 economic crisis massively impacted drug distribution and dealing dynamics around Spain's capital, Valdemingómez still shows little sign of desisting as thousands pour into the sector each day, keeping the drug market buoyant. The few families that now run the drug operations in the sector each own between five to eight properties in the area to avoid major legal consequences, keeping only around 200 grams of both cocaine and heroin in each sales point, while larger quantities are securely located in bunkers – so the families buy drugs in bulk and distribute them to smaller sales points in the area. Indeed, the most popular *fumaderos* can make between €6,000 to €10,000 each day, and for this reason, the social hierarchy among the *gitanos* is determined by the most successful in the drug businesses (see Chapter 6).

The drugs are sold directly in various quantities from the *kiosks* and *fumaderos*, predominantly in small doses, although VIP clients come and buy in bulk at discounted rates. It is possible to buy a hit of heroin and cocaine for €5, which is often mixed and smoked in a *pipa* (or pipe) or on *plata* (foil) as well as available to be mixed for a *chuta* (injection). Other drugs are available such as cannabis, as well as various types of pills. Since the economic crisis, the quality of drugs has reduced considerably as the *gitanos* seek to retain decent profit margins, meaning that they increasingly cut their drugs with a range of hazardous products, which has inevitably increased the probability of overdoses as well as health problems among the drug users.

The people charged with dealing with these kinds of situations, as well as the day-to-day support for people like Juan and Julia, are the harm reduction team, made up of between 15–20 social workers, educators, doctors and nurses. Each day of the year, they arrive at about 10.30 in the morning in several buses, and over the course of seven hours or so, give food, clothes and advice, trying as best they can to persuade a permanent population of drug users to change their lives. Their other remit is to subtly convince another much larger group of people who come intermittently to the area to buy and take drugs to take advantage of their presence and collect clean drug paraphernalia, and to perhaps reconsider the potential pathway they may be taking towards problematic drug use. There is a real demand for their intervention, as each month the team distributes around 35,000 syringes for injecting and 20,000 condoms. When they are not there after 6pm, there is no support mechanism, food, clean water, nor emergency treatment. Indeed, it is common for the team to return the next day and find people dead in the area having overdosed or having got into disputes and been killed. For the police, and even the medical emergency services, there is little motivation to go out to Valdemingómez because it is considered off limits at night.

The case for a new form of analysis

Aside from numerous sensationalised media reports, limited attention has been given to the development of Valdemingómez in the Cañada Real Galiana and the kind of activities that take place there. Previous studies have done admirably well to highlight criminogenic aspects of the Cañada Real Galiana (ACCEM and Fundación Secretariado Gitano, 2010; Ministerio de Formento, 2010) and surrounding communities (Soleares, 2011; Gutíerrez Sánchez, 2015) using an established approach in the social sciences that strips down the complexity of social life into things like 'variables' and 'risk factors'. In doing so, these studies lack a structural appreciation of the processes that perpetuate misery and suffering in the area, and a comprehension of the cultural norms that thus support it. The same research also endeavours to propose policy remedies and further study to determine potential solutions but, as we will show, the problems incumbent to Valdemingómez are far beyond any recommendations urban town planners can offer and the pretty-sounding policy promises politicians can put forward.

Our work tries to go a step further by examining in detail how the precise moot point of political and social intervention is bound to wider processes of ideological, political and economic visions of the city space, combined with an all-out offensive against the swathes of immobilised and disenfranchised poor people who are seen to obstruct these very ambitions. It could be termed thus as a form of 'structural violence'. Our work not only documents aspects of the zone's criminogenic activity, but also examines the role of other forms of illegal activity in the historical and cultural development of various types of different social groups, seemingly coexisting in such a concentrated suburban area. Few serious studies have been done, less so over time, which have tried to understand how it has come to happen that there is such a high level of illegal activity as spatially concentrated as it is here. For that, we also consult urban and geographical studies that place the evolution of Valdemingómez in a context that exposes how commercial desires and economic interests have reorganised the spatial concentration of these social groups (see Chapter 3; see also Requeña, 2014). Moreover, it seems to be evident, from what we can find in the current literature about drug markets and drug use in Spain, that there is a need to provide a new form of nuanced analysis to explain how and why drug use takes place in the Spanish context. Many studies fail to consider historical socio-cultural processes that explain attitudes to drug use as well as structural processes that have, over time, attempted to deal in different ways with the consequential fallout of the normalisation of drug use (see Chapter 4).

While there exist some international studies that have already ethnographically documented problematic drug use and drug markets (Bourgois and Schonberg, 2009; Wacquant, 2009; Briggs, 2012a), there are very few detailed, photo ethnographic studies that offer an insight into how hard drug use is experienced by thousands of people, showing the visual ramifications of the structural violence that takes place against these groups, which results in a cyclical victimisation and permanent fatalism. For this reason, photos complement our observations and interviews, and serve to invite the reader to empathise with the experiences of the people in the book. We have been inside drug dens, in and around derelict sites, on police raids, attended demolitions, been with the harm reduction team, and, most importantly, have been with the people who live in this area. We have watched them inject themselves in all sorts of places/parts of their body, accompanied them in the substandard conditions in which they live, and witnessed life-threatening moments and death. In short, these experiences shine through in the data, as we want to reify the reality that exists in Valdemingómez.

Our study is personally motivated and unfunded after we spent 18 months trying to secure money from the Spanish government by writing three failed research proposals. The Ministry of Social Services rejected the first as the observational and visual methodology was considered to be too 'risky'. When we resubmitted the second to another funding call within the same Ministry, having toned down our methodological approach to a more cross-sectional qualitative analysis, the proposal was accepted: the problem was that when it came to funding it, the government claimed it had spent the money allocated for the project. In a last-ditch effort, a third proposal was submitted to the Ministry of Health that was outright rejected as it was considered 'irrelevant to its remit'.

So when Rubén proposed to initiate a pilot project in the area for his undergraduate degree dissertation on organised crime and police operations, Daniel was charged with supervising him. As Rubén's study progressed, Daniel started to visit the area with Rúben, and to sit in on some of the interviews with the police. These brief experiences were enough to convince us to just do the study without official financing; indeed, had we been awarded money from the government, almost half of any funding would have been lost to the 'institutional costs' of the university anyway. The average cost of our three proposals was €55,000 to undertake a one-year project. Over a two-year period (from November 2014 to November 2016) we spent less than €1,000 of our own money between us to complete our ethnographic study. During that time, we undertook 50 recorded interviews with drug users, *gitanos*, police officers, educational workers, harm reduction and medical staff, and with other associations working in the area of drugs and social services. The next section explains how we obtained our data.

An honest justification of our methodology

We chose Valdemingómez in the Cañada Real Galiana because it is the most problematic area in Spain in terms of drugs, crime and violence, and for this reason, an obvious challenge in researching it was the elevated levels of illegal activity and organised crime. This is compounded by the misperception and misrepresentation of the area in the media, which presents it to the average Spanish citizen as a 'no-go area', a 'lawless place of deprivation' where people who can't get their lives together engage in calculated behaviours that result in police detention (see, for example, Álvarez, 2016, and Telemadrid, 2016). These depictions have created immense caution and mistrust to the point that, even throughout our fieldwork period, regular visits by the media were met with insults from drug users, and stones and rocks being thrown by the *gitanos*.

As we have described, the area is also spatially separated from Madrid and from most neighbouring towns bar Rivas and Coslada, and it is this spatial partition – even from the other five sectors – which assists in the fruition and sustenance of its very specific cultural norms. Naturally, the different populations who visit and live in the area have their own cultural attributes, and we examine these in Chapter 6, but the zone's lack of infrastructure, combined with the symbiosis of the *gitano* culture with the drug trade, and a thriving and varied drug-using community complemented by other illicit businesses, makes it unlike any other place in the country.

These dynamics therefore had implications for how we had to go about our study. We chose ethnographic methods as we were interested in learning about how the people who visit and live in Valdemingómez experience it. Given that high proportions of drug use, drug dealing and crime take place in the area, it makes it difficult to research. The area is controlled by powerful *gitano* families who are unafraid to use firearms and do not hesitate to ward off potential threats with force – even if many disputes and violence take place between them. Their homes as well as the *kiosks* and *fumaderos* are secure places, and almost all the families have firearms. Add to this a high level of mistrust about strangers or new people who come to the area that is amplified by the general caution the *gitano* community have towards people who do not originate from their culture. There is also the ever-present threat of disputes and violence between the drug users, and public fighting is common, which is why, in a few cases, they, too, carry weapons, from knives to guns; if not, then among the rubbish there are usually improvised weapons they can find in the surrounding area such as broken bottles or metal bars. Naturally, the fact that they possess these weapons is made worse by their fragile mental states and varying levels of paranoia and anxiety that are triggered by the relentless use of heroin and cocaine. This is further problematised by the corrosion of their mental, emotional and physical states over time.

Such high levels of drug use also mean that there are constant public health risks, and the risk of catching disease or viruses is high because piles of rotting rubbish surround the area. Between the shacks, or shanty improvised constructions known as *chabolas*, are derelict sites, and scattered in and around them, as well as almost everywhere, are broken bottles, used condoms, shit, and perhaps more than anything else, strewn drug paraphernalia:

> As we return, we see a man with his sleeve rolled up next to an orange tent: he stands up and moves a chair with the syringe hanging from his upper arm. Very damaged and thin women pass us from time to time with very heavy looks on their faces as they trudge up to the harm reduction bus. We decide to take a walk around the back of the church area and pass more testimonies of love made by Juan to Julia written on the church wall. A metre or so away is the sleeping place of the man who we saw injecting the other day. Next to his rags lie used syringes, piss stains and shit. Further on, mostly concentrated around trees or large bushes, are collections of injecting paraphernalia and evidence of fires having been lit ... some ashes are still warm in cinder from the night before. Behind the church, a man stoops to inject himself in the legs, and even as we look just behind the harm reduction bus, two cars sit full of people smoking heroin and cocaine. Around them are small mountains of rubbish and a wild grassland peppered with more unwanted debris.

You cannot simply walk into this area and start asking questions or even attempt to expect to immediately get the trust of these people. We had to work out where was relatively safe (by the church in the *plaza*) in comparison to the locations more likely to be risky (improvised buildings in rubbish dumps) and those that were more dangerous (the *kiosks* and *fumaderos*). In this respect, our exposure to risk changed situationally within the research terrain – the risks we potentially encountered standing around in the *plaza* were minimal compared to those that we took when we scaled the rubbish and derelict sites and those that we took when we entered the *kiosks* and *fumaderos*.

Ethnography is precisely about getting to know the people under study, making them feel comfortable, observing what they do and how they do it, and at times, questioning them about why they think they may do it. Even after nine months into our study we had not undertaken a single interview with the people who visited or lived there, instead, spending our time observing and familiarising ourselves with how things work. The advantage of doing this was that we were also able to establish ourselves as regular visitors to the area. Gradually, as we were seen with increased frequency, we gained some acceptance, and at the same time, obtained a level of confidence about where we could go, what we could say and what we could do. For example, in the initial months we drove to one place on the main *plaza* and sat in the car, getting out for short walks, and by the end of the fieldwork, we were having coffee in *gitanos'* houses and were privy to the display of firearms and drugs. In this period, we made informal exchanges with the harm reduction team, the police and the drug users, often helping them out in times of need to demonstrate our neutral presence, helping them look for items for their tents/huts, for example.

It was then, in the summer of 2015, after about nine months of the fieldwork, that we formally approached Roberto, one of the harm reduction workers who we had come to know quite well. We explained how we wanted to start to undertake more detailed interviews with some of the people, and although we had managed to obtain some trust among some of the drug users, we wanted a more secure place to talk with them. Perhaps, as one can imagine, the dynamics of Valdemingómez made it difficult to find private places to undertake interviews, especially when those were precisely the kinds of places drug users sought out to smoke and/ or inject heroin and cocaine. At first, we undertook two interviews in the harm reduction team bus with both Juan and Julia, and although fruitful for us, this caused problems among the drug workers, some feeling that it was a breach of their health and safety protocols. Roberto then advised us to do the interviews in and around the church area, which was normally where the harm reduction team bus parked, so that if there were problems, he could intervene (although he was not formally required to). This was how we were able to record our interviews using a mobile phone, and the fact that there were two of us enabled us to monitor other activity around us – although it didn't hinder the potential for interruption.

The interviews broadly covered how these people had come to use drugs, in what circumstances and why; perspectives of visiting/living/working in Valdemingómez; experiences of the police and harm reduction team; as well as attempts to get clean from drugs. In almost all of our interviews, like Juan and Julia, people were either preparing to take heroin and cocaine, were actually using them (smoking/injecting), or had recently taken them. In this respect, we have no doubt that the use of these drugs – in terms of their pharmacological effects – had some bearing on our data, but in an area where drug use is part of the everyday fabric of these people's lives, there was little other choice. In any case, the richness of our data should prove that when researching drug cultures such immersion is necessary (see Bourgois and Schonberg, 2009; Mars et al, 2014). We soon realised that the most ideal period to do interviews was late morning to early afternoon, once Valdemingómez residents had been able to cure their withdrawal symptoms (*mono*) by using heroin or methadone or both, and had had something to eat. This was also an ideal time as many worked during the nights for the *gitanos* as *machacas*, and it often gave them some respite to rest before starting their shifts again.

There is no such thing as an ethics committee in Spain, which meant that those who were unfamiliar with ethnographic research would be spared the bureaucracy of filling in long forms; we also avoided the need to justify our fieldwork approach, including having to dumb down (or even lie about) the potential risks to which we were exposed. We therefore took what measures we could when it came to our own safety and that of our participants, and anonymised names and any identifying aspects of our participants' identities. Where they permitted us, we took photos, concealing in this publication the identities of those who didn't want to be recognised. We offered no money to our participants,[2] giving them clothes, shoes and cigarettes from time to time as well as helping them out when they most needed it. When formal, recorded interviews were done, as a gesture of goodwill we offered them a pack of cigarettes, and while in general this was accepted, they often turned it down, preferring to talk without receiving anything. Our questioning style was informal and empathetic. The main interview period in our two-year study lasted six months, from November 2015 to May 2016, and it was this process that cemented our trust with the research population, to the point where we could arrive at the area, speak to them with no fear, and be privy to intimate thoughts before, during and after drug use had taken place.

To complement this data collection, we also undertook a series of interviews with the police, harm reduction workers, educational and drug experts and *gitanos*. The topic of these interviews broadly covered the changes and organisation of the regional drug market as well as the ones local to Valdemingómez, *gitano* drug operations, social and criminal policy with regard to drugs in the city, as well as processes of addiction and recovery. These interviews allowed us to contextualise drug use and attitudes to consumption, experiences of violence and victimisation, and in general, provide a more holistic picture of the social scenery of Valdemingómez.

Structure of the book

In these brief notes about what takes place in Valdemingómez, there are hidden experiences and untold stories about people's lives, and throughout the book we intend to unpack these narratives and to dig deeper into how and why it came to be that they were doing these things, in these places, at this time. Chapter 2 offers the theoretical contextualisation to our study. Here we emphasise the kinds of processes that are displacing problem populations and dumping them outside of cities, as a way of managing them and rendering them obsolete from social consciousness. We ask how and why this is happening, and put this all in to a wider political economic context by covering the recent global economic crisis and how it has influenced Spanish politics, state withdrawal from community support and crumbling community cohesion. For this reason, we also look at urban studies and contemporary work that has theorised the city.

In Chapter 3 we emphasise the historical evolution of the area and how it evolved as a settlement. Using what little is available that documents the early life of the Cañada Real Galiana, we complement this with a narrative history of the evolution of the six sectors. To bolster this, we delve into economic change and population movement in Spain as well as migration to the country. The persecution of social groups in these marginalised areas, particularly the *gitanos*, is also explored, how their livelihoods and *poblados* were essentially banished from the city centre while, at the same time, other areas of Madrid flourished in economic and social growth and value. Our focus here is to draw attention to the expansive growth in inequality in Spanish society.

Valdemingómez's reputation as Spain's principal drug market requires us to consider how drug markets have evolved in the country as a consequence of globalisation, and the evolution of producer and consumer countries (such as

Spain). Therefore, in Chapter 4, we chart the social policy and law enforcement processes that have taken place from the early 1990s in Madrid, as well as in other Spanish cities, which has seen the slow extinction of visible hard drug use (such as smoking crack cocaine and injecting heroin) in public city spaces. We frame this against the spatial dimensions of inequality in the city and the increasingly punitive approaches to drug use that were taken in the 1980s onwards, which essentially guaranteed the multiplication of the drug problem. We also consider cultural attitudes to drug use that were accelerated as Spain entered its democratic era and embraced consumerism. Such was the drug boom, in particular, the use of heroin, that this caused major social problems, triggering political alarm and resulting in harsher laws, which led to long prison sentences. The drug prevention campaigns and rehabilitation programmes that followed had some success, as we point out, but were further damaged by a constant pillaging of public service funding and the economic crash of 2008.

Thereafter begin our data chapters, and Chapter 5 seeks to present the journeys these people take to drug dependence, showing how people like Juan and Julia arrive at living homeless and drug-dependent in Valdemingómez. We point out that dependence doesn't happen overnight, and how, although most people try drugs, the route to dependence is complicated and relies on a personal investment being made on using drugs as a response to structurally predetermined circumstances, that is, growing up in poverty, lacking an education, long spells of unemployment, etc. Crucially, we show how the aggressive spatial displacement of drug markets in Madrid has had a detrimental impact on these drug users' lives in terms of modes of consumption, and elevated their exposure to risk.

Chapter 6 examines the cultural day-to-day dynamics of Valdemingómez, and discusses the social status of each of the different groups of people in the area. For this reason, the role of identity and labour become central concepts to understanding how power is embedded in social relationships, with a focus on the *gitanos*, their employees (the *machacas*), the drug users who live in the area and illegal taxis drivers (*cundas*) who bring drug users to and from Valdemingómez. Here we focus on how the micro dynamics of the drug economy interplay with other forms of illicit and informal economies that thrive as a consequence of the former.

In Chapter 7 we consider the structural framework in operation around Valdemingómez, such as the role of the local councils (predominantly implicated in the management of the area are Madrid and Rivas), the National and Local Police and Civil Guard, and the harm reduction team and other forms of social support. Aside from these institutions' conflicting agendas, the spatial distribution of Valdemingómez immediately poses problems for intervention from both law enforcement and social support. At various levels, corruption among law enforcement and inept political factions problematises formal responses to the drug market, rendering impotent police efforts to contain the problem within Valdemingómez. While from time to time the internal operations of the drug market are temporarily destabilised by police raids and demolishing drug houses, kingpins in the *gitano* clans are replaced by other family members who quickly occupy the available positions.

We also show the consequences of the brutal reduction in state support and investment condensing drug treatment to a very basic version of harm reduction, while other non-governmental organisations (NGOs) such as Cruz Roja (Red Cross) are simply left to chip in as they can. Some, albeit very few, manage to start the path of recovery but often find themselves back in Valdemingómez as their problems are so entrenched and they are so damaged that no service or protocol can dedicate sufficient time to their recovery. So it is rare for the police or drug agencies to see improvements, especially when the raids that are made result in other drug houses opening, and the very few addicts who navigate the bureaucratic support system often return to the area. Moreover, there is little anyone can do about the thousands of people who continue to arrive every day to buy and use drugs. This leaves these workers, like the police and drug agency staff, feeling similarly redundant – which we call 'professional impotence'.

The penultimate data chapter introduces the concept of 'post dependency' along with presenting various accounts and images of how accumulation of these experiences manifests itself in harmful drug use practices. In the main, the people who end up as drug-dependents living in Valdemingómez face an almost impossible task of recovery. This is in part linked to their own self-destruction through the use of drugs, as it is related to the structural processes that initially rendered them marginal in the first place which, over time, additionally exacerbated their vulnerability. So, regardless of fleeting intentions to fix themselves, the 'windows of opportunity' around which the support services base their philosophy have almost shut for someone who is living in their own 'personal abandon', with various sexually transmitted diseases, surviving in substandard conditions and addicted to heroin and cocaine. And even when the 'window of opportunity' may come around – often as a consequence of flirtations with their own death – their past often overwhelms their present, and brittle moments of changing their attitudes towards consumption quickly fade and disappear. Many simply return to drugs, and some return to Valdemingómez.

In the final chapter, we draw the findings together with our theoretical and empirical baseline. We call this chapter 'Not really the conclusion' because, given the complexity of this particular problem, it would be fairly pointless for us to offer recommendations to policy-makers, practitioners and the police, as they seem to be completely complicit to the problem. Studies have already done this, and nothing has changed. It would also be pointless regurgitating a lot of current liberal studies around issues such as drugs and social exclusion by suggesting that 'more education' or 'more resources' would do much to resolve the situation. Perhaps this is why a philosophy of mustering self-motivation is the motif on which the current institutions rely, even if it only consolidates the very problem in which they attempt to intervene, because, as we show, when meritocratic initiative is enduringly internalised by people who are continually blocked by structural impediments, it just simply destroys them.

Notes

[1]   Our research is mainly situated with Spanish-born *gitanos*.

[2]   Not only because we had no budget for it, but also because it would have attracted the wrong form of attention to our presence. Had we declared we were paying people for interviews, we would simply have attracted people just so they could get money, and we knew this from experience (see, for example, Briggs, 2012a).

2

Politics, 'democracy' and the ideology of the postmodern city

Photo 5: Mario's 'map of society' in the sand

After 50 minutes of the interview, a dog jogs past us, and from time to time, other forlorn drug addicts start to drift over to beg for cigarettes or greet us. Mario then draws in the sand his 'map of society'. He sketches out two circles: one he names *"society"* and places his plastic cup in it and the other he labels *"people like gitanos and us"*. First, at this circle he points, saying how *"the blame is put on us"* when it is *"society who does the damage"* and points at the cup. Suddenly, he then scrubs out the circle of *"gypsies and us"* before proceeding to prepare a few cocaine pipes and thereafter recites poetry he wrote when he was young. Soon after he reaches in his pocket and pulls out a small heroin package and sprinkles it into the pipe, before he inhales and lights it at the same time. It is all gone, just like half of his 'map of society'.

Introduction

Mario's understanding of his own predicament is emblematic of precisely the processes we want to address in this chapter: a structural and social exclusion that has spatial dimensions. Mario comes from a large family who lived in a poor urban area of south Madrid, very much exposed to the diminishing industrial economies and increased urban poverty that rendered redundant much of the urban working class in Spanish cities (see Chapter 3). Here, however, he goes a step further in not only describing the social and structural exclusion of people like him, but also their spatial exclusion: the two different maps making reference to the physical separation between them reflective of the proximity of the capital city and Valdemingómez on the outskirts. The other interesting aspect of Mario's map is that he draws two circles that refer to two very different populations, neither of which come out of their circle – they never encounter each other, and thus their realities are detached from each other. In one are the people of the city, and in the other are people like him.

Lastly, the action of erasing the circle where he had identified himself and the *gitanos* is also illustrative of attempts to dispose and eradicate people like him from public consciousness.

In this chapter, we explore why this may be the case by contextualising the political and economic changes over the last 40 years that have characterised the experience for the urban poor in places like Madrid. While we examine in detail the precise nature of how city planners and politicians have engaged in urban cleansing programmes that relegate problem groups like drug users to the city margins, here, we first discuss the global structural undercurrents that have led to greater inequality, unemployment and poverty before showing how a politics of distraction dilutes our collective consciousness to these issues. We show the consequences of this in the final part of the chapter, when we discuss the implications this has for the city and for its urban outcasts.

A world in perpetual crisis

From the mid-1970s onwards, the world advanced into uncharted territory: into one of uncertainty, risk and precariousness. From this period onwards an increasing global, neoliberal agenda – based, in principle, on free market economics and individualism – led to the dismantling of the post-war golden age of high employment, welfare, stable family structures and consensual norms and attitudes. It left in its place market and economic instability, 'risk', potential ecological catastrophe, high unemployment and increasing social inequality sharpened by welfare reduction and criminalisation of the 'underclass' (Standing, 2011; Briggs, 2012b). These are neoliberal economics that are concerned with deregulation and removing perceived restraints that impede profit, resulting in the downsizing of traditional industries, the dominance of global markets and rising unemployment and the growth of low-paid work.

The new consumer-oriented economies – evolving as a consequence of new technological advancement – require lower numbers of employees, and so work production and industry is downsized. Perhaps the most alarming aspect of neoliberal global capitalism relates to how the remedial project has generated social structures that are inherently discordant because corporate profitability has become a function of capital gain rather than economic productivity (Piketty, 2013). This generates surplus populations or 'wasted lives' (Bauman, 2003) – large groups of people who lack a role in the social system and who are stuck in perpetual unemployment and disadvantage.

All this has been drastically exacerbated by the global crisis of 2008 that has exposed rampant irregularities among the banking sector as well as political corruption. However, instead of prompting a reconsideration of capitalism's limitations, we witness the implementation of an aggressive politics of austerity starting to widen the pool of people at the bottom of society. Yet cuts in public spending, the privatisation of services and deregulation of labour markets have done little to reduce global economic problems, despite the continued calls to make governments change tax laws so that corporations and companies become accountable to pay their taxes instead of everyday citizens shouldering the debt burden. While the rich and poor divide continues to grow at the expense of people living in poverty, deprivation and unemployment, people have taken to the streets in protest, and social unrest has evolved in the absence of political and financial stability – largely because of the impotence of a quality politics that works for ordinary people.

This has provoked national and international movements of millions of people in an effort to escape destitution and potential poverty in their homelands, which is why the absence of democratic politics across Western countries – highlighted by growing inequality and continued financial exploitation by political factions – has had a major hand in people movement/displacement across the globe. Economic migrants have left mostly Baltic or Eastern European states, having grown tired of home corruption and botched political mismanagement of their countries that plunged them into debt and unemployment. Others, however, are a growing population of young refugees flocking into Europe, escaping war-torn countries such as Afghanistan, Iraq and Syria: the mobility is prompted by the need for security, the motivation to improve their life circumstances, to have a safe place to live, obtain an education and get a job. Nevertheless, both these groups stumble into new countries as the new 'precariat' (Standing, 2011), and face increasing forms of social rejection, barriers to social mobility and are vulnerable to begin life illegally in their new homelands as a consequence (Briggs and Dobre, 2014).

As voter apathy amasses from the left, an increasingly popular far right places blame on open borders and uncontrolled migration as nations start to implement barriers to people movement. And as the economic conditions and public dissatisfaction with the crisis have intensified, governments in Greece, Ireland, Italy, the Netherlands, Portugal, Slovenia, Slovakia and Spain have collapsed or been voted out of office after calling early elections. Leaders in some of the Eurozone's strongest economies, such as Germany, Finland and the Netherlands, have faced considerable public and political resistance to providing financial support to weaker economies, with critics opposed to the idea of rescuing countries that have not, in their view, exercised adequate budget discipline.

And it is in this political void that the far right has garnered increasing support from voters of diverse political ideologies, primarily because of growing disaffection with the current economic status quo. Many citizens living in 'democratic societies' have begun to feel that their governments are not looking after their own citizens, buying into political cover-up stories that economic woe is related to the problem of unregulated or poorly controlled immigration. At the crux of these explanations is the suggestion that support for radical far right parties comes from citizens who feel threatened by rapid changes in postindustrial societies. Manual workers with low education tend to lose their jobs as a result of changes in modes of production, and often end up competing with migrant workers for scarce resources such as jobs and houses. These 'losers of modernity', as Bauman notes (2003), feel threatened by rapid social change and tend to support radical right-wing parties out of general discontent more than is the case for the established, successful radical right parties.

However, these fringe parties have become quite powerful political entities that have started to have serious influence across the political, social and cultural landscape of Westernised countries. They draw on the economic, political and social fragility of these countries in their post-2008 crisis, and spearheading criticism of the legitimacy of free border movements as nation states exercise a crude paranoia about 'others' supposedly corrupting their economies, sucking off the benefit system, draining national resources and burdening the criminal justice system. This poisonous association is laced by numerous stories in the media that bundle them into the same group with welfare dependants, the disabled or mentally ill or unemployed, immigrants or asylum-seekers; in short, what is created is a sort of social subgroup of people on to which blame is placed when the hard times appear.

Distracting times in liquid modernity

In the wake of all this, permanent jobs and secure family life have liquidised, now replaced by a world of temporary contracts, part-time work and unemployment. Perhaps as a reflection of rampant individualism championed by the Thatcher and Reagan years, today's generation, while resenting the insecurity of the world, want to 'be their own bosses'. Yet these preferences are generally unavailable to many people because they often enter jobs with little employability, receive low wages and fewer benefits (Standing, 2011). Entering at the bottom of the ladder into something temporary or part time limits upward social mobility because permanent job opportunities are disappearing. In addition, work in these service sectors is generally neither productive nor enjoyable; it is 'careerless'. As a consequence, many people in this bracket lack work-based identities, and this generates actions and attitudes towards 'opportunism' and 'seizing the moment' because there is no certainty of future work or a career to guide their commitment; it accelerates an attitude to spend without thinking, to impulsively buy things.

It is into this void of work-based identity that the role of 'play', leisure and consumer culture steps as a means of self-realisation. Traditional 'leisure careers', which would normally run parallel to stabilised labour forms, now look increasingly redundant, and instead, virtual lives, shopping and participation in the night-time economy are the primary means for status generation (Hall and Winlow, 2005). The development of this consumer culture takes capitalism into a new, more sophisticated stage of domination over the masses. Under it, control is accomplished through the 'free' choices made by consumers in leisure and consumption activity (Smith, 2012). These 'choices' are directed by the culture industry to achieve conformity, docility and the reproduction of capitalist hegemony. Increasingly individualised and detached from the fault lines of community, tradition and heritage (Bauman, 2007), people are increasingly vulnerable to commercial persuasion – manufactured as 'desirers', as we have argued – and led to obsess over what is made to be available in this consumer utopia (Briggs, 2016). Those who don't fall into the conventional boundaries of public space or follow such social aspirations appear insignificant and distant from their lifeworlds – much like this subgroup of people, like the homeless person in Paris or the iPhone factory worker in China, their 'otherness needs to be kept at a distance' (Winlow and Hall, 2013, p 136). And this is very much evident in the consumer-oriented centre of Madrid, where fortunate citizens spend money, swan around drinking and celebrating the good life, even if signs of potential malaise are juxtaposed against expensive brand shops, quirky bars and fine-dining restaurants:

> As dinner concludes and our conversations finally pass discussing where we will next go in the centre of Madrid, we then leave into the cold night to look for another bar for a cocktail. It is about 12.30am. We walk only a few metres on Calle de las Huertas from dinner, into a popular bar where finely-dressed people seem to be having deep conversations over cocktails and wine. Daniel orders a sparkling mineral water and passes some time with a few colleagues, soon feeling like he would prefer to be taking a walk somewhere.

> Outside it is that little bit colder as the time approaches 2.40am and the cobbled streets are awkward for the drunken fortunates. Between the fine bars and laughs in the streets, foreign men who seem mostly of Indian descent, stand around at 50m intervals with cardboard boxes propped up by a bag of beer cans. They call out at us or anyone wanting *"one for the road"* ... literally. As we walk, there are even the limp approaches from bar PR workers – who seem to be central or south American – who ask if we are interested in a few *copas* (drinks) in their half-empty bars. They look so tired of standing around and even more tired of their line which starts, *"Hola chicos, ven aquí para tomar algo"* ("Hi guys, come and have something to drink here"), that the level of enthusiasm they transmit easily kills off our remote interest. It's difficult not to assume that they probably have several of these

sorts of jobs in the night-time economy that pay them cash and barely cover their living standards.

On we ponder, old flats in their grandeur, more bars, some fancy restaurants until we get to Plaza de Jacinto Benevente – near the very epicentre of touristic Madrid, Sol. A strong smell of cannabis fills the air as we see takeaways, rubbish and more drunken groups laughing off their evenings of money-spending and alcohol consumption. Life is good.

In Sol, giant trucks clean up the rubbish from the square and the police saunter around while the odd tourist mixes with groups of young drunks. We stop and look around at the flashing lights and brand stores which make up the scenery and start to walk up Calle Montera, one of the prostitute hotpots in the touristic centre. Passing the police station which has its doors firmly closed, we pass numerous prostitutes in the shadows of the branded stores, most of whom are from Eastern Europe and who are working here because of the limited opportunities in their own countries. As we walk up, they increase in their numbers and some even stand in a small group of about 10 in the middle of the pedestrian way. Others from Africa sit crouched near locked toilets eating sandwiches, while a few stand on corners walking up and down in high heels.

As we walk on to Gran Via – the principal site for all the global branded shops and theatres – we are met by more invitations to have drinks from tired PR workers, and start to be given leaflets for strip clubs by even more tired and unmotivated PR workers who have gone beyond speaking and are simply approaching people on a kind of obliged automatic pilot. As we walk down, the traffic whizzes up and down past large electronic banners advertising expensive handbags and top brand make-up. The odd homeless person starts to appear in the large chain stores, where they sprawl out with all their belongings in plastic-bag piles, yet all the while the fortunate people walk on without acknowledging them. In the theatre which shows 'Lion King, The Musical' there is now a high black fence which separates the street from the doors, put in place in the main to stop people sleeping there. We look to the right and not five metres away an old man tinkers around some empty rubbish and cardboard boxes and starts to lay them out on the curb. We continue to walk down past fast food shops including VIPS; at 2.40am, a man in a suit sits drunkenly watching the football as he sips a beer.

As we approach the Plaza de España, the atmosphere changes and the light quality dims in the absence of street lights; the smell of piss, shit and rubbish drifts around as we see the odd homeless person wandering around like a zombie. Under the bridge of Calle de Bailen, more homeless people lie around, cocooned from cold as the loud noise from the cars and taxis echoes against the walls. The streets are thereafter quiet back to Plaza Mayor, and we return to the car. As Daniel drops a colleague off at Moncloa, he notices an old man talking to himself under a statue. The man has in his hand a bottle of wine and a plastic cup and is dressed in rags. He shouts and gesticulates and retreats as the light turns green and Daniel drives past, turning on the radio to a chorus from Imany [a French music artist].

It is these consumer city spaces that keep us readily distracted from our own downfall; real and pressing social problems seem far away because they do not affect us directly. Our time is instead built around the splendour of shopping malls, fancy bars and restaurants and pristine town and city centres or 'non-spaces' (Augé, 2008), places that lack substance, that lack a reflection of the brutal realities of other people's lives. Our spaces are strategically designed to distance us from others. People therefore become unable to connect to the reality of the world's problems or even the potential threats that exist. We are, as Sloterdijk (2011) indicates, increasingly operating in microspheres of subjective space, utilising a form of social distance from the world, plugged into iPods all day long, lost in WhatsApp messaging on iPhones, and persistently updating Facebook statuses on iPads.

Urban outcast in context

The subjects Sloterdijk describes are found in most Western city spaces. These are, we could say, generally educated individuals who participate in the labour market, engage in consumption practices, and are likely to be the 'winners' of globalisation. High-rise condominiums and business centres, 'retail experiences' centred on malls and shopping precincts, gated housing and securitisation also mark the urban landscape in the modern Western city. And the people who live there often seek what Birtchnell and Caletrio (2013) describe as a kind of 'oysterisation' of the world around them that offers security, free-flowing access and closure, whenever these qualities are desired. This 'capsularisation' of social life (de Cauter, 2005) also evokes secure zones, private transport systems and protected leisure destinations, and function to produce privacy and safety as well as prestige. This group of people have access to their own personal transport, have access to the city at the time they want, visit plush malls with manned security guards, live in gated communities and attend well-staffed private leisure and consumption spaces that symbolically or physically block access to potential 'outsiders' (Atkinson and Flint, 2004). This essentially mediates their own experience of the city, making it risk-free and detached from the wider fabric and its services. This facilitates and regulates their relative invisibility and safety, suggests Atkinson (2015, p 1303), as well as:

> The political signal offered from work on cosmopolitanism is that we should encourage

tolerant and open spaces where diverse social encounters can occur, yet the reality remains that contact, respect and citizenship are being recast in many urban contexts where segregation, ethnic and other forms of differentiation and wealth/income inequalities potentially erode any gains that pro-social urban designs and spaces encourage. While the possibilities of exchange and empathy in public space thus remain appealing, they also raise worrisome implications that involve swallowing-back resentments and conflicts indicated by gross urban inequalities and the subjugation of certain urban social groups.

Such gentrification and financification of city public space, then, may create the conditions under which inequality and grievance are either concealed or softened by the apparently democratic nature of urban public life. For example, the typical response of middle and upper classes to threats to security is to seek sanction in these spaces, essentially insulating themselves from the 'threat'. However, populations further down the class scale, that lack the resources and cannot negotiate safety through consumption, have a more enduring experience with violence, and this has a profound effect on how their lives are lived (Hume and Wilding, 2015).

We can also witness in a range of European cities that have experienced much immigration from so-called non-Western countries that ample attention has been given to the (spatial) segregation of migrant and non-migrant population categories, in some contexts referred to as 'ethnic' segregation (often with the idea to distinguish between different places of origin; see Boterman and Musterd, 2016). In the context of vagrant populations – such as homeless people, street drinkers and drug addicts – Mitchell (2016) argues that state aggression on the vulnerable in city spaces is about a general theory of capital circulation, the shifting fortunes of class struggle, and the changing role of the city *within* global capitalism. Mitchell suggests that rather than being a question of 'housing someone' or even 'a housing question', it is more about the continued displacement of the poor and how it is related to how capital proceeds and material processes accumulate in a built urban environment that reproduces city space as 'abstract space' – something that he identified 20 years ago:

> Politicians and managers of the new economy in the late 1980s and early 1990s have turned to what could be called 'the annihilation of space by law.' That is, they have turned to a legal remedy that seeks to cleanse the streets of those left behind by globalization and other secular changes in the economy by simply erasing the spaces in which they must live – by creating a legal fiction in which the rights of the wealthy, of the successful in the global economy, are sufficient for all the rest. (Mitchell, 1997, p 305)

Capital produces misery, and the endless search for capital and profit produces an extension of that suffering. This means that competitive pressures to increase the rate of return means that capital must seek out new sectors for investment. In the context of the city, this means devaluing certain places – perhaps even allowing urban crime to flourish in a certain area – only for it to be repurchased at a low cost for the purpose of more capital generation, even if it fails (see Chapter 10 ... but not yet!). And it is precisely these neoliberal socio-spatial manifestations of gentrification combined with urban and institutional ghettoisation that creates elite cities (Davidson and Ward, 2014). This is amplified by the politics of austerity, as fiscal pain associated with state retrenchment is passed on to its citizens.

So, taken together, the financial crisis, austerity policies and neoliberalisation have eroded strong welfare states that used to buffer social inequality (Boterman and Musterd, 2016) and replaced it with a spatial inequality that is ghettoised and concentrated (Wacquant, 2008, 2009; Peck, 2012). For example, Rae (2011) shows how gentrification in London has produced a dispersal or outward movement of the capital's poorer residents, concentrating poverty into particular suburban areas as urban marginalisation becomes intersected by class, gender, inter-generational and racial inequality (Bourgois, 1995; Davis, 2006; Bourgois and Schonberg, 2009; Butcher, 2016; Mitchell, 2016).

The deep industrial decline of cities coupled with austerity has also meant that social institutions have had to find ways to financially survive cutbacks, and have therefore changed their operational philosophies to ones that revolve around 'filtering' out the most deserving, risk-free, seeking to invest in those who will take advantage of what is on offer (Callinicos, 2012). Therefore the replication and circulation of modes of urban planning results in a discourse that renders urban neighbourhoods and their residents as 'deserving' and 'undeserving', based on their uptake of the 'opportunities' available to them. Governments are happy to develop policies to support people to attain higher levels of education, and provide equal access to education and health because social-cultural practices in the field of consumption, education and housing are associated with individual choice, are traditionally understood to be private choices, and lie outside the realm of government. However, by comparison, given these emerging spatial dimensions and concentration of deprivation, the resources in the hyperghettos lack investment for the very same reason – education and schooling, health services, law enforcement are increasingly sparse, and this directly impacts on the chances these groups have of 'working themselves out of their disadvantage' because neoliberalism underscores mantras of individual choice and individual responsibility.

Failure to comply with these expectations means that government intervention in these domains is even less likely (Boterman and Musterd, 2016). Which is why to be born in a particular urban space such as a hyperghetto is to potentially suffer irreversible lifelong defeat, and instead, to be susceptible to a truncation of opportunity, of education, of access to power, of life expectancy (Lanchester, 2016). This city precariousness is amplified by the reshaping of other processes such as public service reform, which results in many residents in these areas developing new, and sometimes antagonistic, relationships with state services (Rae, 2011), while third sector organisations pick up the pieces and act as a basic safety net for some (Briggs, 2012a). 'Enhanced precarity' of urban life ensues as employment, pensions and healthcare relations become more fragile, and this fractures collective relations and individualises urban life (Davidson and Ward, 2014) into a form of tribal politics (Mitchell, 2016).

The social and structural consequences of these processes are felt most in working-class communities, and derive from a combination of (a) mass unemployment (resulting in family hardship, temporal uncertainty, material deprivation and personal anxiety); (b) relegation to decaying neighbourhoods (in which private and public resources diminish and a competitive intensification takes place for scarce public services); and (c) heightened stigmatisation in daily life, which transcends ethnic and class contours as well as decaying, high-crime neighbourhoods (Wacquant, 2008). And even if the same groups such as homeless drug users regress to the city and are seen to threaten the visual fabric of the newly cleansed spaces of the city centre, ambiguous policies of 'anti-social behaviour' are used against them (Briggs, 2012a). Even in resistance movements in the form of social protest or cityscape squatting made in an effort for the poor to reclaim their former spaces, class power is easily restored by law enforcement agencies (Hall, 2012; Mitchell, 2016), as urban landscapes maintain their campaigns of attractive, modern and neat places (Butcher, 2016).

The political economy of social suffering

The political economy analysis has experienced resurgence since the 1970s, especially since Western cities have become state-led targets as sites for the development of entrepreneurial and competitive practices. It is characterised by an expansion of governance mechanisms through a variety of public–private partnerships, infrastructure development as well as urban, social and cultural policies, and zero-tolerance policing. As we note, this is often at the political, economic and social disregard of certain populations (Bauman, 2003; Wacquant, 2002) such as drug users (Bourgois, 2003). At the hub of this political and social abandonment are increased punitive attitudes and policies to crime, which is linked to political and moralistic motives to invoke fear and the perceived potential threat 'problematic populations' pose to middle-class values and dominant political ideologies (Briggs, 2012a), the protagonists appearing less as victims of a 'structural recalibration of social life' and more as 'disordered and disorderly individuals' (Mitchell, 2016).

The urban violence that then evolves in these urban periphery areas is consequently generated as such, disproportionately impacting the most disadvantaged populations (Auyero and Kilanski, 2015), manifested in high-crime rates and destructive levels of drug use, to the point where addicts are even further marginalised and may pursue drugs with a self-destructive intensity akin to devotion, as if 'they had nothing left to lose' (Mars et al, 2015). On a daily level, victims perpetuate interpersonal violence, usually against their friends and loved ones, as well as against themselves (Bourgois and Schonberg, 2009).

This form of structural violence is not only experienced individually, but also collectively as common forms of 'lived oppression' or 'social suffering' (Bourgois et al, 1997). Social suffering is said to be the result of the devastating injuries that social forces inflict on the human experience. It is this 'traumatic stress disorder' that is produced by the combined effects of being subject over time to intense social oppression such as racial hatred, sexism, class discrimination or homophobia, which is subsequently individually internalised into depression, stigma, self-hatred and a sense of powerlessness (Briggs, 2012a). These experiences are further amplified against perceptions of 'social failure' in cultures of personal achievement (Agar, 2003; Bauman, 2007; Young, 2007). Consequently, Singer (2001, p 205) posits that both:

> Social suffering and the hidden injuries of oppression are emotionally damaging and pressure the sufferers to seek relief. Drug use, in an action-oriented culture that forcefully emphasizes (through the media and elsewhere) instant gratification, pain intolerance, and chemical intervention, is a commonly selected solution.

This results in a fear of inadequacy or failure that can 'haunt' people for life (Bauman, 2007, p 58). Thus:

> Whereas illness, addiction, unemployment and other deviations from the norm used to count as blows of fate, the emphasis today is on individual blame and responsibility. [Consequently] your own life – your own failure. Social crisis phenomena such as structural unemployment can

be shifted as a burden of risk onto the shoulders of individuals. (Beck and Beck-Gernsheim, 2002, p 22)

For example, some argue that the 'responsibilisation of health' 'represents the extension of techniques of social regulation to an unprecedented extent' (Petersen, 1997, p 696), which brings back into the discussion risk determinants frequently obscured by an ideology of individual responsibility (Mars et al, 2015). That is, in a society that expects its citizens to take care of their health, those who do not do everything they can for their health become 'irresponsible citizens' (Rimke, 2000). Such citizens might be accused of being in breach of a 'social contract of health' and, individually, they may experience this breach as a form of personal or 'moral failure'. The social expectancy of groups like drug users, therefore, is that they should 'rise up', 'against all odds', and this is embedded in societal moral standards. Therefore drug users are responsible for their harms and the harm to others (O'Malley, 2008), and much of this rhetoric is embedded in drug treatment and harm reduction philosophies (see Chapter 7) that preach ideologies of personal responsibility.

These forms of social fracturing stemming from the retraction of state investment, budget cuts to state services and political disenfranchisement change citizen relations in marginal areas (Mars et al, 2014). Consequently, this uncharacteristically changes subjectivity, and perversely transforms the very ways in which marginalised individuals – such as Mario at the beginning of the chapter, with his 'map of society' – come to view and feel about their very own exploitation (see Butcher, 2016), therefore negatively marking social relationships with each other (Zubillaga et al, 2015). This sets in motion a pervasive set of reforms that alter subjectivity, creating new and deeper social divisions and, often at times, are seen to have been carried out in the service of the most marginal (see also Wacquant, 2009). This is then further exacerbated by state inaction in these zones, which contributes to a 'permanent state of animosity and competition between people in precarious living conditions who are struggling for a basic right' (Zubillaga et al, 2015, p 183), which often fosters violence in such communities.

3

Madrid: History, social processes and the growth in inequality

The evolution of Valdemingómez should not just simply be seen as some organic process whereby working-class and immigrant people have somehow ended up congregating there in search of economic security and work in the city, but as a consequence of macro processes of economic growth and technological advancement as rural domestic economies submitted to urban industrialisation in Spain. Equally, its configuration as a ghetto, compounded by drug markets, should not be viewed as a consequence of some kind of poverty saturation, but of spatial and structural processes that have rendered people in the urban metropolis increasingly socially redundant, resulting in their destitution and political disaffection. Here, in this chapter, we look at these processes, charting the evolution of the Cañada Real Galiana, and how economic change in Spain, which led to the growth of the

Photo 6: Rubbish, *chabolas* and the *plaza*

suburbs, collided with the economic crisis, increasing zonal inequalities in the capital and expanding drug markets.

Historical evolution of the Cañada Real Galiana

Dating back to the 13th century, the Cañada Real Galiana was a route for goods being transported from the north of the Spanish peninsula to its centre, connecting four autonomous communities (La Rioja, Castilla and León, Comunidad de Madrid and Castilla la Mancha). Known as a 'cattle path', these *cañadas* became increasingly significant during the Middle Ages to transport livestock; their function was to permit farmers and shepherds to move their cattle across the land to take advantage of the best climate for the time of year. Indeed, such was their domestic economic significance for agriculture and farming industries, that this was reflected by laws set out by the Spanish crown to protect them. As a consequence, there was high competition and rivalry between the shepherds and farmers that caused much conflict, as lawful protection from the crown brought significant earnings and profit (ACCEM and Fundación Secretariado Gitano, 2010).

This continued up until its peak during the 19th century, at which point over 5 million cattle owners were using the *cañadas* each spring and autumn to transport livestock. Although the agricultural industry gathered increasing economic importance during the 19th century, by the second part of the 20th century, they had practically been abandoned because of advances in technology, and transport had led to the construction of rail networks and roads. As their use dwindled, large sections of the *cañadas* across the country fell into disuse. This included the area where we undertook our research, which remained largely deserted until about the 1950s, before it began to attract rural migrants looking for economical housing near the capital to be able to look for work in Madrid or its expanding outskirts (ACCEM and

Fundación Secretariado Gitano, 2010). The very processes that had given way to a shift in the rural domestic economy essentially uprooted thousands of people in search of work in the city.

These early residents of the Cañada Real Galiana took advantage of free amenities such as water, electricity and gas, and the earliest settlement was populated closest to Coslada (where the present Sectors 1 and 2 sit), a town which had also grown exponentially in the wake of the growth of industry around it. These early residents, who were mostly rural Spanish families, illegally constructed improvised housing on the *cañada*.[1] From the 1950s to the mid-1970s, the population grew and the sectors extended. New ethnic groups such as Spanish *gitanos* started to occupy the sectors along with other working-class Spanish families in Sector 3, and as Sector 4 expanded, Moroccans and Romanians, along with increasing numbers of Spanish families,[2] which represented an early form of gentrification in the city, contributed to the formation of new communities, all taking advantage of the financial benefits and close proximity to the capital (ACCEM and Fundación Secretariado Gitano, 2010; Ministerio de Formento, 2010). Indeed, the spatial juxtaposition coupled with the fertility of the land made it beneficial to have property or land there, and these new residents in Sectors 3 and 4 also came in the hope that they, too, would be given land like others had been in Sectors 1 and 2[3] (Mbomío Rubio, 2012).

This growth gradually continued with the formation of Sector 5 and a partial Sector 6, or Valdemingómez, until the mid-to-late 1990s, when Madrid started to instigate large-scale changes to the urban landscape. During this period, similar groups to those that had occupied Sector 4 moved in – Moroccans and Romanians, along with a scattering of Sub-Saharan Africans and a sprinkling of Eastern Europeans, although *gitanos* remained the dominant population (Soleares,

2011). However, a series of aggressive social policy efforts initiated by the Operación Barrios en Remodelación (Operation Remodelation of Neighbourhoods) marked the spatial displacement of the city's main *poblados* where already socially excluded *gitano* families engaged in drug sales were pushed to the outskirts.[4] Although the Operación was designed to relocate *gitano* families, many didn't qualify for support or were sidelined from housing opportunities (Lago Ávila, 2014). As noted in other research on the spatial exclusion and attempted forced inclusion of *gitanos* (see Briggs, 2010), the *Plan Nacional de Erradicar del Chabolismo* (*National Plan to Erradicate Chabolismo*) had the reverse effect since, from its inception in 1991 up until 1995, major failings resulted in almost no social support for relocated *gitano* families and, as a consequence, many simply congregated in other *poblados* in Madrid. One of the main problems of this strategy was that it did not anticipate the potential resistance from the *gitano* communities, which made each family relocation complicated, expensive and drawn out; for example, it cost the authorities more than €110 million to relocate 499 families from three *poblado* districts during the mid-to-late 1990s (Lago Ávila, 2014). As the years passed, the respective institutions lost motivation to fund the initiative. The more this was neglected, the more these very *poblados* developed crime problems such as those we describe in this book related to drug use and drug markets. As these administrational problems and lack of strategic intervention continued, eventually, in 1998, the whole Operación disbanded (Lago Ávila, 2014).

All this was taking place as a consequence of massive growth in the city that the authorities had to balance: mainly because, at the end of the 1980s and through to the mid-1990s, these spaces that the *gitanos* occupied were considered to be necessary to the government to allow for the city to grow and expand. However, at the same rate at which the city had expanded, coupled with the authorities' slow progress with relocating the improvised housing known as *chabolas*, this only made for the continuing appearance of more *chabolas*. When the Instituto de Realojamiento e Inserción (IRIS) (Relocation and Insertion Institute) was established in 1998, to continue the battle against the improvised housing that most *gitanos* used, or *chabolismo*, it was never given sufficient direction or funding to make any difference, even in 1999, when a new federation was established to assist with this process and more promises were made by the respective municipal mayors to avoid the creation of ghettos and the growth of *chabolas* (Lago Ávila, 2014).

Table 1: Evolution and devolution of some of the main *poblados* in Madrid

District	*Poblado* name	Year occupied	Year of dismantling	No of years occupied
Fuencarral	La Quinta	1992	2006	14
	Las Liebres	1989	2003	14
Latina	Juaja	1991	1999	8
	Las Miembreras	1995	2009	14
Puente de Vallecas	La Celsa	1992	2000	8
Usera	San Fermín	1990	1998	8
Vicalvaro	El Cañaveral	1986	2006	20
Villa de Vallecas	La Rosilla	1992	2000	8
Villaverde	Plata y Castañar	1986	2006	20

Yet year after year, the *chabolas* were dismantled. From 1999 to 2010, IRIS assisted in the relocation of 1,700 *gitano* families and the dismantling of 60 *chabolismo* zones (Lago Ávila, 2014). Perhaps regarded as some sort of success, this resulted instead in the increased inhabitation towards the end of the 1990s of the sector most recently formed and least developed of the Cañada Real Galiana at Valdemingómez, and this is one of the main reasons why it became one of the main bastions from where drug sales took place. Dozens of houses, flats, caravans and warehouses were bought, occupied and, in some cases, forcibly taken by these *gitano* families who had been moved from *poblado* to *poblado* in Madrid: their motivation for occupying Valdemingómez mainly involved making it the base for new drug-dealing networks. So the closure of these old *poblados* was significant because they assisted in their spatial mutation in other areas of the city.

As *gitano* families installed themselves in Valdemingómez, it took little time to attract the thousands of drug addicts and consumers who had become reliant on other *poblados* for drug purchases. Not only did this then converge the drug market on the outskirts of Madrid, but it also concentrated the marginality associated with it such as the relocation of thousands of people with a range of health, drug and practical problems and other unemployed groups already living in precarious circumstances, of which the majority were working-class Spanish or immigrants. This led to the exponential growth of Valdemingómez, making it the main drug market in Madrid. With ideal connections to the M50 (which practically circumnavigates the capital) and the A3 (linking Madrid to the coastal city of Valencia), the new settlement in Valdemingómez could be accessed easily by customers and *cundas* alike, from almost any point in the capital. It was also advantageous in that it was on the periphery of Madrid, far from major urban residential settlements, and even further from the political focal point of the city centre.

Indeed, Valdemingómez's rapid evolution in the late 1990s was also testament to the historical tolerance by law enforcement agencies – although for centuries, it had been illegal to construct buildings and properties on the *cañadas* as national and local government attention had been minimal.

There the *gitano* clans set up their businesses without any police intervention, at almost no cost, paid no taxes, and were even able to hijack electricity and water from public mains sources. The construction of dozens of makeshift buildings dedicated to the sale and consumption of drugs at the turn of the 21st century made its transformation irreversible. Indeed, the period from 2002 to 2010 became known as the 'golden era' of Valdemingómez as it was calculated that there were about 80 different drug sales points operating at the same time.[5] Over this period, there was also a mass exodus from the area, with many *gitano* and Spanish families leaving the sector because of its social and physical deterioration.

During this very same period at the turn of the century, the *Gallinero* (henhouse) was formed on the other side of the M50 motorway. Although founded by Spanish *gitanos* in the early 1990s, Romanian *gitano* families took over the land in 2002, and it was named thus because of the proximity of the ruins of an old bird farm. Like areas of the Cañada Real Galiana, those living in the Gallinero have had to fight for basic state assistance yet it is still bereft of adequate healthcare, housing and educational intervention. Families do not live there through choice, as almost all have been excluded by the increasing gentrification of city spaces, finding it impossible to survive, and even failing to get help from homeless hostels (Gómez Ciriano, 2011). To this day, around 500 people live there, half of whom are minors living in extremely vulnerable situations, exposed to the high risk of getting involved in criminal activities such as robbery and theft (Gutíerrez Sánchez, 2015). Social exclusion is high, and some of the constructions are in worse condition than in Valdemingómez; the winter rain often destroys the community's improvised buildings, and there is only one water supply to the area and no sewage or water system (ACCEM and Fundación Secretariado Gitano, 2010).

How was it, then, that the Cañada Real Galiana was occupied, given that laws set out in the 1950s – made as a consequence of the *cañadas* becoming redundant – protected them from 'threat' and 'deterioration'? It wasn't until national legislation was made in 1995[6] which declared that the autonomous (local) communities (in this case, the local council of Madrid) could protect their 'integrity and conservation' by allowing them for public use such as cycling, horse riding or hiking. By 1998, the local council in Madrid had finally managed to apply this law, essentially making the terrain protected while at the same time prohibiting the construction of buildings. Naturally, by the time the law was applied, it was too late to deter already-established drug and crime networks that had started to further problematise the application of the law. Deteriorating physical and social conditions and an absence of adequate social support systems had already complicated other formal responses because it involved the collaboration of the regional council of Madrid and the local councils of Coslada and Rivas. This was extremely challenging as it took six years for each of the councils to agree to convene to start the process of designing an intervention for each of the families in Valdemingómez. During this time it was agreed that the respective government institutions share the cost and responsibility for intervention (ACCEM and Fundación Secretariado Gitano, 2010) before the initiative ground to a halt because of a 'conflict of interests' between the different administrations (Gómez Ciriano, 2011), and because of disputed urban commercial and economic interest in the land (Soleares, 2011; see Chapter 7 for a more in-depth discussion).

Currently, 3,500 people live in Valdemingómez, which is only 4km in length, and spread over around 50 hectares. Its position as a sort of no man's land between Madrid, Coslada and Rivas generates numerous problems related to:

- substandard housing or even people living in derelict sites;
- scarcity of basic amenities such as water, electricity, public transport and rubbish collections;
- almost no infrastructure such as asphalt roads, pavements or public space;
- the absence of basic social services such as schools, health institutions, hospitals, cultural centres or sports facilities;
- problematic access to basic public services;
- significant levels of drug dealing and drug use and related issues;
- high levels of crime, violence and low levels of reporting.

In 2007, the police and other law enforcement agencies began a campaign of monitoring and control of Vademingómez, with the aim of eradicating the sale of drugs from the sector. The units, composing of the National Police, Local Police and the Civil Guard, attempted a series of coordinated raids and intervention procedures that centred on tackling the *gitano* families' grip on the drug market, organised robbery, scrapping of vehicles and general illegal dumping and the robbery of copper. However, there was little attention to the repercussions of a raid and the subsequent demolition of a building, with almost no attention given to the human rights of the people inside or immediate alternative housing solutions. This therefore only increased the risks to those made homeless as well as amplifying the dangerous and neglected accumulation of rubbish and dire sanitary conditions. Much of this was continually broadcast by the media and the subsequent attention triggered high levels of social stigma and rejection: many of the other families living in the other sectors have faced discrimination, been blacklisted from possible work opportunities, and struggle to register their children in nearby schools precisely because they 'come from the Cañada Real Galiana'. The tendency for people living in this area, predominantly *gitanos*, is to have low educational levels, difficulty with interpreting and understanding formalised state processes, and lack of knowledge about their human rights (Soleares, 2011).

The constant presence of these agencies combined with the seemingly endless raids conducted over the last decade cannot be correlated with any reduction in crime, only that numerous arrests were made. Between 2012 and 2014, while the collaboration of the law enforcement authorities led to 1,927 arrests and the knocking down of 108 *kiosks* and *fumaderos*, and it is estimated that in the last seven years, drug dealing has been reduced by more than 50% (Barroso, 2014), as we will point out in this book, the detention and/ or displacement of these families has only resulted in their collaboration with other families in the area or operating out of other areas of Madrid – in particular, the *barrios* where drugs were initially sold during the drugs boom of the 1980s (see Chapter 10). Yet nowadays, of the six sectors, Valdemingómez is the most extensive of the Cañada Real Galiana, largely because of the persistent flow of people who come and go to buy and use drugs.

Economic change in Spain

The assembly of the Cañada Real Galiana must therefore be seen as a historical process in which various elements of social change interweave with each other. In this case, we examine the reasons why so many rural workers and immigrants established these communities, and for that, we need to delve further back into history and consider how Spain has been prized open by industrialisation and, consequently, capitalistic forces over the last 40 years.

Early signs of industrialisation

Spain's rapid introduction to industrialisation was hampered by the advent of General Franco's ascension in 1936, which saw the country ruled as a totalitarian state, where only one party was legal, and for some years the Monarchy were not permitted to rule. The Civil War that thereafter followed until 1939 crushed economic infrastructure and strangled business, as many workers were killed. During Franco's early rule, the country was also locked out of international development, had rigid emigration restrictions and promoted an aggressive form of nationalism, essentially repressing cultural diversity and social and economic growth. Instrumental forms of propaganda were introduced in many social institutions, for example, language politics was used to repress local dialects in schools, and the Catholic Church was the central institution used to ensure religion dominated cultural life.

By the end of the Second World War, Spain was starting to suffer from the economic consequences of political isolation. However, Cold War tensions in the 1950s opened up political relations with the US. The subsequent *Plan de Estabilización (Stabilisation Plan)*, published in 1959, enabled US companies to extract petroleum as well as make investments (Burbano Trimiño, 2013). This was then followed by the *Primer Plan de Desarrollo (First Development Plan)*, which went about identifying new investment opportunities along with new industrial districts in Spanish cities, and this was to mark Spain's gradual exposure to mass industry. The main economic drive began through tourism that required imports, engineering and machinery, and this led to the expansion of infrastructure and industry. When both Seat (the car company) and Empresa Nacional Bazán (a shipbuilding firm) began operations,[7] old industrial areas were reinvigorated, and this led to the development of the service sector, thereafter enabling economic prosperity (Gonzalez, 2008).

At first, the intention was to expand the urban areas that lacked development, such as Valencia, Vigo, Sevilla, Zaragoza, Cádiz, Ferrol and Pamplona, with an emphasis on continuing to invest in already industrial areas in Barcelona and Madrid. The rapid growth of opportunity and work in these areas – known as the *Milagro Economico Español* (*Spanish Economic Miracle*) – produced throughout the 1960s and into the early 1970s a massive exodus of rural populations. Between 1960 and 1985, 12 million people emigrated to the cities, which equates to 360,000 per year over 25 years (Burbano Trimiño, 2013). As technology modernised, rural businesses and in general local domestic economies became redundant and inefficient, and low in productivity because they used machinery and could not compete with diversifying their products in line with the new industrial equivalents in the cities. During this time, the Spanish economy was performing so well it was second only to Japan in the global economy, and this movement marked the development of advanced capitalism in Spain. This initiated major structural change in the economy, as people left the country for the city in search of better salaries and stable work. The city, according to Sánchez Jiménez (2001), was also idealised as an 'illusion', and advertised by new forms of media, which promoted it as 'an attractive form of life'.

Class stratification, economic growth and immigration

The evaporation of rural economies concentrated industry and population growth in Spanish cities. In the case of Madrid, the south of the city became largely where rural workers came to escape chronic unemployment caused as a consequence of the diminishing importance of domestic economies such as agriculture. However, in general, Madrid could not absorb such a population influx throughout the

1960s and 1970s, as the demand for forced labour beckoned hundreds of thousands to new urban neighbourhoods. For example, by the end of 1975, almost half of Madrid's population was made up of rural families who had emigrated from the country (Burbano Trimiño, 2013). Such a population influx, however, was not anticipated, for while living standards improved for a rapidly emerging middle class, a new class of industrial workers in Spanish cities was confined to another set of conditions. Such was the inflow of people that Spanish cities such as Barcelona and Madrid could not keep up with the frequency of new workers, and nor could the infrastructure, even though measures had been taken to accommodate the new workforce. The emergence of unplanned ghettos and slums evolved around the south of Madrid,[8] in and around the large, industrial estates.

However, it was not only rural populations that were attracted by the promise of work, for as a higher proportion of people emigrated from the country, other groups immigrated from Romania as well as Latin American countries such as Ecuador, Colombia and Bolivia, as Spain's political, social, cultural and economic modernisation accelerated. These people, equally affected by globalisation and corruption in their home countries, were seeking new labour opportunities. By the mid-1980s, Spain had become a member of the European Union (EU), and although wealth increased and the economy expanded, inequalities sharpened and stable jobs decreased. Agriculture diminished from 23% in 1975 to 9% in 2014 and construction from 39% to 23% in the same period, while the service sector increased from 52% to 74% as a consequence of the increased presence of global companies and corporations. This essentially created scores of unappealing, low-paid, temporary seasonal jobs in which middle- to upper-class Spanish citizens had little interest, considering the type of work inferior to their skillset. It was these opportunities that many working-class Spanish citizens and the new immigrants seized, finding in the main temporary and/or seasonal jobs in construction, the hotel trade, agriculture and in the domestic sphere. For example, by 2006, the share of temporary employment among Spanish workers was 30.2%, yet it was 60.6% among foreigners (Pérez Infante, 2009).

From 1998 to 2008, the national population rose by 10.4 million to 46.4 million, mostly as a result of an unprecedented influx of legal as well as illegal immigrants,[9] reflected in the 8 million jobs that were created between 1995 and 2007. In the same period, in Madrid, the number of immigrants rose exponentially, from 796,979 to 1,071,292. In 2007 alone, the construction industry had built 865,000 properties more than Germany, France and the UK combined, and this was made possible by continuous immigration (Elteto, 2011). However, the journey from economic isolation to European powerhouse was to practically disappear in 2008.

'La crisis'

The decade-long growth, known in Spanish as *vacas gordas* or 'fat cows', ended in 2008 with the collapse of sub-prime mortgages in the US, which had a knock-on snowball effect for the global community. In Spain, savings banks were burdened with unpaid mortgages from people who had lost their jobs, and some real estate agents went bust. Although almost tolerated in the past, significant corruption was exposed, and even though it continues to flourish, it was particularly highlighted in the interface between politicians and social institutions, essentially highlighting the failed diversification of the economy and significant reliance on industry and construction (Soleares, 2011). Wages dropped and/or were suspended, and jobs evaporated as quickly as they had come about – first in line were temporary contracts, to which were attached immigrants as well as other unaccounted people who worked in grey areas of the economy, and young working-class men in the construction sector, many of whom had left school at 16 with a basic education. Indeed, early school leavers peaked at 31% in 2009 – more than double the EU average – and thousands of unqualified young Spanish people who would have hoped to assume the jobs their parents did were suddenly without work (Izquierdo et al, 2015).

The unemployment rate jumped to 20% in the spring of 2010, leaving a mass of immigrants without jobs, and by the beginning of 2013, it had peaked at 26.9%, remaining high among the young (over 55%) and the immigrant population (almost 40%) (Izquierdo et al, 2015). At the same time, the tolerance Spanish people had towards immigrants waned, as 'foreigners' were politically ostracised as the cause of the economic malaise (Briggs and Dobre, 2014). Indeed, political factors were also very much at the root of Spain's crisis, particularly the degeneration of key institutions (the judiciary, regulatory bodies, the Court of Auditors, etc) that were colonised (along with the savings banks) mainly by the two largest political parties, the Popular Party (PP) and the Socialist Party (PSOE). In the process, these institutions were discredited and lost legitimacy, and the political classes were exposed as an extractive elite that was inherently corrupt and bent. Not that this has since changed anything and this situation remains today.

The at-the-time leftist socialist party in power, PSOE, that had previously dominated the political arena since the inception of 'democracy', struggled to deal with the fallout and instead enacted various labour and housing reforms that removed security from working-class families and increased their precariaty. Tens of billions of Euros were borrowed from Europe, and Spanish citizens were charged with the bill. Meanwhile, the bankers and insurance brokers escaped unscathed. In fact, the inequality gap has widened as Spain's super-rich have profited. Recent data from the Spanish Tax Agency Hacienda revealed that 508 people declared assets worth over €30 million in 2014, an 8% rise from the previous year (Sérvulo, 2016a). On the other hand, some 13 million people – a third of the population – are at risk of falling into poverty (Sérvulo, 2016b).

The mishandling of all this essentially catapulted the socialist party into a slow and torturous death spiral as a consequence of its instigation of impoverishment and despair that resulted from the party's servile deference to the Troika's commands. This deeply eroded trust in the political left due to its poor management of the economic downturn and the resulting adjustment measures it imposed on Spanish workers instead of tackling problematic corruption and high-risk banking procedures. Although protests and social unrest ensued, and new leftist parties such as Podemos (meaning 'We can') have since challenged the political establishments, many Spaniards turned their back on the politics of old, and many more simply walked away from the socialists after this latest capitulation (Winlow et al, 2015).

The consequences of this were devastating for residents of the Cañada Real Galiana since many had come to rely on temporary means of work, particularly in the domestic and construction industries. Indeed, the majority of people had, over the years – often because they could not afford a living space among increasingly prime urban spaces – found themselves severed from work and labour alternatives, sharpening their poverty and precarity (Soleares, 2011), and many more, as we shall see, have been made homeless since moving there. While Spanish officials claim that Spain is now very slowly edging out of this long recession, it has yet to recover to the pre-crisis level of economic output. Jobs are being created, albeit mainly precarious ones, partly thanks to the 2012 labour market reforms that made it easier for companies to fire employees and hire people with no-strings-attached contracts. Indeed, the use of short-term contracts has also increased dramatically since 2006. In August 2016, 80,000 short-term contracts were signed in Madrid, but research shows that 42% of those people in Madrid who had short-term contracts were working less than six days at a time (Luque, 2016). This highlights immense labour insecurity.

As we write these words in 2017, the unemployment rate is still more than 20% and hundreds of thousands are leaving the country every year. Coupled with Spain's notoriously low birth rate, this shift means that Spain is shedding residents at an alarming pace. However, not everyone has the resources to leave, and must survive by other means in the cities, much of this through illicit economies such as drug markets. The lack of social mobility coupled with the spatial concentration of poverty has only multiplied levels of inequality in already-decaying *barrios*.

Madrid, inequality and space

Valdemingómez is situated in one of the poorest areas of suburban Madrid, and its immediate surroundings – or the *barrios* such as Vicalvaro, Villa de Vallecas and Puente de Vallecas – are also similarly deprived (IECD, 2014). In these areas, indices of youth and general unemployment are high and life expectancy is somewhat lower by comparison with the wealthier centre and northern part of the capital (see Figure 1). So people living in and around Valdemingómez have a far more precarious existence. Thus, north of these areas in the city centre is where we find high numbers of professionals and fewer unemployed groups, while in the south is where there are higher levels of crime, unemployment and immigration (Clemente, 2015). While it is clear that there have been historical differences between the north and south, and in the periphery, the arrival of the construction boom followed by the labour market vacuum

Figure 1: Indices of geo-spatial inequality in Madrid

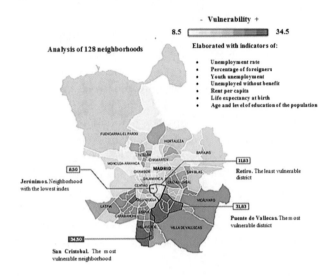

post 2008 only sharpened geo-spatial inequality (Rivas, 2014; Rojas, 2014). It is fairly safe to say that there exists an invisible dividing line between these two parts of Madrid that determine quite significantly a citizen's socioeconomic status, and as a consequence, the urban experience. This is reflected in the high levels of unemployment in the south of the capital (DE, 2016), with many *barrios* averaging unemployment levels around 30% compared to around 15% in their northern equivalents (Leal and Sorando, 2015).

The metropolitan area therefore reflects serious levels of inequality, and this situation of spatial polarisation and social segregation has been aggravated by the economic crisis of 2008 that essentially exacerbated the gap between the two social poles. This has been worsened further by the sale of 96% of the social housing stock – only 29,760 properties – constructed over the last decade by the Madrid government to private companies to make a profit while essentially at the same time blocking access to housing to thousands of people, despite, in the words of the Mayor, 'not to sell social housing to these types of people [business people]' (Martiarena, 2016). It seems that the social strata in Madrid is increasingly separated and remote, and this increases the social fracturing of the urban landscape; Madrid is now the European city with the highest levels of social segregation (Tammaru et al, 2015).

This social division and obvious spatial separation is further swollen by drastically high levels of corruption that continue to damage the Spanish economy and drain valuable resources from public services. Researchers estimate corruption to cost the Spanish economy €40,000 million each year, and it was recently estimated (2013) that there were still 1,700 open cases, while only 20 people had been sent to prison (León et al, 2013).[10] Corrupt institutions massively impact on a host of different sectors including public services, the education system, judicial powers, the police and armed forces (Villoria and Jiménez, 2012). The fact that these fraudulent irregularities are endemic to keeping the political elite in power has resulted in a 'politics of austerity', whereby citizens essentially absorb the debt generated by the banks and other financial institutions. To therefore prop up the economy, citizens pay more for public services, higher taxes, and so on, and for this reason, people in low-paid work struggle. They can't access social housing, have benefits cut, can't access mortgages and their rents increase, which puts pressure on maintaining housing payments, utility charges and costs for children, which has led to families being made homeless and having to stay with other family or friends or to illegally occupy houses/flats.

In the poorer areas of Madrid in particular this is felt more than anywhere else. From 1998 to 2008, a consolidated gentrification of the city has taken place, which has separated the city by financial resources and socioeconomic status: those with fewer assets have had no choice but to move to or stay in the southern areas of the capital, where property and standard of living is cheaper (Delgado, 2008; Leal and Sorando, 2015). At the turn of the 21st century, the Madrid government identified four *barrios* to be those most in need of investment, with an aim to reduce inequality between the north and south of the city over a 10-year period. The *barrios* identified were Tetuán, San Blas, Carabanchel and Vicálvaro (see Comunidad de Madrid, 2009). However, a report published by the Socialist Party in Madrid found that unoccupied properties rose from 49% in 2004 to 56% to 2013, and that, of the €1,117 million available to be invested in those areas, only 61% of the funds had been spent (Belber, 2014).

The creation of these quite separate spaces has been by led by strategic private investment and bolstered with other social policies that are associated with maintaining the rank and organisation of those very spaces; that is, once a *barrio* can peel off symbols of deprivation and destitution – for example, crappy housing, grubby public spaces, problem populations, etc – it can flourish economically and therefore attract further investment. Naturally, this creates other problems because it merely concentrates the poorer groups in other areas, rendering them more vulnerable. Moreover, this very experience is intensified by the disappearance of public policy for the most unprotected, and a political failure to make public institutions respond efficiently to the very process of spatial inequality to which they have generated, essentially multiplying the difficulties people experience in these areas. This is because the social policies are designed to support the accumulation of capital and economic growth of the city (see Chapter 2) rather than the needs of the collective urban population.

For the people in the economically advantaged areas, this poses few problems as public institutions function better and their sense of individual responsibility is in line with the neoliberal expectations of their personal responsibility. However, for families in the poorer areas south of the capital, it is the reverse: public services such as education, health and housing struggle under the weight and demand for their assistance while, at the same time, the personal resources to be responsible are somewhat dented by the experience of deprivation and social exclusion. In particular, there is a massive shortage of affordable social housing in the south of Madrid, so it is perhaps unsurprising to learn that this area of the city reflects the majority of the concentration of illegally occupied housing (see Chapter 10).

In this context of wealth accumulation, increase of poverty and political abandonment of swathes of the urban populace, Madrid is a clear example of the neoliberal city, characterised by the continual search for competitiveness and new forms of business and profit, which sadly shows the power the market has over a society (Requeña, 2014). However, the context of our study is exemplified by the spatial and political abandon of the southern hemisphere of the capital. This only allows for fertile ground for unemployment and crime, which is why places like Valdemingómez and Polígono Marconi in Villaverde (also among the most deprived *barrios* of Madrid) are abundant in organised crime, drugs and prostitution.

The motivation to reverse these trends continues to be piecemeal, and city policy-makers and politicians have taken few effective measures to reduce the growth of inequality let alone reduce its concentration in the peripheries of the city. The precarious situation of the domestic economy and the labour market in deficit tends to therefore aggravate this spatial separation. The centre and north of Madrid are areas for business investment given their touristic appeal, and represent international opportunities for capital investment, reflecting a cosmopolitan city, global and modern in orientation, even if it has clear problems of homelessness, drug dependence and socially vulnerable families. Perhaps it is no surprise to learn that the majority of people with serious drug addiction problems who live/stay in and around the south of the city end up as 'disposable populations' (Bourgois, 2015, p 315), where:

> Huge reservoirs of desperately poor urban and rural populations, [are] shunted into the geographic wastelands with no useful participation in the legal economy, [which] produce inelastic demands for heroin, cocaine, methamphetamine.

Notes

[1] It wasn't until 1988 that the local government finally agreed to allow the improvised constructions to be replaced by legal housing, and therefore the land was made legal to the owners of the properties – a legal battle led by the Residents' Association that took 14 years to resolve. Since then, many poor-quality structures have been rebuilt and replaced by stronger, more robust buildings (see Ministerio de Formento, 2010, pp 12-16).

[2] It is suggested that these families were either 'expelled from the city' or 'had significant wealth to be able to build country residences' (see ACCEM and Fundación Secretariado Gitano, 2010).

[3] Spanish families were able to legally acquire the land over a period of time.

[4] Interestingly, it is almost impossible to know which part of the Cañada Real Galiana falls under which government entity, since the six sectors were demarcated and separated by the Residents' Associations in each of the sectors. Over time, this has led to ambiguity in relation to institutional responsibility.

[5] This figure has been generated as a consequence of our data and interviews with the Local Police in Madrid.

[6] See *La Ley 3/1995, de 23 de marzo De Vías Pecuarias de la Comunidad de Madrid* and *La Ley 8/1998, de 15 de junio, De Vías Pecuarias de la Comunidad de Madrid*.

[7] Fundamentally, it was established for the purpose of constructing naval battle craft, as well as other types of engines.

[8] Similar to those of the French *banlieue*; see, for example, Wacquant (2008).

[9] Pérez Infante (2009) estimates this number to be around 650,000 in 2008.

[10] See also cases like Caso Gürtel, in which 187 people have been implicated for alleged political corruption (Otero, 2014), 77 of whom are from the Partido Popular (Conservative government), and Operación Púnica, which found 100 politicians to have created criminal networks that assisted in the deliberate allocation of €250 million in exchange for illegal commission (Campos, 2015).

4

Drugs, cultural change and drug markets

Photo 7: Raul finalising his heroin injection

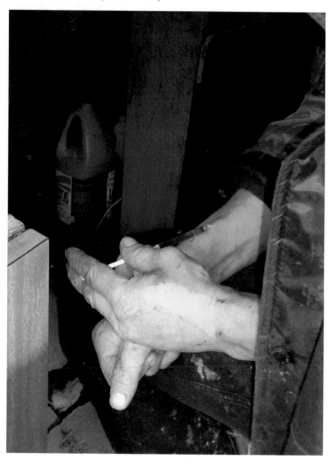

In his *chabola*, Raul moves around, picking at his scarred face; he takes a cigarette with blood stains on it out of his pocket, lights it up and furiously sucks what he can from it before realising that Daniel is not the man from the media which he accused him of the other day. He holds out his scabby blood-stained hands and clasps his, saying *"lo siento amigo"* ("I'm sorry friend"). Raul is 38 and estimates half of his life he has taken *"this shit"*, referring to heroin and cocaine, becoming homeless at the age of 22. He remembers *"all the poblados"*, having visited them one by one before they were closed when the *"police started to come down hard on drugs in the centre"*. He says he started taking drugs because *"everything accumulated"* when he couldn't find work and fell out with his family. When he became homeless it got worse until he said he *"ended up here* [Valdemingómez]*"*. The quality of the drugs has deteriorated, he reflects, as he prepares a heroin injection for his wrist or wherever he finds a vein. Though we crouch inside a hut, he currently has no home, no tent, no shelter and sleeps on thrown-away mattresses. He says it's difficult to get by in Valdemingómez as he often begs or does favours for money, but rarely enters into exchanges with people as it generates disagreements. As he makes the injection, he reflects *"normally I have a friend who injects me in the neck as my veins are getting worse"* before applying it slowly into a ready vein. He sits back and looks up, saying how he is *"on the waiting list"* for a rehabilitation centre; *"let's see if I get there and get clean of this shit and move on"*; he has already tried twice before and relapsed.

Introduction

In these field notes we can see why Raul finds himself in this situation: the collapse of family relationships as a consequence of his unemployment rendering him financially powerless and, in the wake of searching for new work, he found nothing. With the increasing prevalence of drug use as a means of escape, he became homeless, and his mental and physical state deteriorated. Thereafter he found himself swept up by wider structural processes that were concerned with ridding people like him from the streets of Madrid in the city centre. This is why certain areas of Madrid have become prime locations for real estate investment, hence the motivation to cleanse them of potential signs of poverty. So Raul's situation, and those of others in Valdemingómez, becomes about their spatial exclusion, which demands, says Loic Wacquant, a consideration that:

> ... internecine violence 'from below' must be analysed not as an expression of senseless 'pathology' of residents of the hyperghetto but as a function of the degree of penetration and mode of regulation of this territory of the State. It is a reasoned response to various kinds of violence 'from above' and an intelligible by-product of the policy of abandonment of the urban core. (Wacquant, 2008, p 54)

People like Raul have also spent significant time in prison; almost everyone we got to know had done time in one or more Spanish prisons over the last 30 years. This is not necessarily because they have committed some heinous crime that warranted their incarceration – although a few did commit very serious, violent crimes – but in the main was because the political preoccupation for their visibility and circumstances was directed at treating the symptoms of their behaviours rather than the causes, that is, it is easy to put someone in prison who fails to 'behave conventionally'. This, perhaps, does reduce their propensity to commit petty crime, but in the never-ending cycle of prison and homelessness, it makes them a kind of 'lumpenproletariat' (Bourgois and Schonberg, 2009) or disposable population with no real social use. In this chapter, we look at how people like Raul have become exposed to drugs, and why drugs might be something they return to in times of uncertainty.

Photo 8: Used drug paraphernalia strewn on the ground in Valdemingómez

Drug use and cultural change in Spain

Drug markets thrive where there is high demand, and Spain is characterised as one of the principal countries of drug consumption in Europe. The night-time economy, inherited directly from the commercialisation of countercultural movements as a consequence of the transition into a neoliberal democracy, emphasises the realisation of consumption experiences as a mode of being (see Chapter 2). Consequently, excesses related to supposed personal liberation and individual choices normalise the use of drugs and alcohol in nightlife venues such as clubs and bars. It should therefore be no surprise that things like drugs are very much integrated into Spanish culture, and their open access and toleration in the night-time economy means that the people we spent time with in Valdemingómez were open to trying them.

According to the Observatorio Español de la Droga y las Toxicomanías (OEDT) (2015), the drugs most consumed in Spain are cannabis, cocaine, ecstasy, hallucinogenic drugs, amphetamines and new designer drugs. The majority of these substances are initially consumed in bars and clubs and in social situations with friends; however, drugs such as cannabis are generally reserved for domestic environments, often only in the company of close friends, and so it is rare that consumers of such drugs would venture to Valdemingómez, where the main drugs available are heroin and cocaine.

The culture of stimulant drug consumption in the night-time economy derives in the main from the La Ruta del Bakalao or 'The Cod Route' (*Ruta* hereafter), which was a phenomenon that followed the Movida Madrileña (*Movida* hereafter), the artistic and social movement that signalled the end of *Franquismo*, and marked the beginning of a new period in the country's history. There was a feeling of 'freedom' coupled with rebellious attitudes after years of dictatorship. While the *Movida* was more of a middle- to upper-class cultural movement led by artists, photographers, musicians and cinematographers towards the latter stages of the 1970s and early 1980s, the *Ruta* was celebrated in the main by a middle- to lower-class bracket that also celebrated their supposed new liberty over long weekends and indulged in techno/dance music and the availability of numerous substances. The *Ruta* – made up of numerous bars and clubs – developed over a 30km stretch in El Saler in Valencia, where businesses permitted the use and sale of drugs, and minors were allowed to enter clubs. In those times, drug legislation was ambiguous and law enforcement attitudes were lax and negligent. This was the boom of dance and techno music, top DJs and the development of a clubbing culture, made famous by the *macrodiscotecas* or *superdiscos* in industrial estates and the phenomenon of *Botellón*[1] and *Parking*[2] (drinking with music playing in cars before going into clubs) as extensions of the night-time economy.

The *Ruta* movement differentiates from the *Movida* because it was centred on a style of music played in industrial complexes, and a culture of drug consumption that was limited to the weekend. It propelled a whole new industry, clothing style and musical temples built in and around Valencia. Young people started their excesses on the weekends along the 30km route, and went on for days, moving from party to party, musical venue to musical venue, to celebrate hardcore partying. Framed as the time in which 'anything was possible', the unlimited partying was united by music and the experimentation with new drugs and a supposed 'new freedom' (Rivera, 2016). However, the *Ruta* was halted in the early 1990s when the law enforcement agencies started to impose controls on people exiting clubs. This time was also marked by hundreds of deaths on the roads given the excessive consumption of drugs and alcohol – something that continues to happen today, despite prevention campaigns.

The night-time culture continues to show characteristics of this movement, proving problematic because drug use continues to play a pivotal role in the night-time experience, and some of these young people, aside from knowing about the risks of what they take and do, move from recreational drug use at the weekends to drugs becoming precisely the problem that separates them from their families and thereafter ruins their lives. The combination of supposed 'new freedoms' for the lower-class bracket recalibrated around neoliberal ideologies of 'live now, think tomorrow', however, mixed crudely with the dismantling of Madrid's industrial economies that started to increase inequality and make larger numbers of them unemployed. As this happened, the drug markets were securing themselves in deprived areas south of the capital, such as San Blas, Carabanchel and Vallecas:

Roberto: *You needed to have known the barrios of*
             San Blas [north of Vallecas]*, Caño Roto*
             [near Carabanchel] *and Vallecas during the*
             1980s.

Daniel: *How were they?*

Roberto: *How were they? Well, imagine what you*
             see in Valdemingómez, but in your barrio.
             People on the corners, injecting four or five
             syringes in themselves, throwing the syringes
             on the floor. Syringes all over the place. If
             you were to enter the door of your house, the
             porch, they would have broken in, and would
             be inside taking drugs. That was the reality
             of drugs in the 1980s. If you were going to
             the barrios of San Blas, Vallecas and Caño
             Roto, there would be a flood of junkies on one
             side, and on the other waiting to come down
             a drug dealer from the sales point, people
             injecting between cars. It was unbelievable. In
             my time, you either died or went to prison.

Those with few economic resources, living in poor conditions, caught up in these changes in the late 1980s and early 1990s were those who suffered with devastating consequences. The appearance of HIV, tuberculosis (TB), various forms of hepatitis and infectious illnesses among thousands of heroin users resulted in a generation caught up in a vicious cycle of continuous drug use, involvement in crime such as robbery, burglary, car theft and other methods of generating money (Associació Lliure Prohibicionista, 2004). It was therefore routine to find young people in these *barrios* consuming drugs like heroin separately as well as experimenting with mixing drugs. While it was normal to inhale these drugs, a lack of information about drug use, modes of consumption and risks associated with drug-use techniques meant that it was not long before many young people were injecting them. This is what concerned a young Juan at the time – the man we introduced in Chapter 1 – who said there was next to no knowledge about drugs and/or harm reduction:

> *These days, there is a lot of information about drugs, on the television they warn you about it and the doctors tell you. They know about HIV and the transmission of these viruses and illnesses. Now people who get addicted and consume drugs because they want to. It's not like 'I can't know nothing', you can't deny you don't know the risks now these days. In those times [1980s and 1990s], it was a new product that came out and well … I tried it. I liked it and little by little when I realised I was needing it and needing it, there was no way to leave it.*

As a result, many young people in poorer districts of the capital became addicted to heroin, and later, cocaine, buying them in the main from the *poblados* where they went to consume, mix and share drug-using equipment. Our interviewees refer to these young people as *la generación perdida* or 'the lost generation', because many died of HIV and overdoses during these times, and/or contracted viruses that eventually killed them. In this respect, the drug boom also refers to the rapid spread of HIV and other viruses between this young drug-using population, which Roberto – a former user himself during these times – recalls:

> *Yes, look, I can tell you this because I lived in those times when Spain went through hard times with the drugs. In this period, I could be walking around the*

city, and see a syringe on the floor, take it, clean it and I would use it to inject. I was in prison sharing syringes and needles with half the people on the wing and I am one of the few to be lucky enough not to have caught those illnesses. Don't ask me how I never got them, I will never understand. But I am from that era that it was easy to contract and somehow I survived.

This experienced policeman from one of the poorer areas of Madrid, Vallecas, also concurred:

I am from Vallecas, I was born and raised there and in my barrio, we call them 'the lost generation', those of us who are now 50-odd but in the 80s we were like 20 and 25. I know countless numbers of people who died from heroin overdoses. In my class at school, we were about 20 kids but 10 of them died early into their 20s. All for heroin and doing things to get heroin. It was terrible; it ruined a whole generation of us. (Diego)

Indeed, although it was thought to be consumed by high proportions of young people, marginalised *barrios* were hit worst, suffered the highest levels of HIV and health-related illnesses, and were the areas that became ghettos, as Ana, a former addict, reflected:

Carabanchel and Aluche were the barrios in the 1980s which were most affected by the heroin. The boom of heroin. I was born there in 1980 and although I was young I remember people who had been born in the 1960s and 70s, got addicted quickly to the drug. I remember seeing them all around me in my barrio. When I was young and I went to the park, I saw people injecting and smoking heroin there. Of course, when my mother saw this, she took us home but it was

> *unavoidable because you saw it all the time. Not only*
> *at night time, they did it [used drugs] at any time,*
> *smoking base or injecting in the park, no problems. I*
> *saw the consequences of this addiction, people 20, 25*
> *and 30 who were fucked. And I am talking about a*
> *high percentage of people, some 60% of people in these*
> *barrios in the south of Madrid, Villaverde, Orcasitas*
> *and Panbendito.* (Ana)

The proliferation of drugs, the expanding of the *poblados* and the associated crime and health problems, especially HIV and hepatitis, forced the Spanish government to initiate ineffective prevention campaigns at the beginning of the 1990s. The campaigns promised to inform people about the risks and consequences of drugs as well as ways to avoid contracting infectious illnesses. In the same vein, law enforcement agencies started to make their presence known in the main *poblados* until they had managed to dislocate some *gitano* families and drug users from the centre of Madrid. This measure merely moved the problem to the periphery of the city where, in reality, it was less visible, although, as we will point out, this amplified the problem while, at the same time, reduced its immediate visibility. These *poblados* were destroyed and cleared in the name of commercial and residential opportunity (such as in Avenida de Guadalajara, for example), as well as the expansion of transport infrastructure (such as in Pitis or La Quinta). While the regional government tried to relocate, and in some ways, culturally assimilate, the *gitanos* in official housing (free of charge) and thereafter into a conventional way of life, the *gitanos* sold the properties, preferring to live in *poblados* because the new vertical buildings made it difficult to sell drugs efficiently. This, some argued, justified their continuing involvement as major players in the drug market, said one of the local policemen:

> *These people [*gitanos*] like to live in poblados, on the streets because there are no neighbours, or anyone and aside from that it is a lot easier to sell drugs when no one around you impedes it.* (Diego)

With the displacement of the *poblados* to the outskirts of Madrid and an increasing social policy cleansing of the streets came further market innovation with the illegal taxi system of the *cundas*, which operated day and night from the centre of Madrid, and went to and from the main *poblados* as a way of solving new issues of distance and access to the drug markets (see Chapters 5 and 6).

A la cárcel: The shortcomings of punitive laws in the 1980s and 1990s

Unsurprisingly, during the 1980s and early 1990s, drug use increased as well as levels of crime, and the state, with little other solution because there was little recognition of drug use as a symptom of wider social problems, started to fill the prisons with drug users. In prison there was very little knowledge about HIV, other viruses and dangerous drug-using practices. Indeed, there were very few drug programmes that were operating in prison, and post-prison resettlement at this time was non-existent (ACAIP, 2016). Many who entered without drug problems therefore tended to come out with new addictions, and those who were using drugs increased their exposure to risky drug-using practices in the absence of clean equipment or knowledge about what they were doing. For example, it was common that the same syringe was used among prisoners, cleaned, sharpened and reused among others:

Javier: *I spent 17 years in prison.*
Daniel: *Why?*

85

Javier: *Because I killed a man. I was carrying 3kg and half a kilo of gold but the police caught me. I had recently sold drugs to the army and they gave me 22 years. My friend escaped, he got free in Corte Ingles near Arguelles.*

Daniel: *And did you manage to quit drugs in prison?*

Javier: *I continued to use drugs, but ended up taking more pills. I used to inject sometimes. One time a mother of a friend of mine caught someone throwing away drugs in the rubbish at the airport. 'Son, look what I got' and at first she thought it was cocaine. They put her in prison because in the end it was pure heroin. In the end, we injected a bit and liked it. We sent half a gram to 'El gigante real' in Caño Roto, and the bastard injected it all and went straight to hospital. Overdosed in Alcalá Meco. And he thought it was heroin, he was throwing away in the street, and the clever one put half a gram in himself and boom. They found him in the toilet, foaming in the mouth; nearly died, but thank god they saved him.*

Rubén: *Was it easy to find drugs in prison?*

Javier: *No, it wasn't easy. We used to steal from the nurses' first aid cupboards. We went to see them with a small cut and stole the drugs. We shared them between three of us because other workers were coming by because of HIV.*

Daniel: *And during your time in prison in the 80s and 90s, was there a drug programme or something which helped you reduce your dependence?*

Javier: *There was nothing, in those times, nothing existed.*

86

The lack of hygiene and common practices of sharing syringes, water, cotton and filters coupled with the onset of HIV resulted in hundreds of people dying in the prisons of Madrid (Associació Lliure Prohibicionista, 2004). This is why there were more than 70,000 inmates in prison throughout the 1990s, an overpopulation of 119%, while today there are about 61,000 (Caravaca-Sánchez et al, 2015). When these prisoners concluded their sentences in the late 1980s and 1990s, the lack of housing, coupled with the stress of back-to-back sentences, contributed to their physical and mental deterioration, reflected in the high mortality rates in the early 1990s.[3]

So, this generation of generally disadvantaged citizens born in the 1960s and 1970s, who started to see their professional livelihoods in the industrial complexes disappear, often ended up using these drugs, dying at a young age on the streets, in prison or in hospital. Despite this, there were never autopsies, investigations or any type of research study commissioned to examine the extent of this social damage (Associació Lliure Prohibicionista, 2004). This all culminated in social protests on the streets in Madrid, increased media coverage and some attention through *películas quinquis* – films dedicated to presenting the working-class cultural life in the 1970s and 1980s that revolved around drugs and crime. News media relentlessly presented cases of overdoses and robbery resulting in a social campaign against drugs like heroin.

Juan grew up in and around the poverty of Alcorcón in south Madrid. Having left school at an early age, and shortly after, the family home, he was between life on the streets and prison:

Juan: *Yes, between the street and prison. Going in and coming out of prison. Okay, yes, I have worked, I had relationships, and I had times when I left drugs. But bit by bit I have come* back, as the saying goes, 'if you try it once, a fiesta [party] can ruin you'.

Daniel: And in prison did you get any kind of help or did you leave drugs of your own accord?

Juan: In prison yes, well, in prison you can take methadone instead of heroin which sort of keeps you going, but there are drugs in prison, less quantities, but it gets in one way or another. It's more expensive and you get less but there is drugs in prison, the thing is, in prison it is such small quantities for such a high price that it's stupid to take it. I have taken drugs in prison but never got addicted, perhaps during the fiestas. For example, I might have a fiesta to celebrate my wage. In prison, I signed up for the workshops, and with good behaviour, talking to the prison workers, directors, when a post comes up, I get it. I was soldering and they make you a test to start with then you start earning money and at least you are working and doing something rather than nothing. Then I left prison and met my partner and went to Toledo and there I was for 4–5 years without drugging myself but as I said, one fiesta I had and somehow I end up here, my girlfriend leaves me....

By the 1990s, social pressure had resulted in improvements in drug treatment and a methadone maintenance system was introduced. Yet year after year, state public administrations were increasing their spending on the 'drug problem', resulting in further introductions of treatment in prison along with drug-free programmes. Given that the heroin epidemic had practically wiped out a young urban generation, new drug-free campaigns were introduced as a means of prevention as well as educational talks about the possible risks attached to use and the virus that could be caught. Many of these campaigns attempted to be hard-hitting, playing on the idea of a free-choice ideology such as 'just say no' to drugs and that, with education, correct decisions could be taken to avoid problematic drug use (see FAD, 2014). Naturally, these campaigns were also based on the idea that trying drugs led to hard drug use.

A crisis in the perceived cost-benefit of drug treatment (see Chapter 7) resulted in changes to the law. In 1995, the Penal Code reacted in tandem with drug education and prevention by increasing the sentences for drug dealing offences. This only resulted in massive increases in the prison population as the penal state reacted more harshly to drug problems. Unfortunately, given that the main drug problems were located in deprived areas of the urban metropolises such as Madrid, this only ratcheted up suffering on the poor, marginalised and socially disadvantaged (Vázquez, 2012). And with diminishing economic opportunity in these areas, this only resulted in criminal trajectories that revolved around spells of time in prison followed by further criminal activity. Or, as Bourgois (2015, p 314), says:

> ... neoliberal entrenchment of services and subsidies for the poor combined with unemployment ensures the persistence of an artificially large pool of desperate consumers condemned through a hostile deskilling carceral system that produces delinquent subjectivities and eradicates the cultural or symbolic capital necessary to access legal employment.

Since 1985, more than 3,000 people have died in prison of HIV while others have been exonerated only days before their death to live in what remained of community services such as that of Basida, a voluntary-staffed drug rehabilitation unit south of Madrid:

> *We opened this house in 1990. Our first idea was to open a house for people who were HIV positive but it was problematic at that time because it has come about and there was almost no type of response because the illness developed and none of us knew how to react. And so what happened was when the first cases started to arrive we had to put in action a rehabilitation programme because the majority who came, came with an active consumption of heroin via the vein, they had HIV and other viruses like hepatitis. This is what we faced for the first 10–15 years. Now, the profile has changed totally because although we still have these people, you will see that most come from what we call the 'old school' of drugs. They are a totally residual population, in fact, the people who arrive here mainly have problems with alcohol, cannabis and cocaine. No one comes with heroin problems now which is why we have a different perspective to the problem; it's not the same to be working in the Cañada Real Galiana or working in Las Barranquillas, on foot in the harm reduction bus.* (Cristina, Director of Basida)

According to data from the Dirección General de Instituciones Penitenciarias, in 1990, almost half of the prison population used drugs in prison and around one-third had HIV (Vázquez, 2012). The diminishment of heroin, and as a consequence, HIV, over the course of the 1990s, was undoubtedly related to increasing awareness about the risks of hard drug use and policy initiatives such as antiviral treatments. Together with the educational programmes and campaigns, it became normalised to use clean equipment and practices of sharing reduced as drug services developed a harm reduction orientation, working in the deprived communities where drug use was most prevalent (Vázquez, 2012).

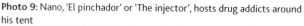

Photo 9: Nano, 'El pinchador' or 'The injector', hosts drug addicts around his tent

In the case of this study, this would be the harm reduction team bus that was commissioned to work in Valdemingómez 365 days a year from 2012. In conversation with the team, they told us that initial efforts in the area to start harm reduction were difficult given the close proximity of the *gitanos*, the continuous flow of clients coming and going, and the obvious conflicts stemming from the politics among the population living there or people like Juan and Julia. The team had relatively little experience and many staff members quit early into the project, struggling with the harsh working conditions, finding it difficult to come to terms with the dishevelled nature of the people and the embedded nature of their problems. However, over time, they have come to establish themselves in Valdemingómez, and now deliver

91

important daily resources to these people such as clean drug paraphernalia, clothes and food as well as offering advice and information about drug treatment engagement processes. This, says Cristina, has resulted in some small successes:

> *Until 2000, there was no such thing as social reinsertion because people arrived in Valdemingómez so deteriorated and so ill that most of them just died. Since we have been here, we have attended more than 1,200 people but seen 275 people die. However, so you have an idea, between 1990 and 1995 175 died of HIV here. So the people that arrive here or end up here somehow, have no perspective of reinsertion, they come to die, to have the best quality of life possible for them the time that they have left. In 1996, new treatments appeared and we started to see results from 2000 onwards, and now we are starting to reinsert people.*

However, to date, many of the most problematic people just don't come to the attention of the services, and drugs remain ever-present in Spanish society. It is currently estimated that there are 1.4 million cocaine users[4] and 95,500 heroin users across the country (European Observatory of Drugs and Drug Addiction, 2016). There also continues to be high demand and a large chain of people working across different countries who make substances like heroin and cocaine available. From what has been detected, the Ministerio del Interior (Ministry of Home Affairs)[5] seized 22 tons of cocaine, 7.3 tons of crack cocaine, 225 kilos of heroin and 400 tons of cannabis in 2016. These are therefore the cultural conditions that frame the lives of the people in this book which, as we will see, are heavily influenced by an oppressive structural system.

Notes

[1] *Botellón* is known as the congregation of young people in public spaces specifically for the purpose of drinking alcohol, listening to music, dancing and socialising. Within the context of the *Botellón*, it is also common to smoke cigarettes and different types of soft drugs like cannabis. This practice has been increasingly seen as deviant over the years and has led to recent clamp-downs on large-scale gatherings, often composed of thousands of young people (Baigorri, 2004).

[2] *Parking* or *Parkineo*, on the other hand, is a version of *Botellón* practised in the main before going on to large nightclubs. Like *Botellón*, the young people principally drink, take drugs, play loud music and dance. This is thought to generate higher levels of substance consumption given that the emphasis is to save money once in the clubs and essentially concentrate it into a short period before going into the discos and clubs. In this respect, *Parking* has greater levels of stigma attached to it. It is also seen as the next step up from doing *Botellón*, as it involves an older group of people who can access clubs.

[3] Reliable statistics on these rates were not available for our study. We found no decent source that could give us some indication of how many people died during the heroin boom of the 1980s and 1990s.

[4] Including those using the drug sporadically, recreationally and habitually.

[5] The equivalent would be the Home Office in the UK and the Department of Homeland Security in the US.

5

Journeys to dependence

Photo 10: Breakfast menu

We amble over to talk to the harm reduction team, and outside the bus there remain a handful of dishevelled figures, standing around, looking nervous and impatient. We wait under a tarpaulin as sit on the table in front of us various needles, syringes and other paraphernalia, as well as a massive black bin full of used syringes and needles, the blood very visible on all of them. As breakfast is served, they queue for biscuits and milk and ham sandwiches. To our right is a ragged man sitting strangely still, and he is almost unrecognisable in a chair with his head in his hands on the dining table; it is as if someone had cast a spell on him to sleep during the day (we later find out he is sleeping because he had spent the whole night selling lighters for drugs and is now resting). Beneath him settles another man in similar rags, and as he lies down, he tries to make himself comfortable to inject himself in the groin, then falls asleep....Then a man, bent by the crippled nature of his back, wanders over. His back is so bent that the bones seem to emerge out of his flesh and through his t-shirt. His dirty trousers hang over his skeletal bum as he extends his hand to reach for the food wrapped in foil; it looks like some feat for him to be able to move. His name is Antonio and he has a withered beard and about four teeth. He calls the place a *"jungle"*, and as he clutches the food and syringes he has just received, he says he is fortunate that his addiction is not as bad.

Introduction

Antonio emphasises the other people being 'worse off' than him as a means of denying the gravity of his current situation, which is that he injects heroin and cocaine, is HIV positive and has hepatitis C. The truth is, however, that someone could not be more unfortunate than him. Antonio's journey to drug dependence to the point where he has lost contact with his friends and family, been made homeless, and accumulated numerous physical, psychological and financial problems is not simple. Have people like Antonio 'fallen victim' to drugs, and subsequently ended up in Valdemingómez, or is their attachment to drug intoxication somewhat more complex? We alluded to this discussion in the previous chapter when we pointed out the various problems with drug campaigns and drug treatments because they hinge on the notion of conscious decision-making, the idea that by equipping someone with knowledge about the risk of drugs and thus educating them, this will therefore result in their capacity to best decide against using them. Essentially the assumption is that given they 'know' the risks and consequences of their use, this then supposedly endows them with a psychological platform to be able to avoid situations in which further use occurs, and thereafter the consequences of dependence and addiction.

But this is simply not how drug dependence works. In conversation after conversation, these people, as well as many of the harm reduction staff, reiterated the damage that the drugs had done to them over the course of their lives. Moreover, a perspective that considers drugs as the cause of someone's demise removes consideration for why the person is motivated to take them in the first place, and why they may want to continue. Addiction, dependence or whatever you want to call living homeless in somewhere like Valdemingómez is bound up with a social process that revolves around the reverse philosophy: rather than what the drugs do to them, it is the investment they make in the drugs as a consequence of wider structural and social pressures that often catapults them into further problematic scenarios in different cultural contexts which facilitates this transition. Almost all the people in our study say they tried drugs for various reasons, but the process attached to their dependence on harder drugs seems somewhat similar; it is therefore important to look at the investment they made in continuing to use drugs, and how, why and when this happened.

Almost all of our cohort either come from seriously deprived zones of urban centres or from poor rural areas and/or are immigrants who have struggled with life in Spain. Many of these people had disrupted families, grew up in poverty and where crime was often all around them, did poorly in school, and often had temporary stints in various types of precarious work industries such as construction and other manual labour posts (see Chapters 2 and 3). Moreover, drugs were readily available in their local, generally poor, neighbourhoods, were a normal thing to try, and were often what was used in their youth as a means of escape from the reality of their lives (see Chapter 4).

These structural and cultural experiences are important because they all play a part in their foreground subjective decisions and actions thereafter. Further investment in drugs does not necessarily occur because of the 'addictive propensity' of the substances – although this is not to deny that drugs have compulsive properties – but because of the motivation these people associate with the need to continue to use drugs to deal with the changing situations of their lives. The contexts, company and places that also arise as a consequence play a part in this transition, as we will show, because as familiar aspects of conventional life start to disappear, and whatever supportive social networks such as family and friends diminish, increased meaning is placed on other relationships and associations with others who are also taking similar sorts of drugs, in different spaces with others who are also involved in delinquent activities.

Importantly, however, the background personal lives of this group, particularly for the women, are often abusive and violent. The turbulent traumas of these experiences – as we will see in this chapter – don't disappear, and are instead revisited as recurrent dreams/flashbacks; essentially, they experience this as a form of 'unpleasure' in the psyche, as Sigmund Freud put it when he observed patients resisting treatment in his clinics. This, as other critical criminologists have indicated (Bollas, 1997; Winlow, 2014; Ellis, 2016), produces a kind of 'death drive' that oscillates around the presence of a pure pain that is neither ejected from, nor neutralised by, the psychic system. This 'unpleasure' refuses resolution, and the psyche is unable to discharge the tension it emits, which only continues to evolve into an emotional 'repetition compulsion' of the trauma, thus providing the basis for subjectively cultivated attitudes towards a perpetual fatalism (see Chapter 8 for how this plays out). This is how the identity transition is facilitated, and in this chapter, we show what exactly contributes to this progression.

Journeys to dependence

Initiation

Mario – the young man from Chapter 2 who drew his 'map of society' in the sand – was only 12 years old when he started trying alcohol and hash. By the age of 14 he had tried Ecstasy, and a year later, he had tried cocaine. At 18 he had smoked a cocaine pipe and then, only two years later, he tried heroin. Like others, he had come to know the *poblados* and was familiar with Las Barranquillas in his late teens (see Chapter 3). He is now only 30 years old, has a host of criminal convictions, and has already spent much of his youth in and out of *"youth correctional facilities"*, as he describes them, *"luckily avoiding prison"*. This gradual trajectory from soft, recreational drug use to experimentation with hard drugs could easily be related as part of Gateway Theory (Goode, 1974), the notion that the probability of trying harder drugs increases after first initiation. Other studies also link this trajectory to the concept of the criminal career, in that, with increasing drug use comes an elevation in delinquency or, quite simply, drugs equal crime (Kandel et al, 1992; Kane and Yacoubian, 1999; Aaron Ginzler et al, 2003). However, these perspectives – largely followed by medical and psychological experts who have never met a drug user in their lives, and who obsess around reality being reflected from complex statistical correlations (Briggs, 2017) – almost always dismiss other cultural, social and psychological processes that elevate attitudes towards drug consumption (see Golub and Johnson, 2002; Briggs, 2012a).

In the case of Mario, therefore, we have to look at how and why he continued to invest himself in drug use, and much of this comes down to growing up in a poor urban area beset with structural unemployment, in difficult family circumstances that truncated opportunities for him from a young age with, at the same time, limited possibilities in a shrinking manual labour economy (see Chapters 2 and 3). His mother and three brothers lived together in Salamanca in Madrid, where he says *"25% of the population were lower middle class"* and the rest were families like his who *"didn't have a cent"*, although most were quite *"devious and scheming"* about how they made money.

This was after his alcoholic father left the family, having regularly beaten up his mother, a trauma that he could never really forget, having witnessed it numerous times. When his father left home, this made financial circumstances more complicated. He recalls how he found himself spending more time *"in the streets"* when his mother bought him and his brothers a football, and he found himself socialising more with *"other young people in the barrio, some of whom were robbing the rich"*. He had a grandfather who sympathised with their poverty and gave him *"5,000 pesetas"* every weekend, or around €25, most of which he spent on video games that he was playing incessantly. At first he spent much of it on chocolate, buying in bulk and selling it to other children. The money was supposed to last him for the week, but it was spent quickly on feeding his video-gaming habit so he started to rob with the other boys in the *barrio* to raise more cash.

School quickly lost its appeal in the excitement and camaraderie of the company of the *barrio*. By the age of 13, he was earning between €150-200 per week from stealing, and much of this early deviant lifestyle was spent with other kids on the *barrio* *"smoking cannabis"*. Drug dealing was a more financially viable solution, since there had been demand in the area for drugs when he was 15, and it had become a normal, integral part of the 'youth experience' in Spain (see Chapter 4). By the age of 15, he had been kicked out of school and was attending *"correctional facilities"*. This continued, and he recalls how he first went down to Las Barranquillas to deal alone with the *gitanos* to then sell on the *barrio*, but when the police started to tear down the *poblado*, he was forced to deviate to Valdemingómez (see Chapter 3). He found it unsafe, and so got to know someone as his *cundero* or driving escort to take him to and from the *poblado*; they ended up protecting each other each time they went to secure higher-quality drugs, as well as smoking some of the profit from their sales.

At the time, he was not able to reckon with the possibility of developing dependence because he didn't see his own consumption as problematic, even though he said he had *"lost all his old friends"* and *"had fights with his mother"*. His expulsion from the correctional facility occurred after he *"beat the shit out of someone"* when he was high on cocaine – although in hindsight he didn't *"feel proud at all"*. He recalls how the *poblados* consolidated into one at Valdemingómez, and how he felt scared, like he *"could shit himself"*, yet at the same time, *"a strange sensation because when you start getting used to the smell of rubbish, it clicks like it gives you a morbid fascination"*, because:

> *My first impression about the surroundings was of the desolation, a city apart, a ghetto, yet at the same time a place of contradictions because people don't leave here, I mean people come who work, people come here in suits, people with all types of consumption … but I was anxious, the children playing in and around the syringes, the rats, and people thought it was normal.*

In addition, Mario continues to fail to recognise his potential dependency when he starts using Valdemingómez as the reference point for problematic dependence: he reasons that as his drug use doesn't compare with what he sees in others, he is able to play down its significance. As his former social ties such as friends and family in the *barrio* diminish in their importance, mostly because of fall-outs, the new environment at Valdemingómez appears as the *"new family"* welcoming him from his disillusion with conventional life:

> *Well, you keep coming down, getting to know people,*
> *the place it is, and regardless of how cruel and dismal*
> *it is, you get used to it. You find yourself liking it*
> *and you get to know more people here than in your*
> *barrio. 'Eh what's happening mate?' they say, and I*
> *suddenly realise that I am like I am at home, only I*
> *miss my mother saying things like 'ah my little boy*
> *Mario'. It is a family feeling but so strange. It's very*
> *fucked up to like it.*

And, between temporary work and robbing expeditions, Mario has continued to come down to Valdemingómez ever since. When we first spoke to him, he had not been in the *poblado* for a week, he said, although he admitted that over the summer that followed he was coming *"every two to three days"*. Concluding, he says he *"likes heroin a lot"* and is *"very tired of all this* [drugs, crime and coming to Valdemingómez]*"*. Looking around as the drug addicts pass us like zombies, he looks at the ground and pauses, before saying:

> *Well, I am going to end up here and I have wasted half*
> *my life already, my youth that is. Many times I saved*
> *money to go away with friends to Ibiza or Amsterdam,*
> *although it would have been another place where I*
> *would have taken drugs, but I end up spending money*
> *here.... I've never had a stable relationship, I have no*
> *school qualifications and some old friends of mine have*
> *a career, a PhD and they have children, a structured*
> *family. My mother is tired of me, the 100 friends I had*
> *are now only 10 if I am lucky. Because people get to a*
> *point when they know so much about you, and even if*
> *you are a 'nice person', they are scared of approaching*
> *you because they know this. Rarely I have hurt people*
> *to get drugs, but people don't understand that.*

Mario has entered a key phase in his drug use, one in which he has almost all but severed licit alternatives. He has no qualifications, poorly paid temporary work is all that is available (see Chapter 2), and he has heroin and cocaine dependency. Social relations are not beyond repair but massively strained, and he risks losing them altogether, even though total abandon has not yet occurred – and he recognises this. Mario is seemingly stuck in periods of cyclical use buttressed by self-evaluations that his failure only has the potential to increase his use, and this is a dangerous subjective state, as we were also to find out when we met Luis.

Cyclical habits

Back in the *plaza*, we get on to the subject of the recent drugs raid, and Roberto remembers only a few weeks ago there was another terrorist raid where two Al Qaida suspects were detained. *"Sometimes people come in who no one knows, rent a house or flat and start doing their thing. They got them for all the things they were preparing, like bombs and that,"* he says (see Chapter 7). As we talk, a thin man wobbles around looking at the ground, picking up small objects; he looks as if he is searching for something he will never find. When we get back to talking to Roberto, he introduces us to Luis, a tall, thin man who speaks eloquently; his sparse stubble sticks out of his chin as we walk off together to chat with him between two cars, as a short, dumpy, fat man drinks milk from a carton and goes away to stroke his cocaine pipe in a corner.

Although he was born in the Middle East, Luis was adopted by a Spanish family. He spent his early life in a local school, but this was complicated when his adoptive parents died in his teenage years. He initially started a relationship with a young woman and they moved in together, but when she left him he moved back with his adoptive parents. When they both died within a short space of time, he struggled to pay the bills, and had few financial resources. Pressures mounted around him, but he found some comfort in friends of his who partied hard on drugs. When he tried and started taking cocaine, he considered it unproblematic, and through expanding drug networks in his local *barrio* he was offered work transporting drugs between La Coruña (a city on the north east coast of Spain that receives substantial quantities of drugs) and Madrid. When he was stopped by the police and found with 3kg of cocaine, he was sent to prison for trafficking charges for nine years, at just the age of 19. He considered himself lucky that he had €36,000 stashed in a secret location, which helped him pay for a good lawyer to have his term reduced.

In prison, he recalled the dire circumstances of seeing fellow inmates die of overdoses and HIV during the early 1990s. Although he quit drugs inside, he complained about the lack of resources in prison to deal with people's addictions, and the absence of clean drug-using equipment (see Chapter 4). He worked and studied hard in prison and, on release in his late 20s, was able to get work in construction and other temporary manual jobs, which was all that seemed to be available. He eventually found work in a drugs agency helping people get clean. He worked there for 15 years and remained drug-free for more than 20 years. During this time, and unbeknown to him, he claims, he was developing depression, and one Saturday night he tried a line of cocaine to see how it felt:

Luis: *I couldn't get over it, didn't know what had
        happened to me. I had known lots of people,
        the director of a therapeutic community,
        families, and ... shame, failure, the world
        came down on me, I wanted to die, I was
        enjoying taking cocaine and I wanted to die,
        I felt dirty. Now I have been using here
        [Valdemingómez] for two years, I had a*

depression, and it started to make it difficult for me to go to work. I carried a feeling of failure and one of self-blame, I was carrying around a little rucksack with all the shit in [drugs and equipment].

Daniel: *So at first you came to Valdemingómez from time to time?*

Luis: *Yes.*

Daniel: *Cunda or how?*

Luis: [Voice starts to stutter in sadness] *Look, the two years I have been consuming drugs like this and there may be 20 days between when I come here.... On that Monday when I had to work, I went to the president and said 'I have no strength, how am I going to go in front of people now?', this enormous feeling of failure. I knew all my colleagues, our clients, their families, I was working with people with heroin and cocaine addictions ... because there were families and young people who used to admire me, I was a reference for them* [Pause, almost crying] *and there was one family who hurt me a lot, they said I had defrauded them and their son, and how I wasn't worth it. And this ... it made me distance myself from my social network and obligated me to hide myself, like a coward.*

Some months later:

On a breezy but sunny spring day, we drive into the main street once again where, quite apparent after the first 500m are the numerous cars on either side of road parked up outside the *fumaderos*. In the *plaza* when we arrive, there are cars on all sides, outside all the *fumaderos*. As we park up, we see a thin figure try to slip inside his car, and as he looks at us, we see that it is Luis. Perhaps feeling obliged, he comes over to talk to us as we get out of the car; he is dressed in the same jumper and trousers he always has, and his greasy hair sticks out in various directions. He firstly embraces us with a strong hug before offering an apology for his lack of contact. He says that his mobile was robbed yet again when he allowed someone to smoke drugs in his car who then robbed him of his phone, National ID and passport. It's the second time he tells us his mobile was robbed. He looks thinner in the face, and has come to Valdemingómez to smoke. His character starts to warm up and he speaks about the recent scandal involving the Panama Papers before starting a tirade against the corrupt nature of the world. *"Imagine how young people see the level of international corruption"* he says, and pulls a sour face of disgust (see Chapter 2). Our laughs echo between the parked cars, and we get a few odd looks from time to time from others who smoke heroin and cocaine from their cars. He laments his temporal work situation that continues to give him an uncertain future and feelings of boredom at work which, we suppose, is why we keep on seeing him in Valdemingómez.

Luis' case is not a standalone – from what we can see since knowing him, he is in the midst of a slow process of potentially relapsing. His work has become increasingly precarious and his boredom levels have increased in and around home, which has resulted in increased visits to Valdemingómez. Yet he does not seem to acknowledge this, and this is another clue to his potential demise – by generating other reasons for being in Valdemingómez, he adds to denial around what he is doing and what is happening to him, all the while convincing himself that he is in control of what he is doing. *Cyclical habits* arise as elements of more conventional life run aground and/or start to close; drugs like heroin and cocaine are sought as a solution, to pass time and/or even to infuse and colour an existence in poorly paid and uncertain, temporal work (see Chapter 2). The habit then becomes extended periods of continuous drug use mixed with binge sessions that push the user into deep contemplative states.

We met Luis numerous times over the course of our fieldwork, and knew him from only these intermittent periods of contact; we saw him turn up in the same clothes and lose more and more weight. We speculate that this is an interim period for Luis, and that within another period of time, his feelings of self-blame may also lead him to commit further to the area. On one of the last occasions we met him, he had been fired from his job. For Luis, the decision to first use drugs was related to its easy availability and kudos in his youth at the time, but his decision to return to drugs seemed to be in an attempt to resolve the onset of depression, and as his subsequent use started to escalate, the sense of personal shame for his actions overcast his ability to recover, setting in motion a series of self-evaluations about his actions. Now, in Valdemingómez, he continues to smoke and inject heroin and cocaine, and looks around in *"sadness at the state of the people"*, as he describes it each time we meet him; he engages with this self-assessment that provokes personal feelings of shame. He distinguishes between a heroin user as *"a socially rejected person"* and how cocaine addiction is more psychological because he reasons that people think *"I only take cocaine, I have my car, my partner"* – he is merely reproducing ideologically and socially constructed concepts around different types of drug use, because encountering the cultural context of Valdemingómez encourages people to ideologically arrange themselves in a social hierarchy (see Chapter 6).

Dependence

Dependence in Luis' case is a process that is still in progress; his intermittent yet potentially lengthy visits to Valdemingómez that we observed becoming more frequent are related to an activity that is growing in prominence in his life. Like almost everyone who lives in Valdemingómez, many who arrive at Luis' position end up coming more frequently, and a high proportion end up staying in the area. We already saw in Mario's case how initial visits to Valdemingómez were exciting, and the irregularity of subsequent visits thereafter are rationalised to represent the control that people like Luis reason they have over their life, confirmed by the fact that they see people, in their view, far worse off who live there, living among rubbish and working for the *gitanos*. This means that the road to dependence has some correlation with perceptions of the self, and this, in turn, is flexibly juxtaposed against supposedly 'worse-off others'.

Julia, who first tried drugs aged 12, increased her use as a teenager, which affected her attendance at school to the point where she stopped attending altogether. Drug use, going out and even drug dealing became a way of life as formal avenues started to disappear in her adolescence. Petty crime became the norm, and along with that came new social relationships with others in other similar delinquent networks. She kept her drug use mostly hidden, especially when she started to try stronger drugs like heroin and cocaine, because it was seen as socially shameful to smoke hard drugs in her *barrio*, which was one reason she visited Valdemingómez, where no one *"bothered"* her, as she describes:

Julia: *Well, I used to have a lot of money and I initially started to take drugs by sniffing them and come here* [Valdemingómez] *because they supposedly gave you more quantity; you know, for the same amount of money than in Madrid. Here, half a gram was, well, anyway, you are going to get more for your money here than any place in Madrid. So I*

	started to come here and it is the environment that gets you hooked.
Daniel:	*The environment? In what sense?*
Julia:	*Well, here [Valdemingómez] no one is looking at you if you take a line or smoke a cocaine pipe; here everyone is like you or worse. When you first start to come, no one bothers you, the police say nothing about the fact you want to drug yourself and, well, you start to come here.*
Daniel:	*Do people bother you if you take drugs in your home barrio?*
Julia:	*Come on, it's not the same to smoke a pipe in your barrio, it's not the same to smoke a pipe in the barrio or smoke on foil in the barrio. I mean, where do you smoke?*
Daniel:	*It's easier, more open here [in Valdemingómez].*
Julia:	*It's better here because it is not badly seen. In Vallecas, it is seen as bad.*

Photo 11: Resting after a shift for the *gitanos*: Julia sleeping (left) on Mitchell (right)

This is important because many of those we spent time with also preferred Valdemingómez with its open availability and social acceptability of taking heroin and cocaine (Chapter 6). As she came to the area more often, Julia learned of the financial benefits of drug trafficking, because *"in this environment, you hear things like 'listen, look what I will offer you to go down to Morocco'"*, and she started to traffic drugs in bulk. This meant that she essentially started to come to Valdemingómez to deal directly with the *gitanos*. Earning most weeks up to €25,000, she got accustomed to an ideological social status attached to her wealth, and came down to spend thousands on long binge nights, *"often treating others"* to drugs in the process. As she started to appear in Valdemingómez more often, disappearing from home for lengthy periods, family relations became further strained. When her long binges started to affect her motivation to continue to traffic drugs from Morocco, she quickly fell into debt with the *gitanos* – to the point where she ended up working for them to pay off the debt she had accumulated. It wasn't long after that, like others around her in the area, that she was wandering around homeless, scavenging among the rubbish and injecting heroin and cocaine by whatever means possible.

Julia's journey to dependence was therefore secured through the social stigma she associated with public use in her local area and her concerns of how it would reflect on her family, coupled with an increasing social status in Valdemingómez that she had started to enjoy. We are therefore describing an identity shift that is increasingly given rank through the use of drugs in a particular place, where liberation on consumption increases the pull of the spatial context, hence her reference to the way Valdemingómez got her *"hooked"*. Although Julia lives locally to the area – Vallecas being only a few kilometres away – these journeys to dependence are harnessed by other processes of displacement from other areas of Madrid.

Dependence displacement: From X to Valdemingómez

Working in tandem with these subjective identity shifts are the processes described in Chapters 2, 3 and 4 related to the social policy and policing initiatives that collectively transferred already problematic drug users from place to place, because the *poblados* in and around Madrid were occupying land that had potential for capital investment. At the same time, there has been a shift towards penal law, giving the police the power to tackle vagrant populations, most recently reflected in the *Ley de la Seguridad Cuidadana* (*Citizen's Security Law*) proposed in 2013, which came into force in 2015. Among the 44 codes, listed as 'grave infractions' are:

- The consumption or possession of illicit drugs, even if they were not destined for trafficking purposes, in public places, and also the neglect of paraphernalia used to take them.
- The transport of people, in any type of vehicle, with the objective of facilitating access to drugs (*cundas*).

The hostile forms of structural and spatial displacement had major ramifications on the people we have come to know in Valdemingómez, because they often had serious implications for their drug-using trajectories, as we shall see.

From poblado to poblado

> *Here, in Madrid, before there were lots of drug distribution points, there was Celsa, Barranquillas, Salobral. Various. Well, bit by bit, the police have destroyed the poblados and in the end, Valdemingómez has become the largest as it has become where most drugs come. So, as the other poblados have closed, the gitanos from the other poblados have come here ...*

smaller poblados that they were clearing and in the end, they all came here, and that's when it started to grow so much. (Juan)

Photo 12: Scattered condom and paper towel debris in Polígono Marconi

The transition people like Juan made from *poblado* to *poblado* was another significant factor in journeys to dependence because, with a shift in physical space comes a shift in personal circumstances and criminal trajectories, as drug-using identities become more prominent as a way of life. For example, Alberto, who grew up the poor *barrio* of Carabanchel in south Madrid during the heroin boom of the 1980s, has used heroin and cocaine for 28 years and first came to Valdemingómez on the *"10th September 2008"* (as he remembers the day). He relays his journey to drug dependence from inception of the first drug, which reflects the popular discourse about soft drugs being the gateway to harder substances (see Briggs, 2012a, for a critique). He began trying drugs in his late teens, even though he can't remember exactly how he developed his habit since, in his words, *"you know, when the company is, like, everyone has a beer, a line of cocaine, you try it and you like it"*. Aged 17 he tried heroin, and within a few days he was *"hooked"*, he says.

The backdrop to this, however, was that with almost no work prospects, having only luck with temporary work contracts and with tense family relationships, he robbed people for money to fund his drug use. It was not long before he was arrested for two *"robbery with intimidation charges"* and received eight years in prison. Within six months of his release, he was charged with *"burglary"* and spent another two years in prison, and on release, robbed another flat and received another two years in custody. Having served three prison sentences in a time when *"drugs were real drugs"*, he ended up without work and homeless, *"robbing and begging on the streets of Madrid"*.

During this time, Alberto came to know numerous *poblados* in Madrid, in particular, Celsa and Las Barranquillas, which, as they were closed, meant he had to go back to Valdemingómez to score drugs. Confused and angry, he says, *"I don't know why they closed Barranquillas because they had drugs rooms which was very important, a clean place to take drugs which was supervised"*. The fact there is no such resource in Valdemingómez is important because it makes the conditions around drug use that much more oppressive: there is no 24-hour drug support, and help is limited to the support of the harm reduction team who come from 10am to 6pm (see Chapter 7).

So when Alberto started coming to Valdemingómez, this change impacted on the circumstances around his drug use and means of generating money for drugs. Nowadays, however, he is *"not in the right condition to rob"* because his physical and mental health has deteriorated since moving to Valdemingómez (because of the dirty conditions and high risk of infectious diseases), and he estimates that he may be lucky to make €15-20 a day compared with five years ago, when he was robbing in Madrid and earning €50-60. These days, he sits and begs in McDonalds, Burger King and the local garage, traversing the A3 on daily basis, having to literally walk across the motorway because of the lack of infrastructure. While the methadone stabilises his need to consume more, he is critical of its side effects, and complains how it is *"worse than heroin"* (see Chapter 8).

From Polígono Marconi to Valdemingómez

> *Sonia, for example, Bea, Beatriz, Gema – Gema I told you earlier – are young women from the Polígono Marconi and they used to come here, all pretty with their tits out, all hair brushed, but they have eventually ended up living here in the rubbish because the pimps have slapped them around and they have nowhere to go so they came to poblado [Valdemingómez] and stayed. The majority of women from Marconi are condemned to this because over there, there are also terrible conditions. Many of these women depend on the pimps, are trafficked, bullied into working, and when it doesn't work out they come here to work it out, prostituting themselves for a little bit of money.* [Roberto]

During the time we spent in the Polígono Marconi – Madrid's prostitution hotspot – we were able to ascertain that it is a space that is controlled by Romanian mafia, where it is estimated that about 300 women work in the area, about 100 at one time, as they often do shifts of up to 10–12 hours. Perhaps it is no surprise that workers such as Roberto and the harm reduction services distribute each month 20,000 condoms to women who come from Marconi. It is also likely that many of those 20,000 condoms end up on the street after they have been used (see Figure 12), as cars incessantly cruise around this wasteland area of Madrid's suburbs. The point about Marconi is that it is also an area of concentrated poverty and advanced marginality in Villaverde, a place that has been left to rot by local government in the wake of the disintegration of Spain's construction industry (see Chapters 2 and 3), the signs of which are ever-present from the rusting factories that surround it. What has historically been a marginal area became increasingly deprived in the wake of the 2008 crisis, coupled with the increased concentration of prostitution after the closure of the other primary sex market in Casa del Campo in 2007 as a consequence of political and commercial gentrification processes (Briggs and Pérez Suárez, 2016). Nowadays, it is the most deprived *barrio* of Madrid because around one-third of its population are unemployed (see Figure 1, under 'Villaverde').

As a consequence, increasing numbers of mainly immigrant and lower-class Spanish women have turned up in an area controlled by mafia, and have fallen victim to organised crime networks. In Marconi, these women sell sex for €20–30. In conversation with one, Dorina – who works every day of the week, 365 days a year – we were told that in the four hours that she has been working she has had eight clients, which gives the reader an idea of how much business she gets. Many of these women take drugs as a means of coping with the oppressive working conditions, and to manage the emotional traumas of the often-twisted demands of their clients, and in our observations, we found used drug paraphernalia in and around the barrio of Villaverde where they work. As Roberto alluded to, outside these oppressive networks, these women have very little else, often either being foreign or having a limited support network. This makes them particularly vulnerable should they try to seek to leave the area, and they either rely on the piecemeal support of prostitution agencies or leave the work by their own accord themselves. Many, like Sonia, were regularly threatened and beaten, and lost the ability to control their drug use, which essentially propelled them into increased intoxication and personal neglect. Mental and physical disintegration resulted in being cast out from the area:

> As the worker drifts off, we move away from the main table area where they distribute the clean paraphernalia. All of a sudden, we start to see someone walking over, crying in desperation; the woman cannot stand up straight nor keep one part of her body

115

still as she struggles with each step towards the water tap. It is Sonia, a woman who used to work in the prostitution hotspot of Marconi and now lives in Valdemingómez. As she approaches, she drops a syringe full of blood on the floor, and stoops under the water container to wash her face and arms – this is one of the two facilities available for people to wash if they don't have an appointment in the church to have a shower. We can't quite work out if she is communicating with us; she sweats and spits as she talks and her body jerks around as it seems she has a nervous system problem. She scratches her skin, and delves her hands below her top to itch herself as she bends around the place: *"they rob me, they took my* [cocaine] *pipe, they treat me as if I'm 30 but I'm nearly 50"*. It seems someone has taken her drug pipe and this has upset her and made her nervous. *"Joder, soy una buena mujer"* ("Fuck it, I'm a good woman") she says, and wiping the tears away from her eyes and the spit and dribble from her mouth, she recounts how she started using drugs because she was abused. Moving from Valladolid after being made redundant, she came to Madrid to live and work in Villaverde, but struggled to find consistent work and got into prostitution. She sits down while at the same time picking up a six-inch nail, and holds it close to her as if she feels that some attack on her is imminent. However, she then throws it away as if she couldn't remember why she had initially picked it up. She leaves unexpectedly, and then two minutes later returns with a pen and wants to give us her telephone number. She searches the floor for paper but instead finds an empty packet of tranquilisers and tries to focus and concentrate as much as possible to write her name and number, spitting and jerking around as she does it. She wanders off again, her tight hair in curly ringlets moving, being thrown everywhere as a consequence of her spasmodic movements.

Sonia charges just a few Euros for a blow job, which is worth a shot of cocaine or heroin in Valdemingómez. Her physical and mental conditions have deteriorated since she abandoned work in Marconi; she has HIV, hepatitis C and a nervous system disorder. Her relocation to Valdemingómez has clearly had a major impact on her drug-using trajectory as well as her route to a different kind of dependence, one that reflects destructive attitudes towards drug use and a disregard for her physical appearance and general health, which seem reflective of the fusion of the 'death drive' and the 'repetition compulsion'.

From cundero to cunda to Valdomingómez

> *Yes, the majority of people who come in cundas take drugs; they either come from families who used to live in places like the Cañada Real Galiana or who, with the crisis of 2008, lost their jobs in construction, they have a few cars and need work. They take drugs as well, yes. So it's like we were saying, the cunderos receive a wage in drugs but are more autonomous, they don't work for gitano families, they risk transporting others to Valdemingómez, so this is also a way of financing drug dependency.* (Marcos)

When the limited prospects of work mix crudely with a developing drug dependency, there is also the possibility that someone may offer driving services or *cundas* to Valdemingómez to other people in their area and/or who are in a similar precarious position. This is potentially profitable, as the driver or *cundero* can earn up to €30 per trip, and this service means the driver either being paid in cash or drugs, to escort people to and from Valdemingómez from various points in Madrid, given that the old *poblados* where drug sales used to take place don't exist any more. One of the principal areas is Embajadores, a marginal-becoming-fashionable area of the city just south of the centre (see Chapter 3 about how certain areas of Madrid are being gentrified). During the early stages of our fieldwork and up until the summer of 2015, it was common to find a very organised system of drug users leaving for Valdemingómez, where *vigilantes* or look-outs lined up addicts on the streets as the *cundas* arrived:

We trudge up the steps of the metro exit at 09.40; there are two groups of drug addicts in view; three stand around as if they are waiting for someone to emerge from the metro while two in the other group hover around, smoking. Another just stands there dazed, as if he had been transported to this place in time to do this thing without being aware of it. One group of three move around arguing between themselves in front of Daniel as other people pass by, seemingly unmoved by this activity. We move into the shade and the three men, having evaluated all the space available to them in the shade, decide to then retreat into the same shade as Daniel. They continue to argue in a low tone, which is something between a half-drugged-up mutter and loud nonsense. The oldest of the three drifts off and starts to cough up blood on the pavement while the others continue to have intermittent conversations. As one stands next to Daniel, another moves behind him and just lingers. Suddenly there is a beep and a small, banged-out silver Toyota pulls up; as the passenger in the car raises two of his fingers, two run off to catch a lift with them.

Two more ragged-looking people come out of the metro exit and embrace each other as they shout at each other. Then the man who coughed up blood walks off down the Calle Embajadores with another as the groups dismantle, disappear and scatter as the National Police pull over and park next to the traffic lights. The police linger around for a while then drive off, and as if by magic, the drug addicts emerge again. We lean against the glass of the bus stop, which is covered in dirt and stains, and smells of urine. To our right, a young woman wobbles out of the metro station, a scar across her face, her eyes half open as she sips a beer and then stuffs a whole packet of crisps into her face. She turns slowly around and thereafter struggles to walk in her stained, white trousers. Then, from nowhere, two other women converge, talking loudly and seemingly arguing, and meet another two men who were in front of Daniel, and they drift off saying *"Nos vamos o nos vamos?"* ("Are we going or what?").

It seems it is the perfect place to meet as there is a constant flow of traffic and the same addicts don't seem to wait around in one area for more than 10 minutes or so. There are six roads which connect the roundabout, which makes it extremely transient, but the busiest area seems to be the road south, Calle de Embajadores, which is on the corner. There, there is a small space for the *cundas* to pull up and then shoot off, and this very road is well connected to the south of Madrid and beyond to the M40, M45 and M50 (all of which circumnavigate the city). On evaluation, the other roads don't seem so appropriate, in particular the main one, which goes horizontally through the roundabout, because there is too much traffic. The roads to the north go in the wrong direction, are either one-way or narrow. The other parallel road to the southbound Calle de Embajadores is too narrow and there is not enough space to pick people up, it seems. Where Daniel stands on this corner seems to be where most of the activity takes place.

Inside the café on the corner right outside where the *cundas* leave from we start up a conversation with the barwoman. As she puts fresh water in the fridge, she reflects on some experiences. She tells us how it is organised, that the drug addicts normally call the *vigilante* to arrange a pick-up, before reflecting on how many addicts come in and use the bathrooms to inject, and how many have threatened her and tried to rob the café when they have been high. It seems that six or seven years ago there was no such activity of drug users, but she shows relief when she reflects on how a new law is being applied which will clamp down on the *cundas*; it will prohibit people stopping to pick up drug addicts as well as returning them to the same or similar areas to commit crime to fund their drug use. Well, this was the intention in any case.

Interestingly, the introduction and development of *cundas* seems to coincide with the closure of many of the last-standing *poblados* at Las Barranquillas. In this way we can see how the evolution of the *cunda* business is related to the spatial mutation of the drugs market along with the fracturing of industrial work, precarious labour and housing and increasing unemployment. Furthermore, we took these notes early in the summer of 2015. The new *Citizens' Security Law*, which came in to force on 1 July 2015, essentially empowered the police to be able to stop and detain *cunderos* and take away their vehicles. What was a busy departure point for drug users connecting the city to Valdemingómez became far more tranquil over the following months, to the point where, one year later, in 2016, it had practically ceased. On one such occasion that summer:

> At Embajadores, from time to time, we pass drug addicts who drift in and out of the busy commuters and ambling retirees, and we also somehow, yet not deliberately, dodge the charity workers who search for financial sponsorship for their cause. Outside one shop sits a gypsy woman with a plastic cup begging, only we have run out of change, having given it to three different people begging on the metro. We cross and wait outside Glorieta de Embajadores where, up until eight months or so ago, numerous *cundas* departed to Valdemingómez. Now there are only a scattering of drug users who mostly sit in the shadows of the metro stop. There is no one organising the *cundas* or any major grouping of drug users, although, while we wait, we see a collection of four thin women huddle together before a van pulls up to collect them – likely destined for Valdemingómez.

In the time we walk around, we see no more than five drug users who look almost lost; one in particular walks around talking to herself as she holds in front of her a brand new iPad, which she hopes to sell. We walk into the nearby café – where we had once talked to the owner who had for years complained at the levels of crime and drug use associated with the area. Yet she is not there, and we are served by a woman who has only been in the job for a few days. We leave shortly after, crossing the road, and order drinks from another café. As the old waiter proudly emerges with his tray, he relays how the numbers of *cundas* started to slowly reduce two years ago, but with the advent of the *Citizens' Security Law* last summer, potential loiterers have all but disappeared. *"Sometimes the odd cunda leaves at night but it's nothing like it was,"* he says, as he shuffles from side to side, *"the mayor is talking about putting on a special bus for them which leaves from here, you know, so they can go to Valdemingómez,"* he adds. A victory for the town planners and the state – it seems as if they have successfully swept the problem under the carpet or, in this case, pushed the problem from the centre of the city to elsewhere.

The point about these initiatives is that they do very little to tackle the problem at its origin, instead focusing more on its consequences: those being the visible outcome of withdrawing localised drug sales points, which leaves a sizeable population of dependent people who are now exposed to Valdemingómez. Essentially, this widens the pool of people dealing directly with the area, and at the same time introduces them to its environment. This partly explains why it can happen that the *cundero* can find him or herself as a passenger in a *cunda*, and sometime later, find themselves living in Valdemingómez as dependence develops. This is further exacerbated by such measures taken by the authorities that essentially truncates some of these people into other means to sustain their drug use, people like Gamal here, who we met wandering around as if he was lost on the main road in Valdemingómez:

> We get talking to a man called Gamal who stands in a ripped, black cloak and moves his feet slowly to the side in his dirty sandals. He shakes his hand with a small collection of Euros and cents to try to interest us to contribute to his cause. As we talk and watch the cars come in and out of Valdemingómez, parking from time to time only metres away, he tells us he has been coming to the area on and off for eight years *"from when the drugs started here"*, and this seems to correspond to other data we have about the exponential growth of Sector 6. Initially he had come to Spain to work, but had only found irregular cash-in-hand jobs and fell into debt and started using drugs. The lack of work meant he quite quickly found alternatives in the informal economy, taking drug users to and from Valdemingómez from Madrid, yet recent laws passed to control *cundas* had meant he had his car confiscated – not that he had a licence, tax or insurance or anything. He is critical and says he has only once managed to get clean from drugs, when he went back to Morocco. He returned, however, last year and passing time with no certain income quickly returned to driving *cundas* and drug use. He says he will not escape, *"there is no salida for me"* ("there is no exit for me"). Maybe not now he has no car, as he is homeless in Valdemingómez.

Dependence acceleration: Living in Valdemingómez

> Gamal knows most people in the area. He reflects on how he looks down on people who inject, saying they are not like him and how he looks after his body – even though he looks like everyone else and is addicted to smoking heroin from the pipe. This is reflected, he says, in the way the drug-taking dens are divided into two types: injecting and smoking. Victimisation is high and commonplace; many times he has been robbed when he was asleep and been

beaten by *gitano* drug dealers and the police, as he shows us bruises under his ripped cloak. Suddenly another *cunda* parks up next to him as he begs them for some money. They wave him off but he says thank you. We continue to talk and he seems to get more fidgety. We ask him about what happens to people here and he says, *"many overdoses"* and *"the more you take resources away from people, the worse they get, the most desperate they get, they rob"*. He then recalls a story from only a few months ago when he witnessed a man being beaten to death by the *gitano* drug dealers.

Gamal continues to describe here a kind of final process into which people pass from a dependence that relies on them visiting Valdemingómez to one that results in them staying there for long periods of time, perhaps even living there. According to Marcos, people pass through 'cycles of use', which not all necessarily result in cases of severe dependence, but more periods of extended use. However, as he alluded to us, once family and networks are exhausted, for many it is just a matter of time before they are visiting Valdemingómez more often. For example:

Daniel: *How would you describe the form of addiction in Valdemingómez?*

Marcos: *I think that drug addiction goes very much in cycles, like, you try something, you go out, you go back to a different environment, another type of drugs, you go out and you are in a poblado like Valdemingómez. The junkie in poblado? How would you say? I suppose it's the moment which comes after various cycles where you break with your family structure, you have no support network and you end up getting more and more hooked on drugs in poblado because the poblado also hooks you.*

Daniel: *Yes, speaking about this environment, many*
          people have said to us in those precise words
          'the environment hooks me'. What does it
          mean?

Marcos: *I see it a little like other environments where*
          the environment hooks you and consuming
          drugs, well, get hooked on them because other
          people are also consuming like you in similar
          situations. If you have a family problem, for
          example, you disconnect and go out to party,
          but in their case it is on a level related to
          their own exclusion, you know, when you
          have nothing you end up there. You see it
          lots, that young people end up there, they are
          a couple of days like that, and they end up
          staying there. They start coming in cundas,
          and a couple of days later they have put up
          their chabola.

Of course, there is no time limit to their more permanent
feature in Valdemingómez, as many people come and go,
disappear, reappear, but a sizeable number pass through this
process. As they do, time and time again, they make reference
to *"el entorno me engancha"* ("the environment gets me
hooked"), suggesting that it is something 'external' to them
that they cannot control that attracts them to the location.
What it actually is, is a way of personally neutralising an
out-of-control drug use in a context of identity recalibration,
which is facilitated by the social acceptance/recognition they
receive from others in a similar position (visiting/staying
there). In many cases, people passing through this process
to staying/living in Valdemingómez change their mode of
drug use and develop new attitudes to consumption that rely
heavily on the cultural operations of the sector. Because they
are almost indefinitely confined to the space, this reduces their

ability to earn money for drugs, therefore truncating their criminal capacity and realigning it to the survival protocols of Valdemingómez (see Chapter 6). Equally, many have amassed significant mental and physical problems related to their consumption by this stage. The fact that they now end up in Valdemingómez means that they are more vulnerable and subject to abuse and manipulation, which we think reflects a 'dependence acceleration':

Roberto: *Fuck, well, let's see, if they are doing a blow job for a guy, one of these gitanos, in disgusting circumstances for a €5 hit or they set themselves up in a fumadero and start sucking off everyone for a hit. It gets to some really low levels.*

Daniel: *I guess they are taking advantage of their vulnerability.*

Roberto: *It is a vicious circle because you end up killing for a hit so you do it, you do what you have to for a hit. And it is worse for women who are valued less, they hit them and everything, rape them daily and there is no problem as it's always the same ones.*

These situations of victimisation, humiliation and abuse layer onto the previous traumas that many of these people seemingly have, enabling a kind of 'death drive' and 'repetition compulsion'. Thereafter, further destructive drug use practices are engaged as many people seem to keep the trauma on a kind of continual playback. Perhaps then self-rationalising that there is nothing worse than their own personal abandon, maintaining dependency thereafter supersedes personal moral boundaries, and new risks are taken that jeopardise personal safety and welfare (see Chapter 8). Among these are those that are clearly linked to emergency and improvised drug use practices, selling sexual services, working in a kind of slavery for the *gitanos* as a *machaca* as well as being subservient to various favours that have the potential to be seen as derogatory in the moral economy (Bourgois and Schonberg, 2009; Wakeman, 2016):

Suddenly, Juan appears from his tent and tightens his thin jogging top to protect him from the wind, and comes over to greet us. Obligingly, we get out into the cold wind and catch up with him as he lights up a cigarette, while in front us a Russian man in his late 20s called Dimitri holds one side of his groin and looks for *chutas* [syringes] on the ground as he has none that are clean. He seems to be in a hurry as he sweats as he searches the floor in the hope a clean one has been discarded, but we can see that among the rubbish are only thrown-away, used syringes. When we take shelter from the wind next to a large metal container, Juan graciously receives the offer of a cigarette from us. When we point to his broken arm, he tells us that a piece of wood fell on it and broke it, and yet, even after he had waited four days in pain, he was reluctant to go to hospital. There they put it in a cast. This is in direct contrast to what Roberto and even Julia had said, which was that he had got into an argument and someone had taken a metal bar to his arm, breaking it in the subsequent fight. We put his reasoning down to the need to retain a form of self-respect; after all, to appear as a victim in this arena is to appear vulnerable. The broken arm also makes it difficult to inject heroin and cocaine, and he sidesteps among the used paraphernalia, trying to keep warm in the cold while suffering from the *mono* (withdrawal symptoms) at the same time. He hopes Julia will finish her shift soon and share her final hit with him. He tells us the *fumadero* where he worked (and where Julia was working inside) is now rented out to another *gitano* family and the *fumadero* business has relocated nearer the *plaza* in an effort to capitalise on more clients driving to the area; its previous location was set down a slope from the *plaza* and clients initially needed to get the all-clear from two *machacas*, one at the entrance of the driveway and another further down who controlled the door. However, the new location is simply one door.

The pressure to get money together for a hit is imminent and continuous: daily life becomes a futile battle to *quitar el mono* (quell the sickness from heroin and cocaine withdrawal), while at the same time avoiding volatile and violent conflict, perhaps, in the process, finding some dignity from the misery around them. Between the coming and going of the *cundas*, the business of going to and from the harm reduction team bus between the rubbish lying around in the wasteland, situations like these are therefore commonplace:

> We retreat from the cold wind back to the car, and as we get in, an extremely thin man in a red puffer jacket walks in front of us and walks over to a shelter by the container where we had been standing to inject in his arm. His face concentrated, he kneels, and carefully inserts the syringe into his arm before injecting as if he were carefully threading a needle. Shortly after, he starts to tremble, looking around in the process in a kind of paranoia that the whole world is judging this very action. Leaving the syringe hanging from his arm, he stands up and starts to scan the floor as his eyes widen. As he stands, the wind blows against his trousers, revealing his emaciated figure, and his thin, fragile legs become apparent. From here it looks like his jaw is broken as he starts to clench it, but it transpires that he has no teeth, so naturally the jaw closes much higher up on his face.

6

Life in the city shadows: Work, identity and social status

Photo 13: *Ruiditos* or 'Little noises'

José is dressed in thick jeans, a brown leather jacket decorated with holes and stains, and a fisherman's hat from under which tumbles out his silvery grey hair. He has two yellow bottom front teeth that jab harmlessly into his gum when he talks; his bushy beard and eyebrows almost hide his strikingly blue eyes. We walk up towards the church in the *plaza*, and sit on the concrete stumps that guard it outside. José, a 56-year-old man from Asturias in northern Spain, starts to talk as a fly buzzes in and out of his nose. He has used heroin and cocaine for the last 20 years, having come to Madrid after being made redundant in the manufacturing industry and in the wake of the collapse of his marriage. Unable to get work, he became homeless and started using drugs. He reflects on life in Valdemingómez as *"brutal"*, suggesting that a major mistake was to close the former drug-dealing area called Las Barranquillas, where there was 24-hour support for drug addicts: *"here, the harm reduction bus goes at 6pm, and people can't wash so they get more infections – the people here live in worse conditions,"* he mumbles (see Chapter 7). He adds that the new law designed to clamp down on *cundas* and *cunderos* has meant that many of those people have drifted into *"robbing or now live here in the Valdemingómez, they take more drugs now"* (see Chapter 5). In Valdemingómez, he says that the drugs are *"between 5–10% pure at best"*. He pauses and then looks down at the floor as he tells us his girlfriend died of an overdose five years ago, before recounting how he has seen the *gitanos* beat someone to death, *"the police came at 4am, then the ambulance was delayed and didn't come, and when it did, he was dead."*

As we conclude the interview, we can't help but ask him about a small blue toy he has dangling from his belt. He holds it gently in his dirty, swollen hands and says it's his *"lucky charm"* called *"ruiditos"* ("little noises"). It doesn't make noises now as it's broken; the bottom plastic bit has fallen out, so when it is squeezed, *"ruiditos"* is silent. He looks at it for some time and smiles before looking up and says, *"you know, I fix toys, I look for them here or anywhere, and give them to people in Atocha train station,"* adding *"I don't do it for money because I don't want to be given money for something I do for people. I do it to see how happy it makes the children".* He smiles broadly as he stands, saying, *"I have to take drugs now ..."* before shaking our hands and drifting off to crouch behind the church where he sits looking over his shoulders as he fills his pipe with cocaine.

Introduction

Like others, José has passed through a similar process of personal collapse, having had key foundations of his life and livelihood severed and, over time, has had to live a more precarious life in and around the streets of Madrid. Like others, he is also a victim of the urban cleansing process we have described, having frequented other *poblados*, and now finds himself living in Valdemingómez, surviving by means of the moral economy (see Chapter 5) and, where possible, trying to carve out a way of life that means he can retain some self-dignity. The place he now frequents in Valdemingómez, however, revolves around its own norms and codes that defy and violate conventional everyday conceptions of what we may consider normative behaviour. This is mainly because Valdemingómez's zonal praxis is assembled on historical notions of law breaking, which, over time, have accommodated other forms of illicit actions and behaviour. Therefore the cultural practices adopted by the people who frequent the area are somewhat distinct because of the structural genetics behind its inception. The area has become host to countless illegal businesses that are in operation alongside the extremely organised nature of the drug market run by the *gitanos* and their workforce (*machacas*), and this attracts around 5,000 clients to the area each day to buy and use heroin and cocaine.

This congregation of crime, violence and victimisation in a spatial and legal no-man's land like Valdemingómez contributes to what Atkinson and Rodgers (2015) call 'zones of exception', like a 'murder box', where grave misdemeanours occur without consequence and violence is a normalised part of the everyday fabric of social life. For this reason, in Valdemingómez, almost anything goes, and as José alludes to in these notes, as a consequence of this there are various tensions in hierarchies attached to cultural interactions in the area that permeate elements of work and labour, the moral economy, daily life and social relations. In this chapter, we take a detailed look at the cultural milieu of Valdemingómez and its operations, and show how people survive there, and how the various players attempt to seek self-respect from these harsh realities.

Zonal containment of illegality

The area of Valdemingómez and the neighbouring five sectors of the Cañada Real Galiana occupy a particular space on the outskirts of Madrid, which is conducive to tolerating various forms of illicit businesses. In some ways, this is somewhat historic in that much of the early residential construction of the area was considered illegal (see Chapter 3). Initial lenience, and the lack of state intervention thereafter, has thus given birth to other illicit ventures – the most recent being the boom of drug businesses and organised crime networks that flourish in the area. However, between the *chabolas*, crumbling structures and *fumaderos* in Valdemingómez there are also other illegal businesses taking advantage of cheap land rent and the absence of clear government rules on tax and business registry. In the other sectors of the Cañada Real Galiana, many of these businesses are dedicated to car workshops and construction. However, as you enter Valdemingómez, the sixth of the sectors, other businesses include furniture warehouses, a transport company (which the local council of Rivas contracts) and several recycling warehouses (white goods such as fridges, freezers and washing machines), and there are even some small cafés and supermarkets, some more secure than others:

> After Juan offers us a tattoo display of his body, we amble down with Julia to a location near the café in the parallel road. We pass the *fumaderos* and *kiosks* on the corner, and turn left down the road, greeting some *gitano* women and children. We approach what we thought was initially a drugs den, only because from the outside it looks like Fort Knox: each window has large, thick bars wedged between them, and as we go in there are two thick front doors, which have between them another iron gate. Inside there is a musty vomit smell and in front of us more iron bars block total access to all the supermarket products on sale in this small grocery store. The irony is that this security structure is managed by a little old *gitano* woman who patters around serving the few drug addicts in front of us; as she walks she talks to herself to remind herself of what she has to get for the customers, only to have to return to ask them again for what they wanted. Behind the bars is a large refrigerated cabinet where there is cheese, yoghurt and other food that needs to stay cool, and against the wall on makeshift shelves are tins of food, biscuits, cereals, fruits and all sorts.

> Julia loses patience and starts to lean through the metal bars, *"Venga ya mujer"* ("Come on woman"), she says. When we are finally seen to, she points up at a piece of cardboard that has on it more cardboard cut-outs of about nine different ice creams. She points through the metal bars at the fruit twister, asking for it, and the little old woman shuffles off to the large freezer and bends down into it. She emerges a minute later with a chocolate cornetto. We chorus *"No"* politely, and say it is the fruit twister that Julia wants. The old woman then acknowledges her mistake

and starts to fish around in the large freezer. She then appears again a minute later with a chocolate ice cream and we say *"Noooo"* and again point out on the cardboard that we want the fruit twister. The old woman returns to the freezer from which the cold mist continues to pour out and emerges again with a chocolate twister. *"¡Qué no! Lo del twister de fruit"* ("No, the fruit twister!") says Julia, before the old woman delves for the last time in the freezer. It seems the chocolate twister is the best she can do and we pay 50 cents.

When we walk out, one of the cars that was parked directly outside has suddenly been swarmed with police and the road has been blocked by a police van. Two officers detain a *gitano* man while two feel around inside a car with special black gloves on. Something has definitely been brewing today, as police activity has been high and constant. We walk out of the road and past the crowds of *gitanos* who look on at the police operation on the parked car, and into the *plaza*.

Indeed, many of the businesses in the area that aren't dedicated to drugs have secure premises, often kitted out with high walls, fences, barbed wire and CCTV cameras. There is clearly is a need for security in an area where disputes can arise quickly between *gitanos* and often result in shooting or violence or both, which means that even in the cafés, weapons are visible and ready to be used. Here, after once again gently trying to convince Julia to present herself to the services to take a pregnancy test, we retreat to a nearby café between the main set of *fumaderos* in Valdemingómez:

Walking down to the parallel road, past the *machacas* and vigilant *gitano* drug dealers, we turn right into a vast puddle before passing several *gitana* women outside their houses. Suddenly Roberto takes a right turn and asks one of the *gitana* women *"¿Podemos tomar café aquí?"* ("Can we get a coffee here?"), before crossing the road. From the outside, it looks like a potential *kiosk* (and maybe it is), but as the short *gitana* peels back the ragged curtains, we enter into a sort of café living room. As we do, we see a large shotgun sitting on the sofa near the dimly-lit living area; a young *gitano* boy about 17–18 comes over, spends a bit of time cleaning it and then gently wraps it in a cloth before taking it away. In the pokey area, there is room for one coffee table and a sort of set of stools against the bar area, which has a small coffee machine and a set of alcoholic drinks. Behind the plastic counter, a set of pastry-like snacks sit awaiting purchase and consumption.

The sheer open availability of weapons, arms and regular eruption of disputes between the *gitanos* and sometimes the *machacas* contributes to a tense and paranoid atmosphere, which is often further amplified by the endless possibility of a police raid. In the next chapter, we show how many of these 'raids' are compromised, but this doesn't mean they don't occur, as we have seen on numerous occasions in Valdemingómez:

In the *plaza* there are 20–30 cars parked up with people smoking and injecting heroin and cocaine. Suddenly, three large black cars appear from nowhere from the second *entrada* and race past us, whipping up dust and all sorts in the process. We squint our eyes as they fly past. It seems they are from the *Grupo Especial de Operaciones* (GEO) (Special Operations Group). The *gitanos* start to emerge from nowhere and converse in the street, making anxious phone calls in the process. A group of them immediately follow the cars as they turn right out of the *plaza* up the road towards the Arab quarter. As we start walking, more and more of the *poblado* emerge to see what is going on. An old *gitano* with no teeth, unable to keep up with the flood of people, stops us and asks what is happening, but we say we don't know. We pick up our pace and continue up the street where already we can see, between the mothers with babies in their arms and children standing around, the road has been closed ahead. It is a raid, but for what reason? It has to be pretty serious as the raids are normally undertaken by the National Police. Given the nature of the GEO's function, we suppose it to be related to terrorism. Only two months ago, three jihadists were arrested in the neighbouring Sector 5 who were *"about to commit attacks,"* we are told. As we approach, more and more flock to the street while the fires burn hard in the cold. As we watch on, policemen come out to cut the road off as the cars surround the property, and soon after another comes out dressed in bullet-proof attire. Meanwhile, other forms of life attempt to go on as normal as we see a man crouch behind a car to smoke a cocaine pipe and outside another *kiosk*, a *machaca* drifts in and out of consciousness.

This illegality inherent in the space, coupled with the surveillance of the *gitanos* and periodic interjections from police raids and 'controls', make them generally distrustful and guarded, but this has a historical context as the *gitanos* have, for some time, lived in precarious circumstances in Spanish society.

Los gitanos: A history of working on the margins

Gitanos have often found themselves living outside other people's cultures, as 'people without a history' (Wolf, 1982). Their difference and the racist treatment toward them can be traced back to the 18th century (Bauman, 1998). As countries across Eastern Europe, the ex-Soviet Union and the developing and third world underwent a process of rapid modernisation, *gitanos* and other nomadic groups found themselves pushed even further to the edges of European society (Cudworth, 2008). Having moved throughout Europe, escaping discrimination and oppressive policing in Eastern Europe, they encountered similar treatment on arrival in parts of Western Europe (Bangieva, 2007). This historic rejection has meant that *gitanos* have become highly capable of cultural adaptation in settings where they have had to survive (Gamella, 1999), interacting in reciprocal contact with hostile host communities in a process of acculturation (Cozzanet et al, 1976). They have, as Sway (1984, p 83) has noted, 'a flexible and successful way of exploiting the economic margins'. This has therefore often promoted unique ways of determining gypsy customs, so much so that some suggest many of the behaviours considered unique to their culture have actually been caused by situations related to social exclusion (Quintero et al, 2007).

In Spain, the *gitanos* have historically suffered varied forms of social persecution, racism and legal discrimination (Poveda and Marcos, 2005) across education, health, employment, housing and the judicial system (Rodríguez et al, 2009). Much of this has been exacerbated by complex urban restructuring processes in city centres over the last 40 years, which has reduced interaction with Spanish communities (Poveda and Marcos, 2005) while confining them to inferior suburban areas with few resources, minimal infrastructure and locking them out of opportunities in city centres (Briggs, 2010). While there have been increased efforts to integrate *gitanos* into Spanish life across Spain (Tomás et al, 2004), they remain confined to the marginal as well as other informal economies that involve the sale of *chatarra* (scrap metal), *cartones* (cardboard boxes) and perhaps *venta ambulante* (street trading) (Jalon and Rivera, 2000). Increasingly, however, these opportunities have become more scant in the wake of new taxation processes and aggressive social policies prohibiting them, which is why, from the mid-1980s onwards, with the advent of large-scale drug distribution in Spain, much of their activity has revolved around the trafficking of drugs (Briggs, 2010).

Drugs, fumaderos and management by fear and violence

Research shows that when drugs started to arrive in bulk in Spain, it was the *gitanos* who started to undercut the competing drug markets by offering high-quality drugs for lower prices (Briggs, 2010). They dealt in the main in heroin in the *barrios* of cities like Madrid and, as a consequence, this has come to define the experience of these particular *poblados*. Indeed, from the 1980s, we can identify 14 large *poblados* as important in Madrid, which include Pitis, Avenida de Guadalajara, Celsa, Las Barranquillas and Valdemingómez in the Cañada Real Galiana.

Figure 2: Spread of the main *poblados* in Madrid

Poblado name	District	Shacks	Poblado name	District	Shacks
1-El Salobral	Villaverde	424	8-Las Barranquillas	Vallecas	120*
2-Mimbreras	La Latina	132	9-Cañada Real	Valdemingómez	2.000
3-Ventorro	Villaverde	?	10-El Aguacate	Carabanchel	30 personas
4-Cañaveral	Vicálvaro	148	11-Puerta de Hierro	Moncloa-Aravaca	16
5-S. Catalina	P. Vallecas	180	12-Las Quinta-Pitis	Fuencarral	12
6-Las Castellanas	S. Fernando	115	13-Plata y Castañar	Villaverde	34*
7-Río Guadarrama	Móstoles	260	14-Valverde	Fuencarral	20

The sale of drugs occurred in each of these *poblados*, often sold from houses, *kiosks*, *fumaderos*, improvised buildings or caravans, 24 hours a day. The main drugs available are heroin, cocaine and various types of amphetamines and cannabis. The *gitano* families manage the drug sales, and operate a strong hierarchy, assigning particular tasks to particular members of the family. Prestige and financial benefits and responsibility are gendered by sex, age and experience. These 'drug clans', as they are known to the media, often have more than one sales point in operation to maximise their profits and to ensure the continuation of business in the event of interruption of their operations. In every sales location there is one person who normally supervises the business with a *mano dura* (tough hand, meaning, to be strict). The success of these families is evident in their ability to transfer their business from place to place. For example, there are key families in Valdemingómez who had initially started some form of drug business in the early 1980s in *poblados* like Pitis, Caño Roto and Salobral (see Figure 2). In this way, the drug business is often inherited, and this is one of the main reasons why social intervention fails in the context of *gitano* families (see Chapter 7).

Relations between families are generally good, and there is cooperation and organisation between them in the trafficking of large amounts of drugs, particularly when it comes to dealing with Colombian cartels (cocaine) and Turkish mafia (heroin). However, when there are disputes between the families or even individuals – which can lead to

Figure 3: Hierarchy of *gitano* relations in Valdemingómez

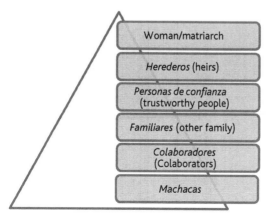

the involvement of the whole family and the patriarch – it is not uncommon for there to be violence, fights and even deaths. *La ley gitana* (the gypsy law) authorises revenge and the use of violence to resolve conflicts between families or, in some cases, whole *poblados*. It is this same law that permits children to grow up and assume the same cultural attitudes and labour roles as their parents – in this case, working in the drug market – and we saw from our time in Valdemingómez that most learn how to drive, fire guns and smoke various substances from a young age.

In each *poblado* there is a hierarchy between the families with respect to the sale of drugs. Those who sell the most carry more social status and because of this, these families have more collective power and influence over collective decisions in the *poblado*. These families are easily identifiable by the visible projection of their wealth, often wearing gold jewellery, expensive designer clothing and driving fast, expensive sports cars. All this was particularly evident in the 'golden age' of heroin and cocaine sales in *poblados* during the 1980s and 1990s, when there seemed to be a collective disinterest on the part of politicians and police in the expansion of drug markets across the country. This is why the arrival and hybridisation of these two drug markets was able to propel the wealth and power to these *poblados*.

For the *gitanos*, drugs are by far the most profitable commodity, and Valdemingómez harbours among the most powerful *gitano* families in Spain. We estimate there to be around 13 main families in the area that own between them around 40 drug-selling points – either *kiosks* or *fumaderos*. The hierarchy is formed of members of the same family, each with between 8–20 people, the matriarch being a woman who has the most important function in managing the organisation while the men tend to manage the labour of sales and security. The younger family members take on important posts when they arrive at adolescence, often being instructed and trained by senior family members to inherit the business, hence their position as *herederos* (heirs). As they are incorporated into the family business, it is common for much younger boys and girls to also assume some small positions such as look-outs, or even to receive clients under the supervision of adults. The *personas de confianza* (trustworthy people) can be either *gitanos* or otherwise, normally recognised for their working reputation in the trafficking and/or sale of the drugs; most commonly, they will buy and sell in bulk or be responsible for taking important players working in drug distribution to and from different places. Even though *gitanos* often have extensive families, priority for working in the drug market is given to those in closer vicinity, and these are called *familiares* (other family members). The *colaboradores* (collaborators) are those who exchange stolen goods/information for drugs and/or can also be involved with laundering money in the local area.

Each *kiosk* and *fumadero* has various employees. The first, who are normally located on the outside door, are the *machacas* who let people in, assist with drug deals, look out and clean up. They are located on the outside door to fill the puddles, maintain the fires and warn of any police presence. Within the inside wall of the venue, another *machaca* will normally open the door after a code word from another on the outside. This person may also help with parking *cundas'* or other clients' cars if the location has a large parking area. Thereafter, to access the *fumadero*, the client will need to pass another *machaca* giving another password to enter the smoking/dealing area:

> Outside one *fumadero* we first get talking to a crowd of four drug users, all of whom practically stand in the fire for warmth. It is quite incredible to look at these people, but most seem fairly harmless as they are in a permanent state of intoxication. Daniel smiles at one in particular, and when he greets him in the same way in return, he counts four teeth. Beneath his beard and the

blackness of his face, he has tanned skin, having spent some time exposed to the elements. He stands with some toes sticking out of his worn trainers, his clothes ragged and worn, and nails almost as long as his fingers. And as he approaches he shakes Daniel's hand as the dirt from his black palm clasps his.

Minutes later, Diego bangs on the gate of the house at which we stand, and the bearded man hurries to him. Diego asks us to be let into the *fumadero* so the bearded man starts whispering through the gate to the guard on the other side. After a minute or so, the gate slowly opens and the supposed guard is another drug addict, half high and half consciously mumbling as his eyes flicker between closed and ajar. We walk into the courtyard of the *fumadero*: in front of the house are two fairly robust doors, and to the right a pile of rubbish and rubble, with a makeshift hut for the *machacas* to sleep in and to the left another hut where some people are permitted to smoke drugs. On the floor, between the dirt and brown puddles, are literally thousands of castaway drug vials. At weekends Diego says the cars pull in here and people come in and stay for the weekend to use drugs. Some, he says, come and spend between €3,000 to €4,000 in a weekend. We turn around at the open gate and the *machaca* stands, leaning against it half asleep, high on a dose of heroin and cocaine.

Clients normally purchase drugs through a gap that is criss-crossed with iron bars, and it is this room that is linked to a high security room known as a bunker. Access to the bunker is impossible from the *fumadero*, and there is normally a specific entrance for *gitano* family members and/or VIP clients. Within the bunker, one person manages the sales with the least amount of drugs as possible, and will normally have enough drugs to last 12 hours of sales, so between 150–200 grams, as a means of minimising losses in the event of a police raid. The protection of the interior varies according to the type of construction and importance of the *gitano* family. For example, some are made up of up to seven armoured doors, reinforced walls and safe boxes. There are also various carbon cookers, drainpipes and corrosive liquids that assist in cutting and preparing the drugs, but also with their elimination. There are never large amounts of money in the bunkers, and funds are emptied regularly every 8–12 hours, with the cash transferred to other locations around the capital before being invested in commodities, property and cars. Less common, although it still happens, is that some *gitano* families will keep the cash in high denomination notes of €200 and €500 in hidden walls and secret locations in and around the property.

Photo 14: Inside a *fumadero* where drugs are mixed and cut

Such is their organisation that it is estimated that within two minutes of a police raid starting, it is possible to have destroyed all the drugs, money and other incriminating material – two minutes being the estimated time it takes to batter down the reinforced walls and doors. All these techniques and measures taken by the *gitanos* have been built up from experience in other *poblados* in Madrid. The *gitanos* will still often physically coax potential clients, in particular, coming up to passing cars, telling them the road has been sealed up ahead and offering free cocaine hits, while the *machaca*'s role in attracting clients is far more passive, largely due to their almost permanent intoxication.

We have no evidence in this study to suggest that the *gitanos* launder money, but this is not to say they don't. What is clear is that money is needed to justify the symbolisms of wealth such as their luxury cars and expensive jewellery. Towards the latter stages of our fieldwork, in the autumn of 2016, some *kiosks* and *fumaderos* started to accept things like gold and precious stones as a means of payment for drugs. This is because the *gitanos* like to show off material trinkets as a means of reflecting a superior social status and how they participate in society like others as competent consumers (see Chapter 2). This also determines the key figures in the *gitano* families: those who are adorned with the most jewels, gold and the like. Key male family members dress in smart suits and hats, perhaps with a gold walking stick, while matriarchs wear gold jewellery, and have often had breast enlargements. Those further down the family hierarchy normally dress in sports and casual clothes. To measure success and social standing in Valdemingómez, the most important families are those who sell the most amounts of drugs, consequently resulting in their ability to display consumer status items, while a more inferior family is one dependent on the former in the sale of drugs.

These power hierarchies are maintained and reproduced at all levels largely because the *gitano* cultural interactions are confined to limited social circles (that is, only fellow *gitanos*) and spatially restricted to the area – there is very little contact between the families in Valdemingómez in Sector 6 and in Sector 5 of the Cañada Real Galiana. This restriction on cultural interactions forces hierarchical relations to revolve around the maintenance of a particular set of symbolic interactions as a means of determining self-respect in a closed space. Taken together, this does not make them socially excluded per se, as they demonstrate all the will to want to be socially included as consumers (Young, 1999; Nightingale, 2012; Winlow and Hall, 2013; see also Chapter 3), only that they are set in ideological competition with each other rather than anyone else. For this to occur, there needs to be a set of norms and codes that place others economically, socially and culturally inferior to them. Those people are the drug users in Valdemingómez, and these power relations are reinforced on a daily basis by the adults as well as the young *gitano* children:

As we talk to Roberto, a chorus of half-asleep drug addicts sit and lounge about at the provided dinner tables. The group of *gitano* boys see Margarita outside one of the *fumaderos* and start to dare each other to approach her before one decides to steal her coat from her back and tosses it into a nearby fire where another *machaca* keeps warm. The coat bursts into flames and Margarita screams and makes one-hand gestures at them. The *machaca* nearby tries to verbally intervene but he can't do anything as these young boys are untouchable – any intervention would mean the quick presence of their parents and would almost certainly end in violence if they had to defend them. As the scene starts to capture the attention of the docile drug addicts in their post-lunch drug taking, the *gitano* kids then steal a blanket from Margarita's back and toss it into the fire. In her fragile state she is helpless and her weak hand gestures only make the children jump up and down in glee. The children then approach her and make faces and insult her as if she was totally alien, before she manages to scare them off temporarily, aided in part by the same *machaca*, who tries to reason with them. As they run off, one falls over in the rubbish and his friends are quick to rescue him, thinking perhaps that he has fallen into some used syringes (the area is strewn with used syringes and other paraphernalia). For young boys no older than five they seem to be aware of these dangers as they strip down the youngest boy, and check for marks. As they dress him again, and in anger, they start to take rocks and throw them in the direction of Margarita.

It is only then that Roberto marches over, waving off the children before shepherding over the bent old woman to the safer territory of the harm reduction team bus. It is only then that we realise how startled she is, as she tos and fros from seat to seat, wondering what to do – she seems to feel violated. As she sits, Roberto rubs her back as she puts her bag full of everything she owns and everything she has to sell on the floor. She sits in a pile and puts her dirty black hands in her face and starts to cry. On top of all her suffering, her most basic things to maintain her daily life in this misery are robbed from her for the short-term and aimless entertainment of some *gitano* children.

As she gathers her strength between some approaches to do business for clean paraphernalia, Yolanda wanders over with four stray pet dogs that follow her, as if she is a magical sage. She has come to collect her medication. All we can gather about this woman is that she lives alone in Valdemingómez after having suffered a bereavement when her husband died. We have seen her wash cars for the *gitanos* for only five Euros. One dog looks like a bear and has with him several friends of lesser size. All the dogs haphazardly follow their graceful master, Yolanda, this resolute woman in her early 50s, with long silver hair and a worn face. The dogs jog around her, in and out of the tables, and in front of cars before circling towards her after she collects her medication.

As they meander off, so do we towards Adrian's *chabola* on the corner, to speak to him. We step up the broken wooden boards, and looking at his collapsing shed, call to him through his wooden structure. He asks us if we are here to cure his dog's leg and it is only then that we see a skinny but quite cute dog limp towards us on three legs, licking its lips with its little pink tongue; the dog is nervous as Adrian shouts at it to come off the road; just as well, for as Yolanda passes, suddenly a *gitano* driver, much to his amusement, emergency brakes as he almost crashes into the large dog. He drives off laughing to himself while Yolanda yells back insults at him.

As we can see in varying intervals of these field notes, the *gitanos* place the drug users at the bottom of the social chain; they are a source of entertainment and ridicule, and often with extreme consequences:

As we come to the conclusion of an interview with Nacho, a local policeman who has worked 25 years in Valdemingómez and many of the surrounding *poblados*, he recalls something quite remarkable as he sits forward, sipping his tall beer. He shakes his head as he remembers how devastating the heroin epidemic was in the 1980s. *"In particular, the poor areas south of Madrid were mostly affected, thousands of people lost, a whole generation,"* he says (see Chapter 2). We can't tell if his eyes well with tears or they squint from the fifth cigarette he smokes. We get on to the subject of prostitution and he starts to fiddle around with his phone as if he has got bored with our questioning. Some seconds later, however, he shows us a video clip recorded by a *gitano* in a *fumadero* where we watch for a few minutes as a woman in her mid-20s dressed in a vest and knickers puts a condom on another drug user, verbally battles off the abuse, jokes and jibes before she starts to suck his dick. As the man exaggerates the pleasure he receives for a few minutes, he turns her around and she drops her knickers. He proceeds to have sex with her quickly and hard, much to the cheers of the other people in the *fumadero*, some of whom are also recording it. A minute or two later, he ejaculates and she walks off, swearing at everyone as they jeer at her, while she tries to restore some dignity by pulling up her knickers and dusting herself down. The clip stops and we really don't know what to say as the policeman lights up his sixth cigarette. Most of his colleagues have sent this to each other via WhatsApp.

Drug users: Working in the margins

Later that day.

As Adrian clutches his dog with his blood-stained hands, he lights up a cigarette. We learn of how he was practically abandoned by his family from the age of nine as he grew up in a reform school. Without much success at school, his life of crime, robbing and living on the streets of south Madrid in Embajadores began shortly after: *"En la calle aprendes como ser delincuente porque no sabes nada más"* ("In the street, you learn how to be a criminal because you don't know anything else") he tells us, and the bone structure on his face becomes apparent while he inhales a cigarette. He regrets it all, he says, and even with his 47 years he has managed to fit 21 of those in prison (see Chapter 5).

Adrian then fiddles around among the mess and used needles in his *chabola* to try and find the dog lead. He then attaches his dog to it, clutches it and recalls how he started to live in one former *poblado*, Las Barranquillas, when it started to open up as a drug-dealing hotspot as a consequence of other *poblado* closures (see Chapter 3). There he worked for one of the major *gitano* families and was paid in drugs as he watched out for the police. He got tired of how they terrorised and beat their staff – the drug addicts – and stopped working for them before the *poblado* closed down. Now he maintains his addiction on a high dosage of methadone, and the €75 he earns from one of the nearby *fumaderos* is spent on cocaine.

He says he needs something from the harm reduction team, so we all walk off together towards the bus. He says his goodbyes before disappearing into the medical bus, and we get talking to Roberto. Ricardo, the man who had a court case last week who we talked to in the *fumadero* the day of the case, got some community service for the string of petty crimes he had committed. He continues to work for the *gitanos* in the *fumadero* and will unlikely do the community service just like the last time and the time before and the time before. Roberto says most of the people from Valdemingómez have numerous criminal histories, saying how one he knows has amassed no fewer than 80 offences. Another, he says, was wanted by the police in different districts of Madrid almost every day: they could never locate him because he was always detained at a different police station each night. He says that the policy of throwing everyone in prison during the 1980s and 1990s had to stop. *"Now the policy is a little more lenient, but it's the same, as these people rack up 10 offences and then go to prison as the community service doesn't work,"* he says.

Here in these field notes that follow on from our observations of the *gitano* kids we get a glimpse into the work opportunities and working conditions available for the people who live in Valdemingómez. Several things are important to note, the first being the brutal reality of working for the *gitanos* that Juan recounts and second, how, in Ricardo's case, the nature of the work – precisely because it is bound to his drug dependence – essentially makes him a 'slave' to the *gitanos*, to the point where he cannot attend a court hearing that determines a sentence for a petty theft he committed. Ricardo is not alone in the work he does, and the work available for people like him varies because in Valdemingómez many have to be creative and manipulative with the meagre resources available to them to sustain their drug dependence while at the same time, grinding out small forms of self-respect.

Machacando: The machaca worker

Esclavo (slave) or *trabajar en esclavitud* (working in slavery) was used numerous times to describe someone working as a *machaca*, a Spanish word deriving from the verb *machacar*, which means to mash, crush, batter or be pounded. We can only conclude that someone working as a *machaca* for the *gitanos* is therefore someone who is seen as completely broken. The work they do often involves police lookouts, acting as doormen, cleaners and/or generally helping inside *fumaderos* with drug dealing, perhaps even minding children or escorting *gitanos* from place to place – although this depends on the 'trust' they have established with the *gitano* family employers:

Daniel: *What is a machaca?*

Marcos: *A consumer who is established in the poblado and already works for the gitano families, selling drugs, doing small jobs, from looking after the children to looking out for the police. Then, within the machacas, there is a mini hierarchy; there are those who are seen as better than others and those who are recommended, and those who escort the family around. More than anything, this comes from the confidence and attitudes that the families may have towards their workers. So there are some who transport people and traffic the drugs.*

Daniel: *And how do I get this trust?*

Marcos: *By how you are related to people in the poblado, your background, your CV.*

Daniel: *So I needed to have been there some years?*

Marcos: *Probably aesthetically and physically you need to look better, probably you are someone who doesn't inject.*

Daniel: *So if I inject it affects my chances of what job I do?*

Marcos: *Of course, injecting demotes you more.*

In our study, we met *machacas* who were consumers but not *personas de confianza* as Marcos had described. In the main we came across those who tended to guard *fumaderos*, look out for the police and do odds tasks that needed doing. The other interesting part of Marcos's discourse is the idea of the CV: the accumulation of experience you can get from working for different *gitano* families, and how, in turn, this can potentially get someone work should their former employees speak well of them. However, in the case of our study, we found little evidence of this; in fact, quite the reverse – almost everyone had been terrorised and victimised by them. The mode of drug use seems also have bearing on social status – injecting is seen as something that carries more stigma and is related to a lack of potential work capacity.

While some *machacas* work day shifts, the majority work nights when more clients tend to come, sleep outside in their own shacks, rest standing up or sleep in rubbish. They are paid wages in drug doses every three or four hours, normally just enough to sustain them. There is no holiday time, no sick pay, no job security, certainly no company car and no bonuses attached to these jobs, and the shifts are normally at least 12 hours. Such is the demand on them that it is common to see them sleeping standing up, a position that over time contributes to some developing arched backs (also as a consequence of frantically searching the ground for strewn drugs, clean syringes and things of value to sell). During our fieldwork, it was estimated that there were between 70 and 100 people working in these circumstances at any one time. To make matters worse, most are subject to almost continuous abuse and violence, often with extreme consequences, as Julia explained to us:

Julia:	*I have worked as a machaca, for one of the toughest gitano families.*
Daniel:	*And how was the experience?*
Julia:	*Until they beat the shit out of me and left me in a coma.*

Daniel: *So then you had to leave, you were in hospital?*

Julia: *Yes, and I left Valdemingómez and came back … but it's because they felt like it, you know, because the gitanos are like that. They never let you explain things. They come over, beat you and that's it. Here [in Valdemingómez] they treat you like dogs, they think like dogs, they think we are dogs. I know a gitano nearby town who sells drugs, there he says nothing, but here they think they are kings.*

Over the period of the fieldwork, both Juan and Julia – among numerous others – were employed as *machacas*. Indeed, in that time, they obtained and lost jobs for differing periods but rarely worked at the same time or for the same employer, often alternating so one could help support the other with their drug dependence (recall Chapter 1 when we were in the *fumadero* with Julia). However, at the same time, this often caused conflict in the relationship because one was seen as having access to 'drugs on tap', and we observed numerous times how they often concealed doses from each other. In these field notes, taken early in 2016, Juan increased his drug consumption when he was employed as a *machaca* and spent days on end in the *fumadero*:

We take extremely small steps against the dusty wind as we heard towards a look-out over a new *fumadero* that has just opened about 3-4 weeks ago. As we stop, several pieces of used *plata* (foil used to smoke heroin) and tissue with blood stains on whisk past us into the air and down into the wasteland plains below, which quickly hoard the rubbish that was on the other side of the *plaza*. As we look behind us, Juan approaches us, kicking rubbish out of the way as he looks at the ground. As he nears, his face looks drawn, his cheeks hug the bone structure of his jaw and we can see he has lost a lot of weight: a tell-tale sign that his drug consumption has increased while his contact with the harm reduction team has dwindled, as he seems malnourished. He lights up a cigarette that smokes itself in the busy wind, and starts to give us an update. It seems he has lost his job as a *machaca* – although he calls it a *"vigilante"* or *"guard"* – probably because *machaca* carries with it a negative social status. *"Better to say you are a vigilante than a machaca,"* as Raul had told us once, even though ideologically speaking they are one and the same.

We try to find an alternative position where there is shelter from the tormenting wind and walk behind the church to the sort of communal washing area; this is the only fresh water source in the area where people can wash or drink water. In the three days without his job for the *gitanos*, he has struggled to find money to support his dependency, although he says he is lucky as he relies on Julia who still has her job inside the *fumadero*, mostly *"cleaning, bagging the drugs in small wraps and serving drugs to the clients"*. She has hardly come out in the time it has been open, working 12-hour shifts from 10am to 10pm or vice versa, from 10pm to 10am, and is paid *"two doses every three hours"* or the equivalent of €10 worth of heroin and cocaine. This was also Juan's wage as a *vigilante*, and although he was also tasked with other forms of work, one of his main roles was to warn about the police coming by shouting *"Fran"* or *"Diego"*; when the police leave, they shout *"clean"*.

As he points across at the driveway where he worked, he seems restless in his sidesteps and points at the blond woman who was his boss – the *gitana* Carmen – as she marches across the *plaza*. He says she had a dispute with her sister with whom she used to sell, so she set up her own house and opened it for clients. Juan lost his job because the police pulled up one day and told him to *"get everyone out of the fumadero"* and he was given a time limit to do it. He couldn't do it in the time as many of the clients inside where half-drugged and half-asleep, so the police then gave an ultimatum to Carmen and said *"sack him* [Juan] *or we will close down your selling operations"*. So she had to sack him.

As we talk, we count four men who come over within a matter of metres of us and urinate against the church and the metal storage container; another wedges himself in a corner to protect himself from the wind before administering a groin injection. Juan moves on to tell us that a women manages the *fumaderos* differently to a man, in that there is generally more order and a stricter regime, *"they don't give you drug advances and lay down the rules more, they get more respect"*. As he says this, a thin woman in only a t-shirt and trousers searches the floor. Daniel asks her if she is looking for *chutas* or syringes before pointing in the direction of about 10 used ones that lie next to the wall. She hurries over and picks them up with her bare hands and puts them in a small plastic box, telling him how she will exchange them with the harm reduction team for tobacco.

Suddenly Carmen summons Juan over to run an errand. He scampers off and finds a ladder before placing it suspiciously against a lamppost that has from it numerous illegally assembled cables connected to one of the large electricity pylons. It seems the *fumadero* has lost power. *"He is also an electrician,"* says Rubén, as Juan cautiously climbs to the top of the ladder as it wobbles, before feeling and fiddling around above his head, in the hope that something he does will return the electricity to the *fumadero*. It seems to have worked and he then receives more instructions from Carmen before starting another search among the rubbish. He then makes up a kind of scarecrow made out of car tyres, a workman's jacket and loads of sticks that we think may indicate that the *fumadero* is open for business, but because of the adverse weather conditions, there is no one to welcome customers at

the entrance of the driveway. It is too fucking cold. Juan may be
unemployed, but he has some sort of temporary task.

Juan may not be under direct employment with Carmen in
the *fumadero*, but it doesn't mean she can't call on his services
in exchange for a hit: after all, there is little else Juan can do
given his situation of needing to maintain his dependency
in Julia's absence. These errands blur the role of the *machaca*
as thereafter we saw him linger around putting wood on the
fire that keeps Carmen warm. Nevertheless, the *machaca's* role
seems to have no concession, there is no end to the demands
on their labour; they must always be available regardless of
the task and irrespective of the time.

For these reasons, the *machaca* is seen as someone who has
reached the lowest stage of their addiction, someone who
has superseded their own personal morals, and for this reason
the work is often seen as socially negative; it carries a degree
of social stigma that is buttressed by the abusive treatment
from the *gitanos*. *Machacas* are seen as people who have lost
everything, they are perceived to have forfeited their own
wellbeing, people who lack interest in their personal dignity
and individual upkeep, and who are prepared to consent to
the violence and control inflicted on them by the *gitanos*. The
fact that they carry this image often acts as a justification for
others to reason that their position or dependence is not as
'bad' as the *machacas*; at least they don't work for the *gitanos*,
and can supposedly carry their head high(er).

In this arena at the bottom of society, which already
carries a social label about the activity that goes on there, the
consequence of these interactions is therefore manifested in
micro-power struggles and identity conflicts. No one wants
to be the lowest of the low living among the low, so the
figure of the *machaca* therefore assists in an *ideological social
ordering*: it ensures the *gitanos* reside as socially superior over
them while, and at the same time, it produces yet also eases

tensions in the identity power struggles among the drug dependents who live and come to the area. This ordering therefore contributes to a form of 'dependence denial' about personal situations that assists in the negation of the gravity of their circumstances (see Chapter 8).

The moral economy

For those who cannot obtain work as a *machaca* – or those who don't qualify and/or have been sacked – a different form of survival entails, which involves *buscar la vida* (find a way by yourself) in the moral economy. In neoliberal terms, we feel this represents the most brutal and challenging form of meritocratic initiative someone could possibly need to show to 'get by'. Drug dependency has become the central feature of these people's lives (see Chapter 5) and, as Julia hinted at earlier, sustaining this revolves around the innovative exploitation of goods/people, resources and opportunities through participation in the *moral economy* (Karandinos et al, 2015; Wakeman, 2016). In the case of how Valdemingómez operates, this seemed to hinge on loans on social security days, sexual services, borrowing, exchanges for cigarettes or syringes or similar artefacts/agreements relative to the value of cultural-specific, thrown-away commodities available in the area (see Mars et al, 2014).

This is not the whole story as the moral economy has some function through the reciprocal relations or 'favours' that developed with these necessities. For example, when Julia returned to Valdemingómez after her hospitalisation, having been beaten by the *gitanos*, she started a relationship with Juan, which was beneficial in supporting their dependence:

Julia: *It's not as if I am dependent on him [Juan], but you see? If you have a partner and it's more or less serious you are not at a loose*

> *end, you are more watched, protected and you won't let the other work in a gitano house and then we come back to the same thing: I don't know why we worked in the house of the gitanos if we earn more together, like that we earn more. It's like you get this dependence because you get up and you have the mono sorted surely and you don't have to give in to anything to solve it.*

Daniel: *It's like some sort of agreement between two people?*

Julia: *Yes, that's it, he helps me and I help him. Or another way is by one being a machaca and another being a prostitute, otherwise there is no other way to drug yourself … or robbing.*

However, there was no real limitation to the way in which these avenues were explored as many of these people demonstrated diverse ways of making use of the waste and rubbish to their dexterous advantage, victimising and manipulating each other, and were unafraid to threaten and use violence on each other. For this reason, these kinds of agreements did not always sustain themselves, mainly because the environment and social interactions in Valdemingómez promote mistrust – even between 'partners'. Furthermore, it was commonplace for there to be situations in which the agreements could not always be honoured, which required emergency improvisation. In these field notes, Nano, a man who had lived for some years in Valdemingómez, offered a kind of injecting service in exchange for his drug purchases. Here, he does not have any spare clean syringes when his services are called on:

Next to the large container, in front of us, a desperate man – in what appears to be his work clothes – runs up to Nano's tent (known as *El jefe de pinchas* or *The injecting boss*). He calls inside while Nano says *"Coge uno en el suelo"* ("Take one from the floor") and the man runs off in something between complete frustration and desperation. He kicks the dust as he runs up to the *fumadero* where he asks them, only for them to shake their heads before running off to another. A few minutes later, he returns to Nano's tent seemingly in success, and opens it, begging him to mix and inject the drugs for him.

The almost terminal nature of these people's physical and social circumstances and their drug dependence combined with the endless financial moot points and incessant conflictive situations requiring improvisation frequently resulted in high-risk behaviour, manipulation and violence. This is further amplified by the dire conditions in Valdemingómez; it is a place littered with rubbish, junk, used syringes, rats and dead animals, and taken together, this impacts on how relationships are managed on a day-to-day basis.

Daily life and relationships

The cultural and structural conditions of Valdemingómez produce a very distinctive set of social conditions that impact on the everyday experience of these people and, coupled with their quite damaged history, makes for an environment that is detrimental to their wellbeing and one that poses constant challenges. While some degree of normality is sought, it is consistently countered by the daily tests of finding enough money for a hit, negotiating the violence from the *gitanos*, the police and other drug users, as well as striving to construct some degree of dignity and respect from their existence. This means that more often than not, the norms and codes of the moral economy are regularly ruptured, which intensifies daily life and social relations.

V is for vendetta

The dust kicks up every few seconds as buyers come and go in cars and Daniel wanders over to Rubén's parked car that sits gathering grit and dirt. Daniel looks at him staring into a space and asks him what's wrong ... only to realise that the space into which he stares is precisely what is wrong. Juan and Julia's tent is no more, and all that remains is a sort of charcoal patch on the ground. We look around for some battered-out green tent but there is none. To our right, we instead see several new large tents which stand in the beating sun, and behind the church a small community of drug addicts taking shelter from the sweltering heat while others amble up to the harm reduction team bus.

We take a short walk to see the open areas almost empty as people take shade where they can from the sun. Today the weather is holding no prisoners, as even the passengers in the *cundas* are all at least half-naked. A woman dressed in a mini skirt curses us as we walk on, thinking we are following her. We aren't though. We are, in fact, looking at the cleaner state of the *plaza*; almost all

Photo 15: Retrieving water from the harm reduction team in sweltering heat

the rotting piles of rubbish have been removed. Across the other side, the wild meadows now feel like jungles as some of the weeds and long grass tower over us. The *fumaderos* have outside them the sweating *machacas*, some of whom wear long-sleeved clothes and even jumpers.

We walk past a road that has been blockaded to stop the *cundas* going down it, then realising that this was the oldest part of the sector where people had initially settled here some 30–40 years ago with their houses and vegetable patches. Even today, among all the grime, drugs and desperation, these houses still exist. Across the *plaza*, on the main road, there are several large paddling pools on the broken road. In them play gypsy children, the day long; the heat is on.

Returning once again to get an update on why we can't find Juan and Julia, we get talking to the ever-reliable harm reduction team. Today they have had to park further from the *plaza* because the frequency of *cunda* arrivals is continually causing dust to blow over. Yet even the extra 100m can make a big difference to those who are engaged with the service: there seems little interest to go the extra distance in the 40° heat. Today, at the communal desk, where the drug addicts eat, drink, sleep and get in to disagreements and fights, Roberto sits and eats a soup dish, nodding and winking at me as Daniel waves. A skinny couple pull up in a battered car, and get out, talking to each other in a senseless slur. They politely ask for food as they falter as they stand half-naked; such is their lack of body weight that you can see their ribs. They sit and eat, and between returning for more soup, bread and water, make sloppy kisses on each other in front of the other half-asleep drug addicts at the table.

We ask the team about Julia and Juan since we have not been able to locate them. A week ago, their tent was burnt down. "*They had too many vendettas*" says Roberto, "*luckily they were not in there sleeping when it happened,"* he adds. The loss of the tent has forced Juan into working for another *gitano* drug clan in the main street, some 500m away. *"We don't know where they live or are staying,"* says Roberto. Julia, who we had tried to help convince several times to get a pregnancy test done despite being almost six months pregnant still works for the *gitanos* on night shifts, but now has a bed inside the *fumadero.* Yesterday, however, she had a constructive conversation with the harm reduction team about pregnancy tests, even though, once again, Juan got violent and had to be sanctioned (in the sense that benefits are withdrawn such as free cigarettes, as the team cannot deny them things like food, drug paraphernalia, etc).

D is for destitute

By now lunch has finished as there sit two drug addicts, both with their heads in their hands on the stained dining table. A man with a scarred and burnt face picks large scabs off his bleeding lips using one of the van's wing mirrors in an effort to make a good job of it. A thin woman gets out of nearby car and demands some of the soup dish before retreating to the back seat of the car to sample it. Perhaps discontent, she then winds down the window and throws it out on to the ground before lighting up some heroin on foil. Some minutes later, she sings peacefully to herself before falling asleep against the car window. Sonia then comes over to collect some water; her body spasms exaggerate her every movement and even the expressions on her face as it looks at times as if someone is applying electrical shocks to her eyes and body. This is as much her motor neurone syndrome as it is the effects of the cocaine she has just taken. We talk to Roberto and he tells us that Gema and Antonio had a close call recently when Gema left a candle burning in their *chabola* overnight and it burnt down. Number 79, Plaza de Valdemingómez, Cañada Real

Photo 16: Mitchell's 'vertical sleeping'

Galiana, Madrid is their address, and their *chabola* now under total reconstruction, it seems.

Suddenly we hear loud but solemn moaning and groaning sounds. It is Mitchell wandering over – the man Daniel had described as having the same walking position as his sitting one, his back being totally bent from hunting and gathering in rubbish and falling asleep standing up. In fact, it is exactly the same as his sleeping one (see Photo 16). He scuffs his slip-on rubber shoes along the floor as the red socks he has on peep out of the small holes in the shoes. As he shuffles along, his long arms drape by the side of his legs that are just about tucked into leggings, and hanging over him is a raggy, quilted jacket, weighed down by a carton of milk he has found. In his black hands he carries a small beer and an empty champagne bottle.

At first he beckons the workers over as if it is an emergency, and there is some concern that perhaps someone has overdosed as Mitchell uses noises to communicate the problem, but it seems it is something minor. They walk away from him with their hands in their pockets, and he then approaches us and looks at us helplessly, as if he had bought a winning lottery ticket but thereafter lost it. He tries to beg a Euro from us with noises before showing us the cracks in his black hands and how they have started to become infected and are scabbing over with pus. Perhaps due to the lack of attention he is getting, he lumbers over to the bus and starts to bang his head against it before collapsing in his standing-up-sleeping pose. The workers usher him away and he returns to stand next to us and resumes his standing-up-resting-sleeping pose, the beer spilling out of his can as he seemingly falls asleep.

When he wakes a few minutes later, he tosses the can and bottle away and starts to fish around in some nearby rubbish, finding quite easily a large sofa. Though he is unable to carry it, and even though he doesn't know exactly what to do with it, he tries to lift it. After no success, someone joins him and they thereafter spend about five minutes trying to work out how they can move the sofa between them. But Mitchell is not strong enough or even stable enough or anything enough, and there is no real communication with his friend. Perhaps in frustration, his friend takes it upon himself to balance the sofa on his head and shoulders, and makes off with it while Mitchell is left to recover his breath as he leans over the rubbish skip. Shortly after he returns to his looting, finding a naked Barbie doll – no doubt to trade or sell to someone for something.

R is for respect

We walk on and into the main drug-dealing area of Valdemingómez, and alongside us walks Antonio, a thin dishevelled man who today wears a cap and is certainly more talkative. Antonio smokes and injects heroin and cocaine, has AIDS, hep C and other physical health problems. We walk and talk and in our conversational amble find ourselves outside two rubbish skips. He starts to reach in and dig around. We ask him what he is looking for as we lean over into where the flies buzz around all manner of rubbish. *"Una puerta"* ("A door") he says, before pulling out a plastic chair and trying it out by sitting on it; though it is broken it barely seems to notice his featherweight body sitting on it. As he sets aside the chair, he continues in his search.

Photos 17 and 18: Antonio (literally) in search of respect

He is looking for a door because last month, Gema, his girlfriend, accidentally set light to their *chabola* and it burnt to the ground. Now, in mid construction of the next one, which sits next door to the former in the rubbish heap, he brushes off old food only to be disappointed that someone has thrown away a good mattress: *"Todos los colchones tienen bichos, es la ley"* ("All the mattresses have bugs, it's the law") he says, as he mixes his grumbling with singing. We help him search as he then reaches for an old wing mirror in the rubbish tip before setting it down on the ground. He looks as it as if he has been sifting for gold for months and finally found it. He reaches into the plastic and tries to wedge out the mirror, taking apart the plastic bolts in the process. As he unhinges the mirror, he dusts it, licking his black hands in the process to assess its quality. Another one for the take-home pile as he puts it on top of the chair.

He then wanders off as if he has forgotten it to get some food, and we say we will look out for it. As we do, we cannot help but notice the high police presence in the area since we came back to the *plaza*. We have counted three Local Police cars, one National Police car and now a Civil Guard car is hovering around our parked car. When they wind down their window and start asking one of the women we know across the *plaza* who is the owner of the car, they then drive up to us before taking a look at us and then driving off – we are not the ones who they are looking for today, it seems.

7

The council, police and health services: An impasse to solutions

Photo 19: 'RIP Public Health'

We sit down and catch up with Julia on some of the concrete stumps outside the church as one of the harm reduction workers comes down from the bus and takes a piss against it. As we move outside into the bright light, drug addicts stagger past us towards the bus to pick up breakfast. It seems warmer outside than in the freezing cold van, and to our gratitude the sun creeps out of the clouds, bringing us some welcome warmth on this bitter winter day. Behind us, next to the church, a man dressed in rags wobbles up to what seems to be the place where he sleeps, which is a series of blankets and a cardboard box. He sifts through everything and finds a syringe, after which he prepares to inject himself. As we sit and talk, a large white van parks next to us and the two thin men inside smoke heroin and cocaine from foil. Julia then tells us about police corruption, and about how some officers receive blow jobs from some of the women in the area, before we then get on to the subject of support for drug users who both live and visit Valdemingómez. As we anticipated, she praises the 365-day service of the harm reduction bus that turns up around 10am and leaves at 6pm, but with one critique:

Daniel: *So what other forms of help are there apart from the harm reduction team?*

Julia: *Well, there is Remar.*

Daniel: *What is that?*

Julia: *Food, no one else brings food, Fridays they come, those Christians, and give us dinner, clothes, but the people that really help us are the harm reduction team who are like saviours to us. But I also think they are doing it badly, like many times when I've been talking to them, I say it because they are accommodating us. I mean, if they weren't here, we wouldn't eat, we wouldn't have breakfast, or anything, and I am grateful to these people. Some time ago, I was a thin 53 kilos but now I am 68 again because I am able to eat, they give me food.*

Daniel: *What do you mean by 'accommodating' you?*

Julia: *They are accommodating us, put it here for us and making it easier to continue to live here. Because now the bus comes and if I say I am hungry, I just wait for the bus. I don't have to go anywhere to eat or wait until tomorrow because the bus will bring me biscuits or sandwiches. Many times when talking to them I think they are facilitating us because giving*

> *us so much help, they are making us more*
> *comfortable here.*

Back at the bus, we get talking to Sergio – another resident who appears from time to time at the harm reduction team bus. He grabs what he can from the table, which includes a ham sandwich and a hot drink, and starts to devour it. Curiously on his t-shirt there is a picture of the grim reaper that resembles the face of the Spanish president Mariano Rajoy, and to the side there is a gravestone that reads *'RIP Sanidad Publica'* ('RIP Public Health').

Introduction

What is precisely contributing to the continued functioning of the drug market in Valdemingómez? How is it so many arrive here at this point in their dependency, yet so few are able to recover? If the council and police know where the problem is, why are they not able to intervene? Here in our discussion with Julia we get some clues as to why this is the case, for it is simply not just the ready availability and demand for drugs (see Chapter 4). Julia talks about police corruption and how the harm reduction team generally seems to 'maintain' people in their misery, and both of these areas are linked to wide political deficiencies (see Chapters 2, 3 and 4). This is important as a moot point arises from potential meaningful intervention because the 'problem' of Valdemingómez – and its complexity, gravity and cultural genetics – carries the same liability as the 'intervention': in essence, the intervention merely sustains the problem.

Various contradictions consequently arise: for example, councils invest time and money in solving the problem of Valdemingómez, yet struggle to agree how best to intervene; the police undertake raids on the *gitanos'* drug businesses, yet some escape prosecution and still their operations flourish;

the harm reduction team builds trust with people, persuades them to take steps towards their rehabilitation, yet many relapse and return to the area (see Chapter 8). Of course, this is all very distant from the public, who are normally fed propaganda success stories about the policing and political promises to mask these tensions. Nevertheless, the different parties involved in intervening in Valdemingómez have different agendas that also contradict each other and make clear solutions problematic. This occurs as a result of shifts in political priorities that never develop further than short-term election promises that soon become forgotten or delayed. Valdemingómez is the shared responsibility of three different councils, which hampers agreement over who is liable for what happens to the thousands of people who occupy this area.

In this chapter, we first show how Valdemingómez is therefore characterised by high levels of 'legal cynicism' (Kirk and Matsuda, 2011) – the shared belief that law enforcement agents are seen as illegitimate, unresponsive and ill equipped to ensure public safety, which emerges out of their perceived unavailability or bias, yet is reinforced by suspected complicity between *gitanos* and drug users. This, we show, has been exacerbated by the recent reorganisation of police responses across the capital, which has had implications for how Valdemingómez is policed – now there are fewer officers making police 'control' check points, and those with specialist investigative knowledge of the area are being retired. With fewer specialised resources, all this has consequences for the people who work within the intervention mechanisms for, given the density of the problem and lack of collective ability to make change, a kind of 'professional impotence' arises – conceding the scale of problem produces feelings of resignation and instead cultivates attitudes that contribute to its cultural milieu, hence the police officers getting blow jobs from female drug users and the harm reduction worker taking a piss against his own bus. This professional resignation can instead also sway them to actually conform to the dynamics of the area, hence the high levels of police corruption, for example. So in some way, like the *gitanos* and drug users, both institutions are complicit in the very problem they are there to resolve.

Drug support at various levels in Spain – from prevention to harm reduction to rehabilitation – is also woefully substandard, with many programmes still devised around medical models of drug dependency that consider drug use an 'illness' and treat the user as a free-will thinker, someone who is able to make clear-cut decisions to use/avoid drugs and who is able to self-regulate consumption regardless of their social and personal circumstances (see Chapter 5). This has not been helped by the reduction in public funding directed at drug-related problems, in the main stemming from widespread misuse of government money and high levels of corruption (see Chapter 2), which essentially means that rather than investing in structural interventions for these people, they instead receive piecemeal advice about how they should responsibilise their personal choices and practices. We have already noted how drug support is drastically thinner on the ground now than it was when it was operating out of the former *poblado*, Las Barranquillas, prior to 2007 (see Alberto in Chapter 5). So, when people arrive at Valdemingómez in the conditions we have shown, a way out is almost impossible (see Chapter 8), which is also why other forms of miscellaneous help evolve in the form of charities and the church. However, despite their good intentions, there is no collaboration with the harm reduction team, even if some of this 'help' appears to exploit them.

Taken together, all this has major consequences for those who live and visit Valdemingómez: aside from the situational challenges they face in their daily life (see Chapter 6), their attitudes, interactions and decisions are directly impacted by these wider institutional and strategic movements. So much so, that the 'accommodation' to which Julia refers underwrites a kind of personal surrender to life and its conditions in Valdemingómez, which we explore in its brutal ramifications in Chapter 8 that follows.

The council

The resulting transfer of other *poblados* to Valdemingómez in the Cañada Real Galiana produced a dilemma for the Madrid regional council. This is first because its spatial location shares boundaries with two other local municipal councils – Rivas and Vallecas – and such is the complexity of the drugs market, the lack of general infrastructure and relative deprivation across the vast part of the Cañada Real Galiana, that no one really wants to take ownership of it and there are disagreements about the correct measures to take to intervene. The main disagreement seems to be around whether or not there should be some sort of support programme, and along with this come issues of funding, support and the logistical relocation of thousands of people. The costs of full support and intervention, claim local governments, are too high, particularly in an era of austerity politics that has forced major cutbacks in welfare spending. And given the millions of Euros spent on bungled *gitano poblado* relocation projects (see Chapter 3), the real political motive seems to be to do nothing. The results are twofold: funds for the inner city are safeguarded and economic wellbeing is secured in those spaces, while at the same time, visible crimes, related to drug offending for example, that threaten disinvestment and/or stimulate social anxiety are removed elsewhere (Atkinson et al, 2016).

Second, old laws pertaining to the terrain as a *via pecuaria* (cattle route) make it difficult for new laws to be passed since these pathways are under state protection. The principal road that passes through Valdemingómez, from the roundabout under the bypass of the A3 to the mudfields of *las moscas* (the flies), where the most impoverished *gitanos* live in *chabolas*, is that of the ancient cattle routes. In 2011, the regional government of Madrid convened meetings to try and rewrite these laws that would essentially dismantle the terrain as cattle routes, thus permitting easier urban and social planning to be made. However, although two years were allowed to enable the respective councils to arrive at a consensus, the deadline passed in 2013 without any agreement being made.

Towards the end of 2016, more constructive conversations have been rekindled between the respective councils (see Chapter 10). Current proposals include coupling the dismantling of Valdemingómez with urban regeneration plans and infrastructure improvements to transport networks. This would, of course, require negotiation with the relevant few residents and their association who still occupy some land in Valdemingómez. In the draft proposal, it is suggested that Sector 3 be dismantled so that a new train tunnel can be constructed. However, this would merely displace thousands of people from all of the sectors elsewhere, and do little to change the root cause of the problem, Valdemingómez. In the same proposals, Madrid council – led by the conservative Popular Party – recommends that the area be urbanised and services be provided to it. However, critics such as Pedro del Cura, an outspoken councillor in Rivas, have said how *"this will only underpin a nucleus of marginality in an inhabitable space"*, given its proximity to the railway lines and the M50 motorway. Others agree in Rivas council, which is now governed by Izquierda Unida (United Left), a new leftist political party that has gathered momentum in the wake of the financial crisis of 2008 and fiscal mismanagement of the country. They see it as consolidating *"the poverty and social exclusion"* of its residents (EFE, 2016). In the main, therefore, the continuing lack of governmental coordination in agreeing what to do with Valdemingómez means that immediate strategic responses rest with law enforcement institutions and the harm reduction team, with periodic support from non-governmental organisations (NGOs) and miscellaneous help.

Law enforcement agencies: The National Police, Local Police and Civil Guard

The role of the law enforcement agencies varies in and around Valdemingómez. However, since the 2008 financial crisis, police resources have been cut considerably. During our fieldwork, specialised law enforcement groups charged with policing Valdemingómez were being slowly cut back. Aside from perhaps the obvious patrolling through 'controls' or stop-and-search practices – which do very little other than confiscate the most battered cars – the police also conduct raids. This is immensely difficult given the complexity of the *gitanos*' drug distribution networks, who have devised measures in the event of a raid (see Chapter 6). Throughout Valdemingómez, there are numerous broken-down mementos of previous raids in the form of rubble and debris. As of 2014, the Local Police can play no role in these raids as much of the responsibility has since fallen to the National Police with the help of the Civil Guard. In the process, various legal representatives have to attend a raid for the purposes of presenting the order for the raid while the evidence is sought to justify it. It is not an easy process, as intelligence needs to be gathered about the location's operations to be able to sanction a legal order to raid and demolish. Moreover, there is always the risk that it can be rendered worthless on the day if the evidence is not found/ or the person/s charged are not caught.

The raid

An obvious consequence of these raids and symbolic acts of livelihood crushing is that many of the operations and networks simply reconsolidate in another area. There is even evidence to suggest that some of the *gitano* families have retreated back to some of the poorer parts of Madrid's suburbs as Valdemingómez experiences a mix between persistent police observation and raids, on the one hand, and total neglect, on the other (see Chapter 10):

> *There is a contradiction because if I am closing the poblados and the sales points where I had allowed them to open, to close street sales points, to leave Madrid a bit more cleaner, well, what happens? Well, people continue taking drugs and the drugs come back to the city barrios, you know. In fact, today, here in Caño Roto [a former poblado in the 1980s that remains poor in south Madrid], there are already drug sales points. People who left Valdemingómez because they were mashing it up so they can sell the land and have started their business here. You see, there are particular interests in Valdemingómez and they want to empty it but they can't. For as much as we may want to live with drugs, if they close the poblados, people will continue to use them because there is demand and people will come back to the city to deal drugs. This is the main problem we have now. What do we do with Valdemingómez? If I close this, where do people go? The idea was that initially it would be a mini-city for drug addicts with minimum police patrol/control.* (Roberto)

As Roberto says, the pressure of shutting down some of the drug operations was being felt in the nearby areas. Over the summer of 2015, six months into our study, we had started to compare drug-dealing activity in Sector 5 – separated only by the A3 – with that of Valdemingómez. We had noticed some activity spilling over from interventions in Valdemingómez, in this case, a small *kiosk* that had started to attract business:

> We park up near the school and walk down past the trees and a local *plaza* under the blazing heat: over the next few days it is to drift towards 40°. We walk past very few people in Rivas town centre and as we walk down to Sector 5, we encounter the improvised house constructions that delineate the 'unconventional world' with the supposed 'conventional' one. When we arrive in Sector 5, there is practically no one in the street. One can even hear the cars on the A3 a mile away, it is that quiet. As we walk around, we pass four *gitanos* outside one place looking suspiciously as if they shouldn't be standing outside the extra-fortified stronghold where they live. One seems to be in charge of swinging the large metal door back and forth, and as we draw closer, a clean car leaves as another arrives. Thereafter, and seemingly uncharacteristic for Sector 5, some drug addicts walk past, as if they are lost.

Valdemingómez boxed in

The next day we attend the impending police raid on a property, but have to wait around at the main entrance to Valdemingómez with the police to catch one of the men who needed to be charged on the property at the same time as the raid; it turns out he had somehow found out about the raid and had disappeared:

> It is 11.15am when we arrive at the roundabout, and Diego waves to us as he stands with a female colleague as they monitor the traffic leaving and entering Sector 6. Without understanding clearly what is going on, it seems they are looking for someone who escaped from the house that is to be raided. They look for

a grey Ford Focus, and every time something passes that is grey, built by Ford, or looks like it could be a Focus, he edges out of the shade. His colleague, however, seems content to roast in the sun.

The *cundas* leave and arrive, mostly full of skeletal figures who have come to score and drift off back to the city. From time to time, young men pass in decent sportswear with rucksacks, a sign that they have come down to buy in bulk to sell in discos. The addicts pass regularly, and most, if not all, seem to have extremely defined calf muscles, probably from the amount of walking they have to do in the absence of a car; in fact, we see one we recognise from an earlier field trip – the man who scratched his arms and brushed his hair and talked to himself walks past [Alberto]. This time, however, he has company. We then see a small Arab woman in numerous layers of clothing pass by loaded with three massive bags; she almost fearlessly crosses the roundabout as if she was blindfolded and crossing a tightrope.

As Diego receives another call, he is told to take a scout in the zone for the runaway car. He mounts the police van with his assistant and they drive off as a bunch of four other colleagues of his arrive. Three of them have sunglasses and don't look too bothered about talking as they hibernate in the shade and watch the road for the car. The other, who is nearest to Daniel, is about his age [38] but with a potbelly. He seems approachable. Daniel starts up a conversation, asking if he thinks it will improve here. He doubts it, and in the eight years he has been an officer here he has seen little change. *"We manage the problem and keep it here* [Valdemingómez],*"* he says. Daniel show his surprise that Sector 5 should have an issue with drugs, and the officer intervenes by saying *"that's why we are doing it, so it doesn't spread"*. The other sectors are not as problematic, he says, before reflecting on some tense moments between *gitanos* and the police when they have arrested or detained someone, and have had to make urgent calls for back-up as they have then been surrounded by other *gitanos*.

When Diego returns, his assistant tells us to get over to Sector 5, as the raid will shortly take place.

As we were to learn, there had been quick and organised behind-the-scenes intelligence-gathering on this potentially evolving matter in Sector 5 for a number of reasons – first, so it didn't get too established and start 'infecting' other areas of the same community, although this is not to say that there is no other drug dealing going on in the same sector, but it is not even remotely open, and it is rare to see *cundas* or drug users in and around the streets. Second, in intervening early, the police and authorities seek to squeeze operations back into the main area where it was initially concentrated in Valdemingómez. Third, the police are seen as acting in the interests of the residents of Rivas – after all, it is a residential area where potential electoral votes can be won, and the residents have long complained about the potential harms of the drug market.

Raid limitations

However, the logistics of the raid are immensely complex as the operational organisation, and police manpower, coupled with problems of access on to the dusty potholed road that cuts through Sector 5, make it even more difficult:

As we drive in off the A3 into Sector 5, the road has been blocked by the police, and there are a ton of cars parked outside the roadblock and some local residents who wait to be able to get back to their houses. Indeed, the giant digger sits patiently in the same space. Daniel gets out while Rubén is directed past the roadblock, given the privileged access we have. Daniel then walks down with the female officer and she tells him that up until a few years ago she was working in traffic, but the unit shut down and two new units were created to respond to drug problems.

As Rubén joins him, the giant digger passes through to knock down another *kiosk* that has opened up in a smaller branch of the Sector 5 community. As Daniel passes the open gate, the residents remain under police command as their property is searched for drugs and money, and the legal documents are signed by the official on site to orchestrate things. We get a glimpse of the *gitanos* we saw yesterday, and feel awkward, thinking they may recognise us.

Professional impotence

Many of the police we met that day, and even over the fieldwork, had grown accustomed to the *gitanos'* activity and had habitualised their own action as officers against it. Even some of the younger officers, it seemed, had quickly surrendered to the status quo of pointless controls, patrolling and raids, to the extent that many had lost the ability to feel that what they were doing was useful, or that it had any impact:

On the corner, looking over the property, we get talking to another local policeman in dark shades; the trees hang over us giving us necessary shade from the burning heat. It is about 12pm. The policeman, again about Daniel's age, reflects on the impossibility of the situation. In the 12 years he has worked in the police, he said, he started with motivation and determination to change the world but, over time, this has become worn. More than anything, he says, he finds it unfair that the *gitanos* pay no taxes, get social benefits worth 1,000 Euros, pay no gas, electricity and water, and this is aside from what they earn in illegal businesses like drugs; conversely, he and his family just get by on his wage, and his wife had to take a part-time contract to look after the children. Moreover, his wage has been reduced as a consequence of police cuts in the wake of the financial crisis. When we ask if his colleagues feel the same, he pulls a face and agrees, adding that the *gitanos* have villas, horses, land, all sorts in other parts of

Spain, so for them to be displaced from a house means nothing: *"they are used to it, they like it,"* he says.

The daily labour of the police coupled with these kinds of attitudes – such as the indignation of the officer – therefore reinforces typical stereotypes about the *gitanos* (see Chapter 6), which is partly why there is such animosity towards the police (particularly demonstrated in art and graffiti in and around Valdemingómez – one giant slab of concrete that was once a wall in a house has on it '*Policia Mierda*', which means 'police shit').

The arrest

Professional impotence enables an emotional distancing from the actions that the police perform and the consequences of those actions. Common phrases they use to justify their interventions echo perceptions of stereotypical associations about *gitano* culture:

> When we start talking to another officer, he explains that it seems the drug dealing was attracting more punters. Inside the building, Diego tells us, they had built a *fumadero* to accommodate people coming and going. The large gate blocked the view of the cars that came in and out to deal. From the inside, it could well have been a normal house, but the construction has been deliberate, it seems, to start to accommodate drug users. We remember from yesterday a few cars coming in and out of the same property; indeed, it seemed to be the only place where there was movement in Sector 5. We cross over the bumpy road as we wait for the civil registry to complete the legal documentation and the search for drugs to be completed, and talk again to the female officer, who now has her glasses removed; the black cap neatly tucks away her long hair. She says she had always wanted to be in the police and, when we ask if this all affects her, turfing people out of their

home, she says *"but it is illegal"*. After an awkward silence, she does then say how she feels sorry for the children, before we spot a large rat running into the nearby wall. She says nothing more as we look around at the flies that buzz around the dirty puddles as the sun gets stronger.

We all loiter around outside the property now, as the neighbours peer over the improvised first floor they have at the impending action. There are council reps, construction experts, gas and electricity consultants, and a bunch of National Police in fluorescent waistcoats guarding the *gitanos*, who sit in plastic chairs fanning themselves. We then hear that a load of cash and about 80 grams of cocaine have been found. The police then find another 200 grams of uncut heroin and cocaine, which we are told equates to a street value of €50,000. They also find a firearm, which, taken together, is more than enough to make the raid some sort of success. Two arrests (a man and a woman) are made, and orders are given to reduce the place to rubble.

The *gitanas* start to bring out clothes and things, and pile them up outside the house, complaining, and tearfully talking to themselves. We ask another police woman if she is affected by all this but she says it's normal and that the *gitanos* *"don't mind it"*; seconds later, a short, tubby *gitana* walks past in a striped dress, fighting back the tears. The *gitanos* who have been ordered to stay in the small side road then try to crowd round as Diego orders them back behind the giant digger, and the police control; *"Niños a casa"* ("Children go home"), he says. The tension increases as the digger gets into position and the fluorescent-jacketed men enter as the civil registrar comes out in tie and shirt, treading carefully over the dirty road in his expensive shoes. Dogs bark as the *gitanos* wait in the road behind the giant digger, and some of the police retreat to the air conditioned van while the team sit in the shade, smoking, waiting for the signal.

Photo 20: The giant digger

Then one police van reverses into the property and two people are bundled in, a man and a woman. There is then a weird few minutes as two of the elder *gitanos* in the property go in to rescue a fridge freezer that they struggle out with, and one grandmother cries out that she needs to pass to give medication to someone. As the two people in the van sit, a boy breaks past the police barrier; it is the son of the man who has been arrested. *"Quiero ver a mi papa"* ("I want to see my father"), he cries, and runs up to the van; almost resigned, he tries to reach out for him, his mum comforting him, also tearful.

The men in the fluorescent jackets try to make the place safe and cut the electricity and gas supplies while the last few *gitanos* are told to leave. One *gitana* leaves with a baby of seven months in her arms, and indignantly sits on a chair she has retrieved, under the shade, opposite the house. She sits with the baby relentlessly moving around in the uncomfortable heat. There is then a moment of reassurance as the policeman who we had talked to, Juan, holds the hands of several *gitanas* as they cry.

Imminent demolition

We take one last look inside the house to see toys and clothes on the floor. Shortly after, the man in the giant digger starts up and positions it outside the gates. When the large digger slowly strikes the gate, it does so with ease, as if it is ripping paper.

Photo 21: *Gitanos* rescue a fridge freezer from the impending demolition

After dispatching with the metal gate, the digger swipes in slow motion at the rubble and moves forward into the courtyard, some baby clothes and toys still evident on the floor. It mounts itself on steel feet to stabilise itself and hacks in slow motion into the walls. The flowers that hang on the wall are quickly buried by the rubble, and the plastic chairs are lost as the roof falls so easily. The neighbours' wall and roof are potentially threatened, but the driver is skilled, and makes his assault painstakingly on the building. It is quite an incredible sound to hear the engine of the digger power up with each strike it makes at the house. Equally it is quite an amazing sight, albeit it very depressing. As one workman takes a piss in the corner, the giant digger brings down the roof and the proudly displayed plates in the kitchen finally fall. It may be illegal, but it was where someone lived.

Photo 22: Enter the giant digger

Photos 23, 24 and 25: Demolition

Law enforcement corruption

Raids like these are commonplace, often coinciding with political pressure stemming from local elections. The wider context to this type of intervention is compromised by widespread corruption among the law enforcement agencies. Throughout our study, internal sources of the Local Police reported corruption cases involving the National Police, in particular, a unit of the police known as the Judicial Police that has a direct role in tackling drugs in Valdemingómez. Conversely, there have also been cases throughout our research where the National Police have spied on the movements of the Local Police to ascertain if they were going to make a particular operation without advising them or if they were investigating a particular *gitano* family; in the case of the latter, this resulted in public castigations of the Local Police through the media and internet forums. In fact, relations became so sour after 2011 that the Local Police stopped collaborating with the National Police after a series of corruption cases impeded their investigations – numerous raids were undertaken and quite suspiciously, no drugs or money were found.

However, while corruption seems to be a fairly common part of Spanish policing culture (see Muñoz and Pérez Ávila, 2016, for examples in Seville; and Boróhorquez, 2016, for examples in Majorca), the wider ramifications of this operational discord contribute to this notion of 'professional impotence' in that it dents inroads into any progress the police can make and instead inverts their strategic vision. The 'legal cynicism' – how law enforcement agents are seen as illegitimate, unresponsive and ill equipped to ensure public safety, which is particularly common in areas of high levels of social exclusion (Kirk and Matsuda, 2011) – which thereafter ensues, completes the general redundancy of law enforcement because its daily function is wedded to the complicity that exists between them and the very agents they are charged with policing. In this context, this is the *gitanos* and drug users. Nevertheless, these apparent squabbles hide numerous clandestine collaborations and agreements between both police forces that the police concede to and drug users in Valdemingómez have noted:

It's clear that there are recorded telephone conversations. There are a lot of interests. There are people and those who we don't agree with, and that is as clear as water. And there are houses [in Valdemingómez] which have never been raided or touched. Nor will be touched or are going to be touched. I understand that information is power and there are people who are benefiting from this information that they give them [gitanos] but there is, of course, more than information. [Diego, Local Police]

Many times I have seen them take away corrupt police. They have taken them and have said what happens, always we come here to do a raid and somehow the gitanos have already been warned. They come, tear down the walls, they come with all the machines, take down the houses and don't get anything. They try to get evidence that there have been drugs but of course there is evidence everywhere around them, but for some reason there is nothing. (Juan)

In addition, some *machacas* told us that members of both police forces had come to the area 'in plain clothes' in their own cars and met with the *gitanos* to receive sums of money. Naturally, a police presence results in caution on the part of the *gitanos*, but at no point do the police interfere in the abuses that take place between the *gitanos* and the *machacas* – or anyone else for that matter:

Some time ago, it happened to me because I was working for a gitano here [in Valdemingómez]. I was on the door and I was opening and closing it so people could come in to buy. I was on the door and someone else was on the inside. The guy on the outside makes a signal for the guy on the inside to open, for example,

'Limpio' or 'Popeye', something like that. So the door is opening and closing constantly. When they leave, the guy on the inside bangs twice and the door opens and when it closes, the outside guy bangs once. But if the police are there, no one bangs or opens and inside everyone is quiet. No one can go out, no one speaks until the police leave. And the gitanos, when a machaca does something bad or careless, the gitanos arrive and insult them, 'son of a bitch, you will get cancer', and they beat them with slaps and punches or they sack them saying, 'get out, get out, don't come back', and so, within two days, this person has no income to get drugs and starts to feel really sick from withdrawal. So he comes back begging on his knees, 'I'm sorry, I didn't realise, I was asleep' because they don't sleep. They put him back to work, 3–4 days straight without sleeping, without eating, and he is just smoking and smoking [heroin and cocaine] so finally he gets sleepy. They are on their feet and sleep on their feet. Many times the gitanos come back, 'hey!', and they beat them up again, 'what are you? Fucking stupid?' Slaps, punches, beatings. (Juan)

The police seem to display a real lack of interest in interfering in these violent exchanges. Moreover, perhaps as a means of maintaining crime figures at a particular rate and avoiding bureaucracy – for there is much unrecorded crime – it is in the police's interest to tolerate/not to respond to certain incidents that they deem to be 'trivial'. We use this word in its relative sense, meaning for officers accustomed to the scale and severity of crime in Valdemingómez, anything from minor cases of open drug dealing to more grave abuses like rape and serious violence. The almost lawlessness of these interactions, coupled with the lack of strategic state intervention, means that at best there are phases of intense patrolling, police checkpoints, raids and arrests as tokenistic responses from public services (like ambulances) so costs are not exceeded (see Chapter 3). However, on the other hand, there are extended periods of total neglect and absolute abandon, and it is from this that a form of 'consented violence' takes precedence, one that is legitimised on the basis of its spatial and contextual circumstances:

> *Buahhh, I have seen things here, my god. I don't know if it is because of drugs that affect people like this but look at this, I am going to tell you what I have seen happen to four people with my eyes. And it was everyone here* [pointing around] *in the plaza. They have come here, scored drugs and started to get high, they were injecting and after a while it gives them like a type of overdose. But it wasn't an overdose because they have taken the drugs and then fallen on the floor as if they had an epileptic fit, 'ahhhhh aaahhhhhh'* [he shouts in imitation], *and people have come along to get hold of them and they were like mad. Another time there was a young guy here that was with his partner and he injected himself and for some reason threw his partner into the camp fire. We were having this camp fire to keep us warm one winter and his partner had been all day with us but had been insulting him, insulting the young guy. And he was dealing with it, 'listen, for fuck's sake, it is not my fault', and the girlfriend, 'you fucking do, you gay fuck, you are no man', all day like this. And the young guy just listening to it and coping with it. Then when he injected I don't know what happened to him but he picked her up and threw her in the fire. Because we were there, we managed to push her off and get her out and the guy is like calling to himself on the floor as if he is possessed. I remember then he started to approach me and I was thinking he*

● DEED SLIP 100% OFFICIAL ●

THIS DEED CONFIRMS OWNERSHIP
OF THE "ARTICLE HEREBY REFERRED
TO AS "THE VERY COMFY PILLOW"
PURCHASED INITIALLY FROM TK MAXX
IN MAY 2017. AT A COST OF £17.

KEVIN IS THE OWNER
LAURA

> *was going to hurt me but he grabbed me by the balls*
> *and started to squeeze them and threw me on the floor.*
> *The police then came and when they got out without*
> *any warning they beat him up.* (Adrian)

Equally this means that because 'it is what it is' and 'it is where it is', there is also no urgency on the part of law enforcement agents to attend major crime scenes in Valdemingómez:

Adrian: *They [the gitanos] killed someone, yes.*
             Beaten to death. They left him there and
             hours passed before the police and ambulance
             came and said he was dead. He was getting
             told off by the gitanos, then three more came
             and started beating and punching him hard,
             constantly, it went on forever. The ambulance
             was very late and when it came he was dead.
Rubén: *When something like this happens, what*
             happens to the gitanos?
Adrian: *Everyone knows who it is, but no one says*
             anything. The police end up knowing, they
             have their contacts, reports and a death is just
             a death. But there are lots of abuses that's why
             I don't like working as a machaca, perhaps
             you can do it for a short while, but no longer.

The *machaca* is also someone who is an insider to *gitano* operations; not only brutally exposed to their violence, but just as much involved in the violence they impose on others. This is confirmed here, in this conversation with Juan:

We get talking to Julia and a very drawn-looking Juan, who sidesteps impatiently as he smokes a cigarette we offer him. They have both just finished a 12-hour shift, 10pm to 10am, in the local *fumadero* (drug house). We get on to the subject of violence and vendettas, and Juan recalls a story from a few months ago whereby a *gitano* was released from prison with a death warrant for someone else. Apparently the man who he wanted to kill had given evidence against him, implicating him in a court case that led to his six-year imprisonment. However, this man also had recorded conversations and photos from the *fumadero* that could further implicate the recently imprisoned man in further offences – which is why he wanted revenge, as well as the phone with the evidence. He came up to the door, knocked on it and asked the *machaca* if the man was there, and he said he would find out. The *machaca* went inside, and told the man, who shrugged his shoulders but went to the door. At that point, the guy just out of prison pulled out a gun and fired it three times in his face; it was totally destroyed. In fact, the police struggled to identify him as a consequence. The phone was stolen at the scene by another female drug user and now this same man is after her: *"he said to the boss of the fumadero, get her here, entertain her and call me and I will make it worth your while,"* says Juan. We get onto the subject of police corruption and Juan recounts several stories of police corruption, explaining how the police will normally receive orders to park up and inspect the *fumaderos* but often do nothing. The *gitanos* close the business, either emptying people into the street or forbidding them to leave until the police have left. However, the police normally linger around until the *gitano* boss comes out and offers them a payment to disappear so business can continue – and so it does.

The area therefore consents to these forms of violence, while at the same time, it allows a sizeable number of *gitano* drug businesses to continue under the auspices of law enforcement corruption, which reduces the potential conflict that could occur between the two parties; perhaps this is why the police indicate that, compared to other *poblados*, this area is generally easier to police. And many times, all the harm reduction team and other helping services can do is look on and watch these things take place, even when these events directly jeopardise the safety of the people to whom they try to offer intervention.

The harm reduction team

In the few years the harm reduction team have been active in and around Valdemingómez, they have been able to establish key trust and rapport with the local population. Their position is somewhat neutral to the violent dynamics we have so far described, although this does not mean they are not affected. If anything, they encounter a similar risk of being threatened and beaten by the *machacas* as their service must provide 365-day provision for whoever comes to their desk to collect food, clean paraphernalia, medical assistance and, if they come to know the staff well, even clothes and cigarettes. The service normally arrives in its large bus which contains computers and is the logistical centre point for the service as well as offering food provision, and is accompanied by two smaller vans: one equipped with medical provisions, medication and the equipment necessary to respond to emergencies such as overdoses, and another that is a sort of people carrier that shuttles drug users to hospital and/or court appointments, which the team also use to go on their lunch shifts.

The harm reduction team is made up of around 15–20 people – educators, social workers, doctors and nurses. The educators are those who have the front-line role on the desk, giving out food and drug paraphernalia to those who stagger up to see them between the hours of 10am to 6pm; they are charged with gaining the trust and confidence of the population, and working on ways to persuade them to engage with the mechanisms of rehabilitation. The social workers, on the other hand, play a more backroom role, interviewing people, making further appointments and updating data on their systems on the progress of the clients.

Every day the bus arrives, turning in off the main road into the second main entrance, navigating the heavily potholed road, and looks for a place to park in the *plaza*. Rarely does it park facing right opposite the three main *fumaderos* opposite the church, to avoid compromising the safety of their clients and to nurture their relationship with them; they tend to park in front of the church or in the desolate land next to it. This is not to say that they avoid contact with the *gitanos*, for on many occasions we have witnessed exchanges and even been with their staff to have coffee in *gitanos'* houses and cafés. Few workers on the team, however, drift from the immediate space of the bus unless there is an emergency such as an overdose or someone who is severely ill.

For us there is a painful irony about all this, which is that, regardless of where the bus parks and how determined they are to save people from this destitution, within a radius of 50m, the people they are charged with persuading to leave their drug use drift in and out of *kiosks* and *fumaderos*. Not more than 25m from them are various tents, *chabolas*, rotten

Photo 26: Respite

mattresses and cardboard boxes where the same people often sleep, and within 10m there is a small camp next to the church where people take shelter; indeed, the church has come to be a useful place during the winter to reduce the impact of the freezing wind and to act as shelter from any breeze that may disturb the process of preparing a heroin and/or cocaine pipe/injection. The team only need to look around where they stand to see used foil, bloody syringes and other rubbish on the floor.

Nevertheless, it is here that the team set up their desks and serve the population of Valdemingómez. The seasons are varied and the temperatures can be as high as 45°C during the summer yet as low as −5°C in winter; there can be a piercing bright sun, which makes it dry (and very dusty as the cars pass incessantly), and there can be a kind of swampy mud when there is torrential rain. In fact, it becomes a sort of day refuge for many people recovering from their night shifts working for the *gitanos* who can only just muster the strength before getting breakfast and falling asleep. Regardless of the weather, the hostility from the people, and the problems they present, the team find a way to deliver a service. In these notes, we record one of our first encounters in Valdemingómez where we first converse with the harm reduction team. Even from this initial visit we were able to gauge the first major strategic hurdle the team face – a reduction in funding and massive under-resourcing of provision:

We pass *kiosks* offering hamburgers and coffees, where really drugs are dealt and smoked, and pull up to the right into an open space which feels like some sort of protest camp: on the right is a small community of houses, with some rubble, rubbish and paraphernalia in between, and on the left more rubble and a handful of tents where Diego says people go to inject heroin and cocaine. There is a real decrepit feeling about the place and as we get out, standing on syringes and paraphernalia, we see a church in the distance where next to it various mobile harm reduction services have pulled up. We greet the crowd of people who have surrounded us: one man staggers around in front of us, his face barely recognisable from the dirt. As they circle around us to try and work out who we are, they are only to be dispersed by a National Police van. Thereafter out get numerous officers next to us, two of whom have their hands on the triggers of their shotguns: they release the safety cap and start to disperse the people, and move in on a particular house where they want to make enquiries about a drug deal.

Trying to avoid as best we can the syringes on the floor, a man suddenly pulls up in a car next to us and quite inconspicuously starts to prepare a syringe to inject himself while he sits in the car. We walk on and there seems to be a congregation of people around the two mobile vans outside the church. As we introduce ourselves to the harm reduction staff and members of the local council social work team, the drug addicts circle quickly from time to time like seagulls, diving down to collect tea, food, clean syringes and the like, before disappearing. The people are mostly dishevelled, half alive, yet they seem fairly harmless and friendly.

We get talking to the head of the harm reduction mobile unit who shows us the type of paraphernalia they give out which ranges from needles, syringes, tissues, water, pipes, etc. The improvised table also has on it a tea machine and water, and sandwiches are also available. While the staff stand around, occasionally talking to the drug users, most seem occupied smoking and/or checking their mobile phones, and we continue to talk to the boss. He explains that the service has had cuts over the last three years, and criticises the way the government keep changing the way they run the initiatives – *"if nothing works in the short term, it is then changed,"* he says. He pauses, frowns, and as he looks us in the eyes, smoking, says, *"the only thing we are doing here, is prolonging their misery"*. This irony is perhaps summarised when a thin and wrinkly woman comes up to us, smiles revealing her brown teeth, and begs a cigarette from him: he gives her two saying, *"Adios guapa"* ("Goodbye beautiful").

The harm reduction bus and team are normally funded on a three-year cycle, but some of their contracts run for a period of 12 months, and the pay is generally low. While they have managed to retain core staff members, others have left because of low prospects, and others because of the work conditions. In our discussions with them as well, they criticise the performance-related and procedural directives made on them to do their job that they have to adapt to the volatile conditions of Valdemingómez. Indeed, for this reason, many staff have left the job, having struggled with the emotional demands of the work. Perhaps this aptly highlights what was written on Sergio's t-shirt at the beginning of the chapter, *'RIP Sanidad Publica'*.

There are also major limitations on what they can do, which is perhaps why Julia said they were 'accommodating' them rather than helping them out of their dependence. First, these limitations relate to their timetable: drug users only come during the daytime, and outside these hours there is no lighting, no electricity, no food, no clean water (apart from the dirty public tap attached to the outside of the church) or access to clean paraphernalia such as injecting equipment. There is no nearby clinic, hospital or anywhere remotely related to offering support to drug users. As we saw earlier in the chapter, the emergency services (as much ambulances as hospitals) have drug dependents low down on their priority lists; after all, they are also running on reduced costs and resources, and consider patient care for this group unimportant given their re-admittance, having either failed in rehabilitation attempts or having caused their own personal downfall to the point that 'more deserving' citizens are more appreciative of their services:

As we clamber down from the *chabolas* into the *plaza*, Roberto gets out of the bus and lights up a cigarette. We greet him and stand with him, behind the harm reduction table, to help distribute food, drink, clothes and new drug injecting and smoking equipment. From time to time, glass smashes in the distance, and intermittent thuds are heard from the bored *gitano* who continues to play baseball with rocks and his homemade bat. We first try and find out what had happened to Alberto, who Juan had said was knocked over by a car. This appears to be true as he was hit two weeks ago, crossing one of the busiest motorways out of Madrid, the A3. When he was taken to Arganda Hospital, they checked him out, saying he *"had nothing"*. He somehow made his way to San Juan homeless hostel, where one of the harm reduction team doctors saw him and said he had severe problems. They took him to another hospital, Infanta Leonor Hospital, where various tests and X-rays showed he had a broken rib and his 5th vertebrae was fractured. As we speak, Roberto says he is waiting for an operation in one of the public hospitals in Madrid, although we don't know which one. *"That's what they think, some of these hospitals, see a drug addict and just get them up out the door as soon as possible; we are going to report Arganda"*, he says. He has been there ever since with periodic visits from the harm reduction team, who, every time they go, pay 10 Euros for him to watch 24 hours of TV. Roberto says this sort of thing has happened to various people, the time before being one man who had staggered up towards the harm reduction bus with his head pouring with blood having been knocked down by a car in the nearby road.

Like the police who arrive late and sometimes don't respond, the priority is low for the emergency services. So outside the times of the harm reduction team, the risks multiply, as provisions like this are just not available. When the bus departs, drug addicts normally make a last-minute flurry to get what they can, and thereafter many make do with the provisions for paraphernalia they have been able to collect, or resort to asking for favours, begging from associates and/ or scavenging – regardless of the condition of the syringe, as we have seen in various field notes and in Chapter 1, when we were trying to convince Julia to take a pregnancy test and engage with the service. High-risk practices such as sharing injecting equipment that can result in the transmission of HIV, hepatitis C and other infections are less commonplace in Valdemingómez these days, with the presence of the bus and improved awareness among the injecting population, although this doesn't mean that the mere presence of the harm reduction team and 'knowledge of the risks' results in less-risky practices, particularly when the attitudes and lifestyles of the people who live in Valdemingómez often sideline concern for their own welfare in times of need (see Chapters 5 and 8):

> Daniel returns to Rubén as a white car pulls up. The man in his mid-30s, who has a dog in the back, opens his car door and prepares a syringe for injecting. After a few minutes of fighting back his dog to the back of the car so he can inject his body, he gets frustrated and tosses the syringe out of the window on to the floor. There it lies, a mixture of blood and heroin. He then seems to doze off at the wheel, nodding from time to time to try and keep himself awake. About 10 minutes later, however, another ragged-looking man dressed in a mixture of grey and black shuffles past in his boots, kicking the dust as he walks, looking obsessively at the floor. To his luck, or perhaps not, he notices the blood-filled syringe which has been thrown away, and picks it up and ambles off.

The entrenched nature of heroin and cocaine dependence displayed by these people make problematic any attempt to coerce them out of their chaotic lifestyles – not that this means that there have been no success cases (see Chapter 8). Yet even if the staff do manage to process someone out of Valdemingómez, their success thereafter hinges on the availability of funding, a place in a rehab unit, continued support, avoiding the risk of arrest and, along the way, a therapeutic process of coming to terms with past actions, before potentially relapsing. And in an era of cuts, austerity and the plundering of public service funding, the last thing on the political radar is a commitment to strategies to deal with problematic drug users who are trying to recover in some faraway place on the outskirts of the capital:

> *Well, they have been reducing them bit by bit [resources to fund drug problems], but this was greatly accelerated with the advent of 2008. The heroin boom was in the 1980s and then they started to create resources for drug dependents, to stop the problem because you can't show off a city with drug problems. However, they are not a problem in Valdemingómez or Quinta – another poblado they had – or they don't bother us if they are in the ghettos which are now forming, I don't send the police there, I don't stop the cundas who leave here [Madrid city centre], so they leave the city and I try to sell the idea that I am doing something to solve the problem and initiate programmes like harm reduction and I give funds to the NGOs, Red Cross although they have already reduced the grants ... people without vital structures that you are attending to, they lose their funding. And you are going to find that the problem will continue to grow, but now that you don't see it and it's not in Madrid, it's not important.* (Imma)

Miscellaneous help

"*No puedo hacer pis con los nervios*" ("I can't take a piss with these nerves"), Julia says, but we manage to persuade her to drink some liquid to be able to go to the toilet to do the pregnancy test. She scuffs her steps over to a religious association to collect some orange juice while Juan berates the attempts he has made to persuade her to get the test done. As Daniel sits on the concrete next to Rúben, a red car pulls up and the man in the front seat pulls it back to smoke some heroin while the thin woman in the back of the car opens the door and bends over to find veins in her ankles, where she then starts to dig around with a loaded syringe. Julia returns with a plastic cup of juice; her pregnant belly wobbling over her tight trousers. When we return to the subject of her pregnancy, she says *"Mi cuerpo demanda la cocaina pero despues me encuentro vomitando"* ("My body demands the cocaine but after I end up vomiting"), before smoking a cigarette. Her dietary pattern has changed as she has started to crave sweet things, evident from the cake she puts into her mouth and the melting chocolate donut she nestles under her armpit.

Between these notes where we, once again, try to convince Julia to present to the services to do a pregnancy test, we pass the other supposed form of support in Valdemingómez. Seemingly posing as NGOs, these services are manned with a few people dressed informally who often hand out small snacks, drinks and in the process of people taking food and drink, they attempt to suggest that their recovery is in the hands of higher powers if they come with them to repent:

As we pass back we stop to talk to another association called Betel that also works with the drug users in Valdemingómez in a more evangelical way. Essentially it is a service that immediately takes people out of the area and places them in a rigid programme of abstinence (even smoking is prohibited) coupled with religious education. We get talking to one of the volunteers, Eduardo, who says some 24 years ago he was injecting heroin on the streets of Madrid. He is reluctant to talk about statistics and the success rates of the service, saying that, *"if we save one it is our work done"*, adding, *"really, this is the last stop for most people before they die."*

The team seem well aware of the problems, noting the closure of other *poblados* around Madrid over the last 20 years, and saying how Valdemingómez is the *"last bastion"* after other *poblados* like Pitis, La Celsa, El Pozo del Tio, Los Pitufos and, last but not least, Las Barranquillas, have been taken down (see Chapter 3). For that reason, they say their work is difficult because of the embeddedness of the drug use in someone's identity (see Chapter 8), noting how the *machacas* are particularly difficult to engage as they are *"slaves to the gitanos"*, which jeopardises any recovery. However, very often, these pep talks into recovery are attempts to 'enlighten them', and the rehabilitation philosophy they endorse has strict religious conditions, as we found out on another occasion when we got talking to a similar association, having been mistaken for drug users in the area because of our shabby appearance; after all, we wore the same clothes day in, day out, when we went to the area:

We amble up towards the car, passing on our right-hand side an open car boot with a box of croissants and other pastries and a tank of orange juice. At their side stand three stocky yet sunburnt men, one Bulgarian and two Greek, who help in the Betel programme. Some addicts stumble up to them and pass polite conversation with them as they take as much food as they can before making excuses to leave. As we talk to them, we learn that the organisation is a Christian one called Remar and, like Asocación Betel, will remove anyone with immediate effect who says they are serious about getting clean, take them to Valencia and put them up in accommodation free of charge. The rehab programme, though unclear to us, revolves around the *"repentance of sins"*. We ask about the programme's success, and Dimitri gives me a hazy answer, saying some people *"take advantage of them"* and perhaps understandably so, but what exactly are they doing?

While at the outset this may appear a feasible option for someone living in Valdemingómez, since those early conversations we were able to form the view that these organisations pose as sects, and that the 'rehabilitation' they offer is like another form of slavery in that people are put to work for the organisation and prevented from leaving. The opportunity for these associations to turn up in a van with some food and drink and approach whoever they like and take them away comes about in the absence of coordinated support and strategic planning of help. This is not to criticise what the harm reduction team does, or any other organisations like the Red Cross that turn up from time to time to distribute aid and resources, but merely to point out that if there was something more formally coordinated that took account of what service did what for who on which days of the week, then there could be improvements to how the intervention was coordinated.

Intervention, as we have noted, was late to be commissioned in Valdemingómez, starting only as recently as 2011, with the introduction of the harm reduction team. There is no clear urgency for the poor, it seems. There were initially some earlier first reports on the conditions in Valdemingómez and the other sectors that had been done in collaboration with the NGOs, Red Cross and Accen, who had been working on the relocation of Romanian groups in the area. The preliminary analysis was about their experiences in each of the sectors of the Cañada Real Galiana: the report was published about the conditions in which they lived and methods of good practice that could improve their wellbeing.

Much of this was kept out of the media because it would have attracted attention as well as the fact that at the same time there were a lot of minors and young people being killed by lorries as they went to and fro from the rubbish dump (which sits behind Valdemingómez). This, too, was documented in reports to the local council, this time by the Red Cross and social workers in Vallecas, who worked with socially excluded groups across the Cañada Real Galiana. However, a senior politician in the council forbade its publication, saying it should not be the responsibility of the local council to intervene. When the workers tried to publish it another way, they approached Amnesty International, but received no formal answer.

As the Cañada Real Galiana expanded and swelled at the turn of the 21st century, and pockets of the drug market started to appear, money confiscated by raids or tax collection in the area was reinvested in social interventions such as Secretariado Gitano and Accen in Sector 5. This money resulted in a two-year study/intervention. In this time, and although there had been no formal commissioning by the local authorities, there was some improvement in Sector 5: perhaps this is one reason why the difference between it and Valdemingómez is significant.

But before this, there had been no intervention. And so, it seems, there were no funds to intervene. Long gone were the public funds available for things like hostels, safe injecting rooms open 24 hours a day, available doctors, educators and showers. There was no service giving out syringes or food; these provisions had been lost under public health cuts. These days, aside from weekly interventions by the Red Cross and an almost dormant office sitting behind the Arab quarter, the harm reduction team is the main tributary of support. However, as we have noted, it has its limits, which opens up the opportunity for potential bogus associations to take advantage of vulnerable people who are stuck in a dead end.

8

Post dependency: What next?

Photos 27, 28 and 29: Juan's 25-hour day

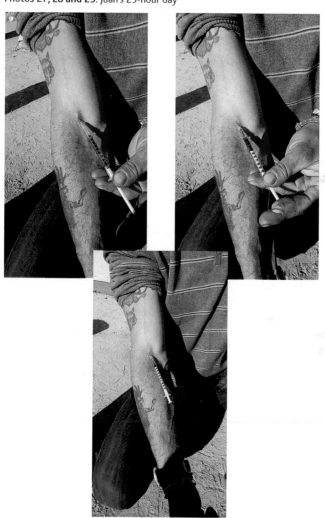

We return to a familiar spot of ours, sitting on the concrete stumps next to the church. Out comes Julia from the tent and removes Juan's rucksack as he wipes his lightly perspiring brow from our long walk around the area. She sits on a stump opposite us and rapidly makes up a heroin injection, placing half the hit in another syringe for Juan. Giving it to him, he places it behind his ear and starts to study her neck as if he were a DIY man making an assessment on where best to drill a hole in the wall. Drilling is what it looks like as he asks her to hold her breath to help summon the vein in her neck. She hugs her arms tight like a little girl might as if she were to receive her first inoculation. Yet this is not her first. As he gently tilts her to one side, her face turns red and he lightly jabs the needle around in her neck only for it to fill slightly with blood. He withdraws from his first attempt and reminds her to keep still – though she hasn't moved – and returns to his position. We peer over looking at the blood trickle down her neck slightly as Juan gently digs around for the vein. No luck. He mops his brow again and looks around the barren landscape for inspiration, takes a breath and returns to his position. We move around the other side watching Julia's eyes fill with fear, yet a kind of trust at the same time. Seconds later, Juan's skill pays off as he injects the bloody solution into her neck.

Juan then sits down on the same stump and pulls up his stained jumper with the syringe between his teeth. Placing it over a very visible vein, within five seconds he has made the injection and even lets it hang there on display for five minutes or so, returning to it from time to time to draw out blood before injecting it back in. He makes a resigned smile at us and the large gaps appear in his mouth where teeth have fallen out through malnutrition. He pauses as he looks at us with the sun glinting in his eyes and says, *"I'm tired of this, I'm tired of being here, and seeing this 24 hours a day. You know I call it 25 hours because it feels like the days are longer"*, as we then watch as a large dog passes us and walks up to their tent and takes a piss on it.

Introduction

This moment, captured in just a few minutes, is indicative of a moot point in Juan and Julia's situation: homeless in Valdemingómez, seemingly beyond formal state help mechanisms, reliant on the daily basics of the harm reduction team, and reliant on their work for the *gitanos* coupled with petty crime and other innovative schemes to fund their drug use. This moment is also indicative of Juan's almost fleeting confession of his submission to drugs and overall fatigue of the lifestyle. This was the moment for intervention – on a Monday afternoon at 16:45 in late December 2015 – but it has to be quick, for the 'window of opportunity' that Prochaska, Norcross and DiClemente (1995) talk about in their cycle of addiction is far more narrow and acute for many of these people. Largely devised for epidemiologists and public health researchers, the model assumes that someone addicted to drugs passes through a conceptual cycle on the path to change, starting at 'pre-contemplation', 'contemplation', 'preparation', 'action', 'maintenance' and 'relapse'. It has since become the philosophical centrepiece for the structure of drug rehabilitation services in Spain and other Western countries.

However, no one in our study came close to following this particular change pattern for various reasons. First and foremost, the wellbeing, confidence and self-esteem of these people has been eroded to the point that attitudes of self-care are replaced by self-neglect (see Chapter 5), and personal markers of the self are measured against the physical and visual degeneration of other people around them and the environment, which is reinforced psychologically through the structural and subjective experience of violence, victimisation and degradation. This is known as the 'spoilt identity' (see Briggs, 2012a), and it is this that invites personal resignation to living in a place such as Valdemingómez, rendering conceptions of self-recovery distant.

Second, the 'accommodating' nature of the harm reduction intervention – as well as the intermittent appearance of other help services – interferes with these sequential thought patterns proposed by Prochaska et al (1995), and instead contributes to a 'personal surrender' to their circumstances (see Chapter 7). Without taking away the success the team have had with some drug dependents – although beyond those who leave Valdomingómez little is known about what happens afterwards – the harm reduction team are generally not perceived as a 'way out' but 'the only way to stay in'. They are actually seen as another component in the assistance of their misery (see Chapter 7). Taken together this means that the subjective progress towards changes that Prochaska et al (1995) propose rarely gets beyond 'contemplation' to arrive at 'action', meaning it continually resets to 'contemplation'. Even then, the dirty drug-using environments, pressure to sustain dependency and tensions in the moral economy (see Chapter 6) lead to risky drug practices that contravene 'clean and healthy' practices heralded by the harm reduction team. This therefore hinders any 'action' that these people can take to turn their lives around.

Other intrusions on these potential reflections that could stimulate change are the imminent and ever-present pressures and risks in and around Valdemingómez, such as the incessant social demands to use drugs and the configuration of alliances made through the moral economy (see Chapter 6). As we have also seen, *machacas* – or those working directly for the *gitanos* – are susceptible to night shifts, which makes most of their day redundant, and this reduces time to approach services as well as impinges on supposed reflection time to 'change behaviour'. Given the area is constantly controlled by the police, and many of these people have delinquent histories and are criminally active, police arrest may also disrupt any intentions to turn their lives around, and this affects their motivation to engage as much as it heightens their risk of overdoses (see Mars et al, 2015). While there is clearly a static population in Valdemingómez, the high turnover of people for differing reasons produces extraordinary transience, and it is common that people appear as quickly as they disappear for no known reason, which also removes opportunities to intervene. In some testimonies, the psychological replay of vivid and traumatic past experiences, which played a part in reasons to take drugs and decisions to continue using, facilitates a form of pure pain that consistently lingers, resists change and manifests itself as more determined attitudes towards personal destruction (see Chapter 5). Therefore, and perhaps more inevitable for most given the embedded nature of such fatalistic attitudes, is the high chance of overdoses and a slow drift towards death. Even in documentaries made about previous *poblados*, in particular, Las Barranquillas, drug addicts are interviewed in similar conditions, one young woman saying *"we have come here to die"* (see FCYC, 2007).[1]

While this is not the complete story, it is the common narrative for those who find themselves living in Valdemingómez. Even if, by some chance, some manage to engage with drug services, their progress relies on a flimsy rehabilitation apparatus beset with cuts and under-resourced staff (see Chapter 7), which is snared with neoliberal ideologies requiring its participants to concede 'personal responsibility', demanding that these people continually summon their inner strength (which very few have) to recover. Thereafter there is the high chance they will remain on long housing waiting lists and somehow adjust themselves to the limited and careerless options for them in the labour market (see Chapter 2). During this process, however, in the absence of filling the psychological void, boredom often sets in and old practices are revisited, as we saw with Luis in Chapter 5. These circumstances have nothing to do with an inherent 'self-motivation to return to drug use' or 'relapse', which Prochaska et al (1995) insinuate, because the structural deficits outlined in Chapters 2 and 7 only assist in resetting the subjective preference to its default mode: harmful forms of intoxication. In many cases, within a short space of time, 'progress made' is negated by the continuous use of drugs, and before long many end up in the very same situation they were hoping to override – homeless and living in Valdemingómez. Taken together, for many, all that is left are fleeting moments – like Juan's – where they flirt with the idea of change before reconciling the absolute impossibility of it.

Dependency denial

The process by which many of these people have come to have lost everything not only relates to the commitment they place on drugs in situations that perpetuate their circumstances (see Chapter 5), but also a self-psychological conditioning over time about what is happening to them: denial of what they do and how and why they do it becomes bound up in conceptions of where and with whom they find themselves. The gravity of being homeless using drugs in Valdemingómez therefore prompts people to engage in self-evaluations against the relative disintegration of others around them as a means of personal reassurance, and this is what adds to 'dependency denial'. For example, the *machacas* are considered socially inferior because of their submission to *gitano* working regimes yet, at the same time, the stagnant population who rely more on the uncertainty of the moral economy are seen as a redundant workforce. Those who inject heroin and cocaine are seen as 'yonkies' or 'junkies' by those who smoke the same drugs from the foil and in the pipe. Yet at the same time, those to whom these labels are given reject them; referring to them represents someone else, often prompting them to reproduce a certain degree of self-assurance about the level of control and stability they have over their lives. These kind of mythical justifications about the conditions of someone else therefore only serve to reaffirm to the self that their circumstances are not as overcast, and, as we saw in Chapter 6, the ideological figure of the *machaca* assists in the management of these personal psychological battles.

In short, when we challenged people about their brutal circumstances and chaotic drug use, some were unable to concede to the gravity of the situation. The broader consequences of dependency denial are, however, more damaging, for not only do many negate aspects of their physical and mental state, but also past actions, feelings and emotions, and traumatic experiences. Others, conversely, made total admission of their destitution. Nevertheless, in the case of our research, it is often only when people start to get into the treatment system that all this starts to unravel: the main problem these people seem to have when they engage in rehabilitation is coming to terms with what they have done and what has happened to them, having denied it for many years:

> *The cycle doesn't end for people; they don't get out of it. What do we have for them to fill their lives? What opportunities are there really for them? You are not incorporating them into change but into a new life. They don't know people outside these networks* [points around at drug addicts sitting next to us in the dust and at the breakfast table under the canopy which protects them from the sun], *they need new work, new life. Otherwise they feel empty, and if they feel empty they just go back to it [drugs].* (Roberto)

Photo 30: Daily meeting

Treatment sequences

José, who we met in Chapter 6, also takes 60 milligrams of methadone because the *"heroin is shit* [quality]*"* and is hoping to go to some drug support accommodation, having tried only once, four years ago, because *"a moment comes when you get tired of all this"*. And it is obligatory to start with methadone regardless:

> You have to start with methadone, then they do a blood analysis, medical check, then you go there for two to three months, then you go to a flat, they support you financially and I don't know what happens then. It's a long-term programme. (José)

José refers to *"a moment"* as if it were some sort of turning point in his life, and in this way this very much echoes the drug treatment philosophy of Prochaska et al (1995) – when someone passes from the first stage of contemplation to action. If this was the case, how is it that four years later José is still in Valdemingómez? How is it that Julia, having tried to engage with the rehabilitation process three times, is still injecting heroin and cocaine and five months pregnant? Most of the people we spent time with had been through rehabilitation or at least tried to get clean from drugs several times yet failed quickly and fallen back into their former lifestyles. This was due to several reasons, but fundamentally because they had been unable to accept the magnitude of what they had done, having been in denial for some years. So, when engaging with a form of therapy that is configured around neoliberal mantras such as 'the drug user taking responsibility', many resisted, struggled and fought against it:

Rubén: *Have you tried to get clean from drugs?*

Adán: *Yes, three or four times with the harm reduction team. I lasted 11 months in the detox centre, the second time it was three months I lasted, and the last time two days.*

Rubén: *Two days?*

Adán: *Then the very last time was one month I think.*

Rubén: *So how come you didn't make it through those three times?*

Adán: *They threw me out twice because of other people, they were insulting me or I was insulting them so they penalised me. Another time I left by my own accord.*

Rubén: *They penalised you for insulting people?*

Adán: *Yes, not the workers, the other drug addicts in recovery.*

Daniel: *And they kicked you out.*

Adán: *Yes.*

Daniel: *And the first time was 11 months? Quite a long time. Where did you go in the end?*

Adán:	*Ambite [a housing and support stage in the rehabilitation process], and they let me have a flat with them, the first time with a flat.*
Daniel:	*All for yourself?*
Adán:	*No I lived with another guy. We lived together for two months and the agency arranged for me to have work, clothes, food, medication, everything.*
Daniel:	*And you were 11 months without drugs?*
Adán:	*But when I was kicked out I didn't know where to go, I had no other place to go.*

However, on reflection, the *"new routine"* Adán refers to, consisting of *"two hours of work a day, watching TV, eating and gardening"*, was somewhat limiting. Half of the small amount of money he earned went to the drug agency to support his costs, which left him little money, not that the alternative was much either, *"around €27 if you didn't work"*. Adán came back to Valdemingómez the same day he was kicked out of the drug support accommodation. This was two years ago. He fell hard back into the lifestyle, injecting heroin and cocaine, yet then managed to stay clean for three months, having detoxified for 15 days, once again taking advantage of help from the harm reduction team before he was again kicked out for arguing in the same support unit. This time, however, he was not so fortunate to have a flat to himself as he shared the accommodation with around 20 other recovering addicts. Arguments led once again to his expulsion. On the third occasion, in 2015, he lasted only two days in detox, asking to check out of the hospital, saying how his *"head wasn't right"*; *"I left to take drugs, and I went"*, he said.

Part of the problem, it seems, is that to qualify for further drug support, these people need to have been 15 days in detox in hospital where there is a waiting list for detox beds. The other alternative is to get drug free in Valdemingómez and take methadone but that, as Adán says, is *"very complicated"* because the *"pressure to take drugs comes from all sides"*. Asking for maintenance on methadone is fairly simple, as is the process to insist on increases in its dosage. Adán had initially started on 35-40 milligrams a day, but at the time of the research was taking 160 milligrams, far above the recommended daily dosage: *"You tell them that you wake up feeling sick, you feel bad, you can't sleep, and they say if you want that you can increase it 5 milligrams, then another week, another 5, another week, another 10 like that,"* he says after confessing he knows someone who is on 250 milligrams. Similarly, others we knew had dosages in the region of 180 to 220 milligrams. However, the recommended dosage of methadone, according to the *Drug Dependents Manual*, is 50 milligrams per 1 gram of heroin, with adjustments permitted between 5 and 10 milligrams (Martínez and Rubio, 2002). This, we hypothesise, is related to the high consumption of heroin and cocaine that is used on top of the methadone prescriptions, which consequently nullifies the dose, thereby requiring higher quantities to be prescribed. While one of the main risks of heroin consumption and associated sharing risks are reduced through methadone prescription, this doesn't eliminate its use. Adán, like others, used heroin on top of his methadone prescriptions; still, he was critical of the side effects of methadone, saying they were worse than heroin.

Adán has been in treatment four times and failed on all four occasions. This is because drug treatment in Spain, and in most other Western countries, is structured around a psychological reasoning around making change, and in a climate of public health cuts, it is easier to demand personal motivation from the client, patient and/or drug user, so the most deserving are funded and treated. Therefore those who appear 'less motivated' don't waste time and precious financial resources. As Prochaska et al (1995) indicate in

Figure 4: Cycle of change

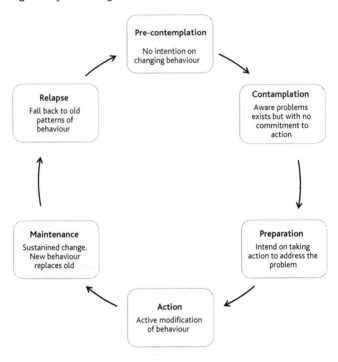

Figure 4, the addict, dependent or patient passes through a series of thought patterns that eventually end in change. What they don't say is how long this will take, and rightly so: each person's dependence cannot be generalised. However, the idea that recovery can be sequential, even after a few rounds in this psychological process, was almost impossible for these people, largely because each time they had tried to take action to come out of such embedded lifestyles, it had backfired. Furthermore, many already overstretched drug services, often overpopulated, were not configured to accommodate complex people with a multitude of mental, physical and financial problems (see Chapter 10). Failure in a culture of personal responsibility (see Chapter 3) only adds further layers of shame to subjectivity (Briggs, 2012a), leading many to return to what has become the default setting – using drugs – and hence the conclusion that ways out are practically impossible.

So between the fleeting ambitions Juan had, real intervention can only take place when something serious happens; in this case, it tends to be a near-death experience, such as that which happened to Alberto. When we first met Alberto in the fieldwork, it was common to see him talking to himself in the *plaza* and brushing his hair in a small portable mirror. His story is similar to others we came to know in Valdemingómez, growing up in a poor area, having little educational opportunity, almost no work and having caved in to the open availability of drugs in his area (see Chapters 4 and 5). Some months later, when we came to know him and interview him, his responses manifest a kind of self-blame for his predicament (see Chapter 2) as well as the dominant ideology of treatment philosophies – that drug use is an illness:

> *I have spent 28 years taking drugs, seven years and three months of those in the streets. I am very sincere* [holding heroin in a syringe], *this is not drugs. From one gram, you take a micro maybe, and the rest is not worth analysing because who knows what it has in it. In the beginning it is like a vice or bad habit then it becomes an illness without your realising. At first you like it, you have a good time, the company makes it. Many people ask me how I started with this and I can't remember, but you know who I blame, the company, because I don't remember how I started, but like everyone you have a beer, then a spliff, then a line of cocaine, and you like it, then it's off we go. From then on, life sets us back, well everyone, but the setback from the drugs I would want for no one. And I speak from knowledge, otherwise I would not say.* (Alberto)

Over the course of our fieldwork we saw Alberto numerous times – even picking him up from a petrol station where he was begging, to take him back to Valdemingómez, otherwise he would have to walk for an hour. He tended to live on the outskirts of Valdemingómez, but came down to access the harm reduction team bus and its facilities, probably because of his mental health illnesses – although we cannot be sure what he is diagnosed with, and nor can he, but suspect it to be schizophrenia. Halfway through our fieldwork, when crossing the A3, Alberto was hit by a car and knocked unconscious. We were to learn this after not having seen him for a month in Valdemingómez. We asked around at hospitals, eventually finding him in Hospital 12 Octubre:

> We walk up from the restaurant towards the hospital. Up the slope, there is rubbish on the pavement and on the left there is a small *chabola* in a vacant building space. We cross towards the hospital before the rush hour traffic starts to pick up. Inside, it is busy yet surprisingly easy to locate Alberto's room as we find the lift and head for the sixth floor. As we exit, several nurses walk on, talking to each other, while another tends to a large machine and presses buttons. The passageway is long and each room seems to have two patients.

> We pass the unmanned reception desk looking on the left and right for 607 where Alberto is staying. 601, 603, 605, and 607.... We peer inside, where two elderly women sit in a concerned manner next to an elderly man who lies fairly motionless in the bed with his leg bandaged up. We excuse ourselves as we pass, and assume that Alberto shares the same room, and is behind the plastic curtain. As we pull it back, a thin figure lies there in a hospital gown and an adult nappie thing. He kind of recognises us as part of the harm reduction team, and reaches out his withered hand to clasp ours, and closing his eyes, he says, *"Me allegro veros, la verdad, gracias por venir"* ("I'm so happy to see you, thanks for

coming"). We hand over mandarins, biscuits and some sweets in a plastic bag and start to listen to his story.

The last time we had seen him, he was heavily dosed with methadone and topping it up with heroin and cocaine in Valdemingómez. We frequently saw him talking to himself in the *plaza* and everyone else we had talked to told us he had *"another fictional friend"*. We had managed to interview him a few months ago, just before his accident, when he was knocked over by a car on the A3 motorway. To cut a long story short, one hospital discharged him because they said he had nothing wrong with him and he was taken to a homeless hostel where the doctor there diagnosed him with severe injuries. When he was taken to another hospital, they found out he had broken ribs and a fractured vertebrae. This is typical treatment for drug users, we have been told by the harm reduction team, who have had to report the hospitals. He said he could hardly walk and the whole of his hip was *"black because of the swelling"*.

He talks us through his injuries, pointing at his thin legs, and at the surgery that the doctors had done on his knee so he could walk. Pulling up his gown, we see his thin but admittedly better-fed stomach. Leaning to the right, and in pain, he shows us where they operated on his hip and vertebrae. He sighs and looks out of the window, laughing to himself, saying how a *"pretty nurse caught me smoking but said she had seen nothing"*. He says he sees clearly: now is the moment to get clean, to move on from drugs. It seems some of his family have come to see him and offered support. *"When I get out of here, I am going straight to rehab,"* he says, and with that, within a few days, he says he hopes to be released.

We are then politely kicked out of the room while the nurses change the sheets and move the other elderly man into a sitting position. As we wait, we talk awkwardly with the other visitors of the elderly man. There is a short silence as we exhaust all possible places to look apart from at each other before Daniel breaks the ice and asks how many days the old man has been here. They say 15. There is another awkward silence because they have been listening in on our conversation about drugs and recovery, and whispering among themselves. We explain that Alberto has had a number of problems, and they look to the floor as we explain, before the younger of the two says, *"well once you get involved with drugs, that's it"*. Daniel pulls a confused face at her. At that moment, the smiling nurses come out of the room.

We go in again and tiptoe around the elderly man's leg to talk to Alberto. As he moves his thin legs, the wasted muscle flaps around under his bones while his feet remain tucked into his reindeer-themed winter socks. He continues to get our names wrong as he looks out of the window and promises himself to beat drugs. *"Lo tengo clarisimo, lo sé lo que voy hacer"* ("I see it clear, I know what I am going to do"), as he looks out of the window as if he can see his own future. Time is getting on and we shake his hand tightly and leave, wishing him all the strength and support. As we leave, we only hope that his family are able to assist him with his recovery – it's been years since they spoke, but at least they have come to see him in hospital.

Alberto managed to get a place in rehab, having also detoxed of heroin in hospital, yet only managed to last a month in a treatment facility:

It is around 11.00 when Daniel arrives at the very muddy Valdemingómez; it is covered in a kind of light slop which isn't deep, but just gets trodden everywhere. It is busy so Daniel finds a space on the right-hand side near the rubbish tip and parks up. In his wing mirror he can see one driver of a *cunda* start to slap around a women he has brought to the Valdemingómez; as he strikes her, she retreats to the car while he threatens her with more from the outside the car. He lumbers off and starts to lecture another driver who is blocking the way, then gets back in. Daniel then gets out into the muddy slop on the ground (because of the heavy rain), and wanders down to the busy harm reduction team bus where there are trivial arguments over the quantity of food being distributed. Juan passes me without noticing me, and gets his biscuits and chocolate milk before disappearing.

Daniel invites Marcos and Roberto for a coffee in one of the *gitano's* cafés, but only Roberto can come. We skid down through the muddy slop past the cars and *machacas* and into a calmer parallel street where a pair of *gitanos* play guitar. In the café, Roberto lights up a cigarette and updates us on affairs. They are proud to have managed to help two people to hospital for detox over the last two weeks. Alberto, Roberto tells me, is alive and well but in a homeless hostel – not completely relapsing, but drinking from time to time and still on his methadone. "*It's a massive step for him, much better he is there than he is here,*" says Roberto.

Towards the end of our fieldwork, Alberto had since left the hostel and was once again sleeping on the streets, drinking heavily and taking drugs. Yet progress is seen as leaving Valdomingómez, which is why in the absence of 'getting out' of the area, ways of 'getting by' are accepted instead (see Chapter 7), and many thereafter remain stabilised on substances such as methadone, which does little to improve their circumstances; every day, they are given free food, clean syringes and clothes from time to time, and in between they raid the rubbish tips for things to improve their *chabolas*.

Photo 31: Stefano salvages a sofa then reads a newspaper outside his *chabola*

Roberto: *The harm reduction team support them a lot with that [methadone].*

Daniel: *For how long?*

Roberto: *Their whole life.*

Rúben: *So they substitute methadone?*

Daniel: *It's a supplement, nothing more.*

Roberto: *The idea is that it gets them off drugs like heroin and that thereafter there is a detoxification process off methadone ...*

Rúben: *But very extended ...*

Roberto: *This is where the process fucks up. Why are so many drug addicts depending on methadone? 90% in fact. How many have come off methadone? They continue with their life but they are just daily dependent on methadone, their family if they have them, and medication. They are not people who are going to form a family, get married, have children, and buy a car.... The process they offer is not serious, there is no real alternative for them [the people of Valdemingómez]. It doesn't depend on simply taking people out of the area. The main problem is that we still consider drug use as an illness, like a virus which we supposedly need to cure and that the cure is the medication like methadone we give them but it is much more a social issue. When you medicate someone with something like methadone, you are controlling them. They are a controlled consumer. Remember the aim is to reduce their criminality and it's true the crime has gone down because these people just go to prison or die.*

Generally, very few escape this lifestyle once they are in it as exiting demands their own navigation of a complex set of violent interactions and systematic obstructions, which holds the way out to ransom. As referred to earlier, ways out are very rare, but 'ways to stay in' are common. By this we refer to the way in which oppressive forms of social control haphazardly direct their lives in ways they cannot control, and keep them either in Valdemingómez, in prison, somewhere on the streets or somewhere in between.

Appearances and disappearances

As we have shown, *gitano* operations, combined with the mechanisms of supervision and intervention, are heavily implicated in what happens to the people of Valdemingómez, to the extent to which they invalidate each other. In these case studies taken from our time in the area, we show several examples of how this is the case, and this often leads to negatively perpetuating their situations.

Always late for court

Ricardo is wanted by the police and needs to attend a court appearance but is working as a *machaca* for the *gitanos*, and the nature of his work impedes his attendance at court and therefore increases the chance of his warrant and imprisonment. He is oblivious to the consequences of his failed court appearance because going to prison means nothing to him any more; he is far gone in his drug dependence, and working under exploitative conditions for the *gitanos*:

> When Roberto is finally able to free himself from the early breakfast scramble, he wanders over, eating a ham roll, and proposes we have a coffee in a part of the sector where we haven't yet been. We agree as he warns us that Telemadrid, the local television company, are hunting around for people to do interviews. Between his animalistic bites of the ham roll, he tells us that a while ago someone came to film in Valdemingómez and *gitanos* came out and threw stones at them and the crew left, running as fast as they could.

> To pass time, we walk with Roberto to see if we can escort one of the *machacas* called Ricardo to a court hearing to receive his sentence for a string of petty crimes. As it approaches 11am, Roberto tells us the hearing was at 10.30am. Sometime shortly after, Ricardo arrives on his bike having cycled from the *fumadero* where he has started to work (the same one where Julia works). He seems unbothered by the court hearing, and proceeds as normal with the preparation of his breakfast, opening the whole packet of biscuits, emptying them crumbled up into his plastic bowl after crushing them in his black hands and then proceeding to cycle off with the bowl in his hand, promising he will return in half an hour. As he leaves, a sleepy Gema wanders over and does the same thing with her biscuits followed by another woman dressed only in a

t-shirt and leggings. Roberto leans over and says *"pobre mujer"* ("poor woman"), before telling us that last year this woman was beaten *"por alguien"* ("by someone") when she was pregnant and she lost the baby and her arm was broken.

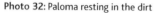

Photo 32: Paloma resting in the dirt

Vanishing act

Help mechanisms cannot intervene with everyone. Many people in Valdemingómez live within a set of complex interactions and relationships and survive in an arena that revolves around violence, with vendettas the daily order. As we have seen from accounts in previous chapters, many people like Paloma simply appear as quickly as they disappear:

> Roberto needs to go, so therefore decides to take a coffee in the middle of one of the most conflictive areas of the sector, a road parallel to the main street, set back, where there are around seven different *fumaderos*. As Roberto lights up yet another cigarette,

we walk across the *plaza* and turn left, passing into the small road. It is certainly a little quieter as fewer cars can enter this more residential area. However, this doesn't mean it is necessarily safer, for on each side of the road are two or three *fumaderos*, some with large metal gates and padlocks installed at the doors. *"Son todos como bunkers"* ("They are like bunkers"), says Roberto referring to the way the buildings are built, secured and guarded, and how the drugs are stored. The road narrows as we pass the main dealing area, and we take a left into a dim-lit café where a few *gitanos* sit inside, smoking cigarettes, sipping coffee and gawping at the TV. It could be any café in Madrid really; it has all the same installations and equipment as it takes me a while to remember what it was like being in a public house where people were smoking. We sit, and Roberto shows us several photos from his phone. One in particular is particularly moving as he shows us a picture of a barefoot prostitute curled up on the floor with a plastic baby toy in her arms. *"Se fue a buscar el bebe en la basura"* ("She went looking for the baby in the rubbish"), he says, before shaking his head, lamenting how she disappeared suddenly last year. We look at the picture as the tone of her skin changes from tanned on her arms and chest to white on her legs to grey on her feet having walked around barefoot. All Roberto knows about her is that she had been working in Marconi and sold sexual services regularly in Valdemingómez. We drink up soon after and walk back up the street as a few clients walk from the *fumaderos*, also passing in the process the *machacas* warming themselves by the fires.

Prison, Valdemingómez, prison, Valdemingómez

The woeful drug support in prison combined with the limited post-custody support provided to people like David very often casts them back out on to the streets, facing the very same barriers that had initially led to more acute problems with drugs. This revolving door, which is very much the experience for this cohort, only normalises an existence in

Valdemingómez, for it becomes the only option for them on release from prison since they have little else:

> In front of us in the queue is a man in purple tracksuit bottoms that don't seem to reach his ankles and a thin jumper; yet he has covering him an oversized coat. We remember we had seen him as we drove in and he had recognised us from our car. When we get talking to him, it transpires his name is David, and it turns out he has been using drugs for 20 years and in that time been in and out of prison for 14 of those, mostly what appear to be for *robos violentos* (violent robbery), although his stature, demeanour and interactions wouldn't suggest he could be this man: he is a short fellow, with thin cheek bones, over which is a layer of messy stubble; his eyes sit back in his head due to his malnourishment. It turns out that he has only been out of prison for 10 days and is already homeless. David, who is 43 years old, was able to stop taking drugs in prison and managed to put on weight. Having left, he found no work and returned to old pressures: boredom, drugs and Valdemingómez. He now lives homeless in a town nearby, where he was making around €50–80. He has eight brothers and sisters who had, in their time, tried to help; the most recent occasion was when they helped him access rehabilitation, but after an argument with a staff member he was kicked out.

Killing me softly: Overdose and death

In a situation which many of these people have come to accept as the status quo, and despite fleeting moments of flirting with the utopia of exiting Valdemingómez, the most probable consequence for most is a personal surrender to a progressive death – much like what happened to Fabian (see Photo 33). The accumulation of health problems related to self-neglect as a consequence of increased investment in a drug-using lifestyle results in a dependence acceleration that is particularly relevant to living in Valdemingómez.

Photo 33: Fabian suffering an overdose

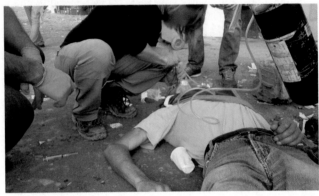

Such is their state that they are often realistically beyond intervention, and this was the case for Gema. She had suffered family abuse, left home at an early age, had a disrupted education and almost no work experience (see Chapter 5), and thereafter had experienced a life of sexual abuse, been in and out of prison, worked directly for violent and abusive mafias who physically raped her, and to this day is still wanted by them. The experience, however, as a sex worker in Marconi, played an important part in the internalisation of her feelings, increased drug use and involvement in sexual activity. It was common for her to have clients who paid her between €100-150 to cuddle her, watch her take a piss, insert things like cucumbers into her arsehole, film her giving them blow jobs, and pay her to take drugs and have sex, and this was how she developed an addiction. Sometimes the clients paid more to avoid using condoms, which she often spent on more drugs to deal with these daily traumas. As we had learned from Roberto, she was beaten and had lost a baby.

In hindsight, she tells us, fighting back the tears, things took their toll on her physical and mental health:

Gema: *Yes, I knew a lot of women* [in Marconi]. *In situations like mine but not quite like mine. They aren't bad. I am dying. I am dying of pneumonia, hepatitis C, HIV and lung cancer. I am dying of four things.*

Dan: *How do you know you have all this?*

Gema: *Because the doctor told me. All the men I am with are also ill with the same. I am already dying. I am poor, I live in poverty. I am dead.*

Over the period of our research, we watched with great sadness as Gema's health, in particular her mental health, disintegrated significantly. In conversations and interviews, she increasingly displayed difficulty in talking clearly, with there often being long silences and broken conversation where it was clear she was suffering from vivid flashbacks (see Chapter 5):

Suddenly Gema appears from nowhere and collects her bowl and yoghurt with chocolate flakes. She sits herself next to the man who is conscious and breaks up her bread carefully into small pieces, before prodding it into the soup with her swollen black hands. We amble up towards the concrete stumps and rest by a fence that overlooks the new *fumadero* (drug house). On the way up, we notice her right hand is bound up in dirty bandages, out of which poke her swollen black hands. When we ask her what the problem is, she tells us that she has an open abscess that has now turned gangerous, and this has infected her whole forearm. Although the harm reduction team clean and dress it daily, she needs hospital treatment, and if she does not get medical help shortly, she will have to have her hand cut off.

Perhaps this is why she will not engage with the harm reduction staff who have tried daily for the last week to persuade her to go to hospital – because she has perhaps given up on herself and decided that there is little way out for her. As she wraps her black hands with her white cotton jumper with streaks of blood down the side, she says goodbye with a customary kiss on each cheek. She then starts to fish around the rubbish for things to sell to the *gitanos*, finding a couple of children's shoes and dusting them down, she approaches the queue, confident of selling them, only to have no luck and to have to return to the rubbish heap to find other things to sell.

In particular, Gema's resistance in the notes is reflective of elements of the 'death drive' mentioned in Chapter 5. Towards the end of the fieldwork period, Gema took a turn for the worse. One day in October 2016, she emerged from her *chabola* looking yellow and almost fainting at breakfast. The team called the ambulance and she has since been in a serious condition in hospital: she was just 28 years of age in 2016. It should therefore be of no surprise that, over the course of our study, we witnessed overdoses and heard accounts of deaths. Indeed, it was not common for these people to have known someone close to them living in the area die of an overdose or health-related complications:

Adán:	*Lots of people have died here, overdoses, freezing in cars, sleeping.*
Daniel:	*Were you with them much?*
Adán:	*Yes, some.*
Daniel:	*Why didn't you call the ambulance?*
Adán:	*The last time someone died here, no one knew about it. After taking a hit, he fell asleep in his car and the next morning when the harm reduction team came they went to move him and he didn't wake up so they thought he*

> *was sleeping. No one knew he was dead and it was just here* [points 10m away].

In the testimonies, these accounts appear quite nonchalant, which very much reflects the work of Jean Comaroff (2007) who talks about how the suffering of victims of HIV is often obliterated from local and national memory, which is a form of negating the social significance of death (Murray, 2006).

Life after death

The heroin boom of the 1980s and early 1990s eventually led to the phasing out of 'drug-free programmes' or 'abstinence programmes' in Spain because of the high costs and low success rates: we suggest that this was because these services were poorly configured in the first place, and lacked a grounding in the circumstances of the new drug-using population coming through with HIV and other associated health problems. Indeed, such was the volume of people passing through and relapsing that when evidence appeared about a new and more economic way of managing drug problems via harm reduction, this idea was borrowed from the US. Harm reduction programmes came about because of concern about high rates of drug-related crime, but were ideologically presented by state health departments as interventions that would reduce the damage people do to themselves through drugs by offering them clean paraphernalia to do it, endowing them with 'knowledge' to reduce harm and offering them a drug equally as addictive (methadone) (Briggs, 2012a).

Since the goal has never really been to solve someone's dependence, less so the related problems that accumulate, as we describe throughout this book, perhaps unsurprisingly retention figures on programmes following harm reduction intervention in Spain with these kinds of groups are low, and completion rates even lower (Sánchez Pardo, 2000; Rodríguez Molina, 2007). A major flaw is also those studies that canvass the approach but only measure participation in programmes after a short period of time, when a true appraisal of success should be considered long term. So the story of 'success' is the mere fact that someone has come onto a drug programme: temporary retention is therefore the index of success (Briggs, 2012a), and this is reflected in numerous studies undertaken by national health agencies in Spain that retain between 18-25% of those who come into the process (Plan Regional sobre Drogas, 1992; Agencia Antidroga 1999; 2004). Yet this tells nothing of what happens after treatment, which is why we would certainly challenge this on the basis of our study.

Now, in a time of austerity politics and budget cuts, much of what should be a robust system supporting the work of the harm reduction team in Valdemingómez has all but disappeared. Waiting lists are long, space on programmes is limited, and such is the demand to get a place that only those 'most motivated' – often with the least complex problems – qualify for help in a system that each year streamlines even more who it claims to help.[2] So, as the people who appear in this book acquire more problems, unfortunately, they inadvertently start to close the door on their own recovery. Into this gap step third sector organisations such as Basida, which more than anything end up providing a service to those who somehow manage to negotiate the process:

> We walk in to the drug service and are welcomed by the director and shown upstairs to get a briefing about the programme. The service is open to anyone who is in need and has substance-related problems, taking old, young, families, illegal immigrants, anyone really. Unfortunately, they can't help everyone, and there is a waiting list of over 200. It transpires that the association receives barely any governmental support, given that much of it has been

cut; in fact, they are still waiting for last year's payment of €13,000 which is overdue. However, they have over 900 members and private donors who make up the funding. Everything everyone does is purely voluntary, no one receives any wage for what they do. The upkeep of the place is undertaken by the residents, some of whom have become educational workers. They say that since the 2008 crisis demand for the service increased and threats were made from the state to withdraw their pitiful funding unless they expanded to offer more help to receive more people. However, they knew that the service worked best when it gave people the time they needed to move on from the service instead of pressuring them. There are six phases to the service, which, at each stage, gradually give residents more autonomy and responsibility, and thereafter links to reintegration back into the community. After our introduction, we are given a tour of the facilities. Walking outside, we walk to another building where some people work on fixing pallets and under the sun we cross the courtyard past a few dogs who are locked up in a kennel, before looking out across the 12 hectare land; in front of us is the old railway station where one of the clients was supposed to have lain down and been hit by a train. The sun shines down as we are shown a theatre, a garage complete with a Basida ambulance, children's adventure playground, meditation room, dentist surgery and hairdressers, separate guest quarters for volunteers and I don't know what else. It is immensely impressive and clean and organised. From time to time on our tour, we bump into the residents who greet us, smiling.

We are here to interview Miguel, a man in his mid-40s, who is not long out of prison. He has been in the programme for two months. Although it seems like he is well on the way to rehabilitation, in recovery terms, he has some way to go:

Opposite Daniel sits Miguel, an ex-convict, who has been in the programme for two months. He sits with spikey hair, two teeth and numerous wrinkles on his face that melt into the contours of his face when he smiles. For him, it is the first time he has been drug-free, and this is the first attempt he has made to get clean. He has spent 22 years of his life going in and out of prison. Drug offence after drug offence, prison term after prison term. Now he is in recovery he has managed to put on weight and has an infectious smile. *"I'm free, I have my life back"*, he says, as he looks around at the people and then winks at Daniel.

Miguel talks about the early periods of his heroin use as a time when people knew nothing about dependence. Like most people, and as we have discussed (see Chapter 5), he talks about a progression from substance to substance, and gives importance to his social company or other factors relevant in his dependence:

> *You start with tobacco when you are you, and you are, like, 11 or 12, a cigarette, like that, and in front of you there is a bar where people meet at night. Spliffs, alcohol and where people used to meet. Then, a few years later, you think you know more about life, but you know nothing, and you start to enjoy things, although you are ignorant. You develop bad habits and you get to know soft drugs until it ends in heroin and cocaine. When you put yourself in the world of drugs it is to avoid yourself, and then you don't understand what is around you, but you attempt to get around people who may understand you and that's how it happens more easily; where you inject, where you smoke. Then there is someone you know who has tried heroin, they offer it to you and then you know someone who sells. You ask for a bit to sell, then you come to Madrid, you come to Valdemingómez for grams: all to be able to have your mind and body well, because at first it hooks you but then your body and mind need it. Then it is not to keep you happy but to forget things, then it is to give*

> *yourself what you need. Then comes a moment that you*
> *have to take it just to get up in the morning.* (Miguel)

Like the dominant ideology around drug addiction and
treatment rhetoric, Miguel constructs his dependence as if it
were a progression from soft to hard drugs (see Chapter 5).
In his hometown of Soria, just 200 km from Madrid, he
says he still knows people taking drugs all of whom are
in rehabilitation programmes for treatment, but *"have not
psychologically been able to recover"*; instead they *"are given
methadone and it is controlled"*. Growing up in poverty, and
surrounded with available drugs, Miguel quickly fell into
street company and started robbing for drugs. When he was
admitted to a youth offending institute, around him were
"people who had problems with society, rebels". By the age of 16
he had already served his first prison sentence, since *"Soria
was a small town where the police knew the criminals"*, and he felt
most guilty about *"playing a part in the expansion of the drug
problem"*, as he was one who dealt drugs to the city.

Miguel was most critical of the way in which drugs
were permitted to be used and sold in prisons, and of the
marginal support for addicts to get clean. Although he says
organisations like the Red Cross offered some help in the
mid to late 1990s, it was not until the turn of the century,
he says, that proper associations appeared with knowledge
about dependency. Although these days treatment is still
limited because *"among the politicians public money disappears
to tax havens"* (see Chapter 2), Miguel recognises the general
failure of a system:

> *But if the government realise what makes a junkie,*
> *in life, from friends, in society, in places that there is*
> *no one, then they should be worried. Behind all this,*
> *the government are responsible. There has always been*
> *crime but never have there been so many people who*

> *wanted to throw away their lives because to arrive at*
> *being a junkie, you are throwing your life away and*
> *you don't realise. When you become a person who*
> *doesn't value themselves as a person or anyone else, it*
> *is not because he or she has failed. There are people*
> *with psychological problems, lots of substances, speed*
> *or whatever, but when a person doesn't value anything,*
> *they can't do anything, they can't recognise the value of*
> *life, something has happened in this process to make you*
> *inject heroin in you and you think 'fuck it'. Something*
> *has failed and they [the government] haven't shown you*
> *what it is. Over the years, something fails in schools, in*
> *prison, in all social institutions.* (Miguel)

Suffering numerous overdoses from the varying and unpredictable quality of some dealing outlets, Miguel now talks about having been *"given life after death"*, that his former self is dying, and in its place is a new self that is replacing the old spoilt self; perhaps evident in his last words is his understanding of a wider context attached to his addiction, imprisonment and now recovery.

Death after life

Such are the conditions of the people in Basida, however, that many end up dying there – either because of their physical or mental state or a combination of both. During the time of our fieldwork there, one man, who was closing out his prison sentence in the service, died of terminal cancer. Another committed suicide when he decided to lie down on the nearby train track – apparently he had not been seen for breakfast and a search party was sent out for him. He was spotted in pieces on the train track 15 minutes later only because someone had recognised his torn clothes in and around the area. Perhaps in this short time available for people like Javier there is time to reconcile with one's actions as well as realise how, at various intervals, the social institutions that Miguel had mentioned fail the poorest people in society:

> When we walk into what seems to be the living room area of one building, some volunteers sit around trying to animate a very mixed crowd of people with a game. A few sit sort of docile and reasonably attentive on the opposite side, while near me, a few sit in wheelchairs. One lady has a missing eye and tries to identify Inma by voice – we are later told she lost the eye when her former pimp beat her; her body to this day is still covered with bruises and scars. Yet there is one figure who is not taking part for some reason; he got angry, it seems, and wheeled himself off to the middle of the room.

> Javier is his name and he sits in a pile, with his left arm bent redundantly into the chair and the left side of his face in a permanent spasm from the stroke he had. Inma wheels him off and talks to him, explaining about our study. *"Sí, no hay problema, me engañaron con la metadona"* ("They cheated me with the methadone"), he repeats several times, as she wheels him outside and across the courtyard to a more discreet place to interview. We enter the dinner hall and turn right into a small corner of the room and begin the interview as Javier looks distant into our eyes.

> A rather disordered conversation starts off as he recalls how his cousin died from drugs during the heroin boom of the 1980s. His first memory of using drugs was when he used to inject morphine when he was 15 and 16, which led to him being kicked out of his home, something he says he always regrets as he becomes tearful. Thereafter in the streets, he learned from street adversaries about crime, robbing banks and jewellery stores from the age of 18 onwards. During this time, his dependency on heroin grew, and as he recalls the quality of the drugs, he starts to dribble. *"Todo fiestas, putas, drogas, todo gastado"* ("All on parties, whores, drugs,

all spent"), he summarises this period of his life in the early 1980s. And like this it continued until in his early 20s he had an encounter with another drug user outside a church. They agree to continue their disagreement in the Casa de Campo, and as they reached the Palacio Real, Javier stabbed the man twice in the heart, killing him, only to earn himself a prison sentence of 28 years.

In prison, he continued to use drugs, and recalls how they were thrown over the prison wall and came in via the prison guards. After serving half his time, on his release in 1996 he went straight back to his robbery operations and teamed up with five associates to rob a jewellery store, each earning about €50,000. With it he bought a house, clothes and returned to heavy heroin use. However, times had changed and so had the quality of the drugs. In one moment, he recalls how he went to a *gitano* area of Madrid and asked for heroin and was confused when he was told that people smoked it on foil. He handed over money and asked for *"heroina para pincharse"* ("heroin to inject") ... as he applied dose after dose, it did nothing for him and he felt no effects.

In an effort to quit the habit that he now saw as pretty useless, he started attending a methadone agency where he was given the drug substitute. He met another woman in the programme who was living on the streets and invited her to live with him. At first, he seemed content to pay for her drug needs, accompanying her to Valdemingómez from time to time in the *cundas* before things started to turn sour. Increasingly immobile because of health complications, he became confined to a wheelchair. She started to demand more money and abuse his trust, on one occasion leaving him in a cold bath for a day and on another occasion destroying his phone so he had no contact with his family or friends. In the end, they separated and he sold the flat to be able to come and stay in the drug programme – the only drug rehabilitation that would take him given his complications.

Javier is only 45 years old and has colon cancer, AIDS, emphysema, and having had a stroke leaving him half paralysed, has only the use of his right arm and the potential to move his right leg with the help of his hand. As he explains this, he tries to rekindle his former glory, boasting how he could take on any man and that if we insulted him he would *"darnos un par de hostias"* ("give us a couple of slaps"). Suddenly he stands in this mini recreation of his former glory only to get his feet stuck in the wheelchair and almost falls over. We help him back into the wheelchair before he then wheels himself closer. He asks for Daniel's hand and clenches it as hard as he can; *"soy fuerte"* ("I'm strong"), he says, before showing us his right arm muscle which sort of limps around under his tracksuit top. Re-evaluating his wheelchair state, he looks at himself, dribbling slightly on to his grey t-shirt that has started to come up revealing his colostomy bag. He lifts his right hand as it trembles and pretends to be holding something. Suddenly he speaks: *"€500 no vale para nada si no puedes andar, yo quemaba notas de €500 pero al final no vale para nada, no puedo andar"* ("€500 is worth nothing if you can't walk, I was burning €500 notes but in the end it is worth nothing, I can't walk"), and with that his face sinks and his eyes water.

Notes

[1] In one short documentary, drug addicts from the former *poblado* are filmed taking drugs and interviewed about life in Las Barranquillas. They reflect how there is 'no support' and lived in a poverty akin to that of Valdemingómez. See www.youtube.com/watch?v=b8Q9va8bmMU

[2] Remember that these agencies also have to justify their funding, and by doing so they have to prove that their programme is efficient by providing statistics on their 'performance outcomes' or basically the number of people they retain on a programme. Whether they are public or third sector, in Spain there is almost no evaluation of how well these interventions work, and in particular, no medium- to long-term evaluations of their impact.

9

Not really the conclusion

Introduction

This is the part of the book where we try and tie things together in an effort to be optimistic about how we can improve the current situation for people who arrive in Valdemingómez. It would normally start with a deep methodological reflection about how we have advanced knowledge before discussing how innovative our methods were. We would then discuss the main findings of the book in relation to the theory outlined, before making some comments on policy improvements and recommendations so we can avoid such situations of desperate poverty and fatalistic drug use, thereafter arriving at some conclusion. Perhaps lots of academics do this to feel good about their work, or maybe it is more about closure. Or maybe it is more that they feel obliged to write something that will, in fact, change nothing – like, for example, that we need to make more investment in harm reduction. Aside from being really obvious, given the current political and economic climate, this is unlikely to happen. Even a significant budget increase to the harm reduction team would at best be tokenistic, and in any case, such gestures would obfuscate the real and meaningful change that needs to take place so that Valdemingómez and the people in that space do not end up destroying themselves.

This is because the problems we describe in this book cannot and will not be totally fixed by the introduction of new bespoke social policies. The Spanish economy is contracting and, because Spain is bound to the Euro, it can't devalue its currency in the hope of encouraging the forms of productive labour that might allow its poorest to move into stable and reasonably remunerative jobs. Social housing is disappearing, and the benefit system is collapsing. The Spanish state is debt-ridden. It is corrupt. The state has capitulated and the market has won, which is why the political will to intervene in the hope of setting things straight appears nowhere. At best, all politicians can hope to do is to tamper with what already exists, and castigate anyone who proposes disrupting the smooth rhythm of capital accumulation, even though the majority of Spaniards have been getting poorer, year on year, for 20 years or so. Spain is now a hideously stretched society, and, unless we make changes at a fundamental level, the gap between rich and poor will only get bigger. So, having presented the gravity of the situation in relation to Valdemingómez and those who live/work there, from what we conclude, this is not really the conclusion, and here is why.

Ethnography in a time of neoliberal politics

Although we undertook this work, it is unlikely that its methods or findings will trigger any immediate rethink about how research on social problems is done in Spain. As in most Western countries, neoliberal politics are increasingly closing off avenues to the acquisition of critical knowledge in the education sphere. It seems that universities employ academics mainly to attract money, market themselves, participate in competitive knowledge economies that prioritise prestigious grants, and foist on them pressure to publish in high-impact journals so they can be cited as a measure of their 'excellence'. Even when the grant calls come around, we have to somehow solder our own, and probably more significant, research intentions into rigid research restrictions. We are then measured on a points system relative, in the main, to where we work and how prestigious it is, and are given the funds according to where we publish our work. Then we have to write a dry report with recommendations for policy-makers to mull over – if they get past the executive summary. To be completely honest, this does very little in helping us move forward to change the status quo described in Chapter 2, and changes little for the people at the bottom of society.

To some extent we tried to play this game. Over 18 months, perhaps stupidly, we tried hard under institutional pressure to obtain research money to get funding to study an issue that in the end cost us relatively little. But in the end, interest in having someone examine the problem in detail was never on the political radar. From what we can see, it seems that the function of the current political arena is not to have to think about real answers or to have someone present them with the right questions about what is currently happening in the city shadows. For us, it is sad that after trying to persuade government institutions to consider our research proposals and to fund them, they seem to have been rejected on the basis of their innovation and precise function to offer something different from current knowledge. This is problematic for politicians and civil servants for several reasons.

First, as it currently stands, the political status quo does not allow there to be too much insight into the mechanisms that inflict social woe on the urban poor, and even less about making public real-life stories of social suffering, because it might reveal its precise complexity as well as compromise powerful people in powerful positions and jeopardise the political apparatus. Second, the new and innovative methods we have supposedly used – which, when considered against the history of the sociological and criminological disciplines are not that pioneering – appear to be somewhat threatening to the way knowledge is constructed for them. Hence, in one research proposal, we were essentially told to 'tone down' our observational methodology and to provide a more interview-based approach. Had it been funded, this would have drastically altered the trajectory of our research and jeopardised a clearer construction of the reality we had come to study. You can perhaps be the judge of that. Last, it is much easier to commission survey studies that dumb down subjective realities associated with exclusion and evade the appreciation of how macro-structural, historical and spatial processes interfere with population movement and isolate poverty from collective conscience. In Spain, it is most common to hear on the radio or see on television the research results of CIS (Centro de Investigaciones Sociologicas; Centre for Sociological Research), which publishes what we consider to be fairly bland data on the labour market, education, crime, politics and how people feel about society. CIS often publish research bulletins that receive inflated press coverage about minor reductions in the unemployment rate – either because of the tourist seasons and/or because of changes to employment law – or those related to the preoccupation Spanish people have about corruption in the country. But that's it, really.

So in the end, we did it on our own, spending our own money and time because we felt it was important. We hope you now concur. Indeed, we think that this kind of research is entirely possible and have shown its benefits, so hereafter encourage other scholars to do the same: carefully and patiently immerse themselves in the complexities of social problems. Although we can apply no new generalisations to our data, no fancy correlations or chi square analysis to impress you, or abstract charts relating to cognitive processes of dependence, instead, we offer you an authentic vista into the lives of a group of people who, increasingly, are massively misunderstood and even blamed for their personal destitution. We have also tried to draw your attention to part of society that is outside the current swank of the city's tourism sites, gated communities and spotless shopping malls, where many of you, including ourselves, spend our time. In the process of this project, we did our best to get to know these people by showing them respect, giving them time to trust us, even though there were times when we could not reveal our study intentions to everyone. We validated what we came to learn about by cross-referencing data, which made it reliable and conclusive. To situate our observations and interviews with drug users, we interviewed other parties involved in Valdemingómez, and made observations in other areas of Madrid to enhance the findings. Even as we wrote it, we went back to clarify small details in an effort to present everything as clearly as possible (see Chapter 1).

This started off as a research study, and along the way morphed into something else related to the welfare of the people we studied. This was something that funding bodies and ethics committees would have frowned on, which was related to our ongoing, personal and intimate contact with these people. Perhaps it may have been patronisingly liberal to have continued to try to persuade Julia to do pregnancy tests and thereafter hopefully embark on a process of recovery, but it is what we ended up doing, having got caught up in the interactions and dilemmas of our participants. Of course, it actually could have had the reverse effect. But there were no institutional, ethical or funding directives attached to our work, so no one or nothing could tell us otherwise how and why we did what we did or how to approach it. Perhaps this was how we were able to do it. Undertaking this kind of research means abandoning objective epistemologies that researchers may have about the terrain they analyse, and thus distance them in the process. By ditching these before we undertook our study, we feel we came closer to finding a way to depict how the realities of Valdemingómez function. And to be honest, to feel that we played some part in someone's decision to come out of that environment is far more rewarding than, for example, receiving notification of having had an article published in a high impact factor journal or being interviewed on television.

The fact that we have been able to do this research has surprised some of our colleagues and, indeed, in Daniel's case, many of his students. In particular, at the height of the fieldwork, Daniel took a group of three criminology students from the private university where he teaches on a tour of Valdemingómez, inviting them to step out into the mud and strewn syringes in the *plaza* where we spent most of our time. One student immediately lit up a cigarette to deal with the sight of carloads of people injecting heroin and cocaine, another got back into the car and refused to come out until we left, and the other started shaking and trembling. These are harsh realities that we have grown accustomed to, and their reactions are perhaps indicative of the lack of exposure everyday people get to these kinds of social injustices that take place in the dark corners of the urban sprawl, while at the same time, this confirms their participation in the other privileged circle labelled 'society' that Mario had drawn for us in Chapter 2. Valdemingómez is far from their secure worlds of iPods, Instagram and Starbucks; it is, as we have written, where the Wild West meets the third world.

People have also expressed shock in online forums where we have blogged about our emerging findings, and audiences have felt moved when we have done conference papers showing images of the people we have come to know on their knees injecting or lying in human heaps, recuperating from long shifts working for the *gitanos*. And it is for this reason we did the research in this way, using ethnographic methods through the use of photography: so you could *see* and *feel* our data, *see* and *feel* the personal stymies of these people, and understand the impotence of the authorities and helping services. We would hope that the ramifications of this book could lead to a political rethink of the way urban problems such as drugs and crime are conceptualised, but remain doubtful given our struggle to stimulate governmental interest in the first place. While we will continue our diffusion of the findings as much as possible, our secondary hope is therefore that this book has impacted on how you may see these people, if only to think twice about what you think about them.

Drugs, the global political economy and personal decision-making

Drugs will continue to play a part in the day-to-day lives of millions of people – as farmers, traffickers, mules, consumers – as long as the global political economy continues to strip away labour markets without providing decent alternatives for people. Secluded pockets of marginalisation, such as Valdemingómez, where chaotic drug use and violence are endemic, will continue to thrive because these communities have thus been politically and spatially manufactured to have no interaction with formal economies other than those that offer them some food and clean syringes, and those that patrol and arrest them. Furthermore, drugs will also continue to be available, tried, used habitually and problematically as long as cultural attitudes towards our mode of being oscillates around consumerist attitudes mixed with a quest for our own self-gratification and supposed freedom to 'experience' what the world has to offer. So long as consumer culture continues to create a nagging discontent in people's lives that can be solved by their purchase of an experience/feeling like drugs to temporarily ease the pang, the marketisation of drug use will continue.

We lack a real sense of why people take drugs and do so to the degree that we expose in this book. A common popular misperception about action attributed to drugs, whether it be dealing or consumption, is that it is some clear-cut choice, made in the acquisition/absence of knowledge about using a particular substance or engaging in dealing. For example, 'I take these drugs knowing/not knowing the consequences of their consumption' or 'I deal drugs taking a calculated risk knowing that there will be repercussions should I be caught'. We have been conditioned to believe that drugs do the damage to us, which embeds in us a sense of passivity of our own agency when it comes to their distribution/consumption. We have shown in our work that this very philosophy is the thrust of treatment mantras, and penal as well as social policy in Spain. Hence, in the wake of the heroin boom of the 1980s and early 1990s, the emphasis was placed on drug education, to make people aware of the risks of certain types of drugs as well as the legal mechanisms that come down on offenders if they are caught. One of the main problems of this perspective is that it simply sidelines the role of wider forces that may influence someone from a particular social cohort to deal/use drugs and thereafter either to return to them, in the process developing dependence, and/or to continue to deal drugs.

Here is where we need an appreciation of the political economy at a time when cultural attitudes to consumption are indiscriminate and excessive, and youthful abandon takes precedence, and it is this which should explain our attitudes to trying substances. The split away from a society that revolved around notions of community, heritage and established cultural norms made possible by the advent of neoliberalism in the 1970s has set society in competition with itself and recalibrated subjective identities around the symbolisms provided to us by corporations and marketing experts. And from this time onwards our cultural attitudes have started to reflect elements of these structural changes as we place emphasis on 'living for the moment' and 'seizing opportunities' – all of which mirror established neoliberal philosophies that cast aside the future and problems like finding work or establishing a career and family, replacing them with the need for personal gratification, risk-taking and pleasure-seeking. Yet at the same time, we are tasked with being responsible for ourselves and for our own health. It is under these cultural circumstances that our research cohort developed consumerist attitudes towards drug use, and it is where their dilemmas remain as they are caught between extreme, flaunting and opportunistic forms of consumption and safe and healthy consumption. In the end, for these people, this personal quandary is not really resolved as many fluctuate between the two states even if and when they try to take steps towards recovery.

The same transition into the neoliberal period, however, also destabilised the social structure and automatically rendered certain social groups at the bottom of society redundant. Failure to evolve as 'responsible citizens' – regardless of socioeconomic status – in a society that ever more gives preference to individual meritocratic initiative, coupled with the stark lack of opportunity and economic and educational limitations for many people described in this book only served up viable options in the illicit economies that had come to revolve around inequalities, such as drugs, prostitution and crime. While these realities are not certainties for everyone born into these conditions, they are severe impediments to any reasonable alternative, especially given the structural and spatial obstructions to a better life in and around this area of Madrid.

These problems – far from being locally born – have global origins. For example, the *gitano* dealers described throughout have become the face of the street drug market in Spain, but this is largely because of the political scapegoating of the way they have to survive. Criminalising marginal activity like recycling copper, reselling old machines, even applying stricter rules to street market licences, only fosters the need to innovate in the search for other opportunities in other illicit economies (see Chapter 3). Even then, the *gitanos* do not simply produce the drugs, but are, instead, part of a global chain of contacts and players in the international drug trade, responding to a market opportunity in a time in which drug consumption has been normalised. Behind the *gitanos* are political pressures in producer countries that result in the need to cultivate drugs, as there exist thousands of other people who, as a consequence of imbalances in the global political economy, work illegally in the same industry – transporting, dealing, cutting and reselling drugs.

Solutions to these exclusionary predicaments are presented to us as if they hinge on individual decision-making. For example, governments are content to develop policies to support those willing and culturally competent to attain higher levels of education, and provide equal access to education and health because social-cultural practices in the field of consumption, education and housing are associated with individual choice: they are realised by private choices that lie outside the realm of government. This is because social institutions now 'filter out' the most deserving, risk-free people in whom to invest: those who will take advantage of what is on offer. However, by comparison, given these emerging spatial dimensions and the concentration of deprivation, the resources in hyperghettos like Valdemingómez lack investment for the very same reason – there is almost zero motivation to invest in a dead cause, reflected in the slow and drawn-out reluctance to spend dedicated funds on these people, who are seen only to squander away their own futures (see Chapters 2 and 10). The money 'goes missing', has somehow been 'miscellaneously and mysteriously spent', just like when we tried to fund our study (see Chapter 1), and this seems to correlate with endemic corruption cases in Spain.

The collapse of the left and the rise of the right

It is this corruption that stifles economic recovery and eats away at social welfare. After nearly a decade of austerity, depression, chronic unemployment and perpetual political submission to the directives of the Troika (the Troika being the International Monetary Fund, European Central Bank and European Commission), tens of thousands of people have been left displaced from work and home, and are left with little choice but to seek refuge in the few parcels of public infrastructure that remain available to them. Throughout Spain, members of the growing reserve army of *ninis* ('neither nors'), the quarter of young Spanish people who are neither in school, nor employed, nor in training programmes – struggle to find food to take home to their squatted apartments. *Los irrecuperables* (unrecoverables), those people over the age of 50 who make up more than half of Spain's long-term unemployed are meanwhile forced to figure out how to subsist on severely reduced pensions and any charity their friends or family can offer. Most of these people fit into the 30% of the Spanish population currently classified by the Unión General de Trabajadores (General Union of Workers, or UGT) as 'at risk' of poverty. No wonder those with the relevant skillset consider joining the estimated 700,000 Spaniards who leave the country each year to find marginal employment elsewhere. However, people like those who you read about in this book are well below this potential threshold, and are locked out of this opportunity.

In this climate, deep indignation has emerged among the population about political and financial corruption, aggravating the perceptions of citizens to the point that they consider corruption to be the result of a systemic deficiency in the political and economic model. So, until a party is able to address the declining economic realities of its country's electorate, we expect more and more traditional political parties to be punished by the electorate and new political movements to be given a chance – and this is what we have seen in the sequential failure of the dominant parties to offer a clear alternative that doesn't ruin the lives of working-class Spanish people.

Populism has sailed on the winds of the financial crisis, and indignation has successfully spread its simple solutions to complex problems without having to worry about demonstrating that these solutions are possible. We must therefore remember that populism is a political narrative, not a programme for government because its proposals are disconnected from reality; they are practically unfeasible, and a departure from politics and real economics are not obstacles to its success but together form a utopian component typical of wishful thinking that only makes populism more attractive to certain sectors of the electorate and public opinion. The failure of any political and economic thinkers to successfully manage their way past the low growth, low inflation and high debt years of austerity following the financial crisis has pushed the electorate towards solutions offered by untried sources. We therefore enter a medium- to long-term period of right-wing governance that will only sharpen the experience of poverty and continue to multiply debt, render people unemployed or precariously employed, and make them homeless.

Space, capital and processes of social cleansing

While global corruption continues to impede steps forward for our future (witness the Panama Papers), and record levels of people displacement continue to reflect the stuttering engine of global capitalism, it is also prising open a realisation that democratic societies supposedly serving ordinary people are perpetuating the inequality they claim to be eradicating. The only escape from this domestic as much as international uprooting for many (see Chapter 3) has been to move to substandard conditions on the city fringes, where the casualties of globalisation blend into temporary work if they are lucky, or more likely into the cracks of the informal economy, the only available opportunities in the fallout of the collapse of industrialisation being the uncertainties of the service sector or other temporary means, which is why inequality is most felt in the urban peripheries, where the experience of unemployment, marginalisation and lack of social mobility has stagnated with various opportunities in the illicit drug trade.

Our work shows the crude ramifications of the global chase for profit; as large industrial complexes and corporations shift their workforces overseas to streamline profits, they leave large landscapes of working-class populations and newly arrived immigrants competing for scarce opportunities in concentrated areas that have been spatially severed from prime city spaces. Not only are they priced out of these areas, but they are vertically blocked because of their class orientation and skillsets. Almost all of these people cannot compete in a global market. As we have shown, the people in this book have experienced the need to move country (such as Adán from Romania and Gamal from Morocco) as well as drift towards the main Spanish cities from rural areas and smaller towns (José from Asturias and Miguel from Soria) in search of opportunities, which puts them on the front line of this process.

Instead, the evidence we present here shows how these processes directly and negatively impact on these people in these areas. As a consequence of the closure and displacement of previous *gitano poblados* and the bungled management of attempts to reintegrate those same families, both drug users and *gitanos* have been forcefully evacuated from city spaces where access to help and support was more available. This highlights the total disinterest capital has in citizen welfare, in particular the welfare of the most vulnerable people in society, because nothing stands in the way of new economic possibility. In removing old *poblados*, new spaces for commercial and residential investment are realised, and with the instigation of new laws to enforce the very people shunned from these areas, like the *Citizens' Security Law*, the urban transformation is increasingly more streamlined towards clean and organised streets where the good citizens who access the shops and work hard for their wages socialise. Gentrification is attained when the poorer groups in the area can't afford to get by as a consequence of the new investment and the new profile of resident entering with more money. Put up a few CCTV cameras and get some police to walk around, and it seems like a nice safe place to be for the happy consumers wearing branded clothing, striding around with their iPhones glued to their hand. The project becomes even more complete when the media project one-sided stories of the misery of the displaced that never get beyond sordid descriptions of detentions as calculated acts by people who are at fault for their own poverty, coupled with online propaganda produced by the authorities about the quantity of drugs seized from raids.

So when commercial ventures are made in the new city spaces, which only assists in the 'capsularising' of our social life, suddenly, against the sterile surroundings, the failed consumers stick out like a sore thumb … if only people noticed them. Instead, the city folk are confused at their destitution and pass by ignoring them, as they only invite attention from the authorities that move them on. The wider political and economic goal of this assault on the poor is threefold. First, it is to socially and spatially amputate the city of surplus people who do not conform to the ideals set out by the very spaces that have been ideologically structured to support a particular kind of citizen, by relegating them into residual spaces that are a physical reflection of their own failure. Places like Valdemingómez as well as Polígono Marconi – the politically forgotten prostitution hotspot – become thriving hyperghettos full of people in competition against each other who end up literally fighting for self-respect. Thus the urban experience becomes far more segregated and unequal (see Chapter 2), but that doesn't matter because the authorities save a bit of cash as well as concentrate the problem in one place, which requires fewer resources to manage.

Secondly, this spatial demotion allows politicians to make use of various 'blame mechanisms' on those people, which often only results in their increased surveillance at opportune moments and the creation of more stringent social policies that mask background commercial interests. Concentrating the drug market with all its associated crime, suffering and victimisation means that blame can collectively be placed on a poor group who can't participate in civic life in the city centre spaces. Indeed, their presence in the city is seen as an invasion. Although governing institutions put forward the supposed opportunity for these people to work themselves out of their situations, the way out is fraught with bureaucratic obstacles and milestones that only register self-determination and personal resistance as the requisites for success. So when it all goes wrong, they can also be expected to be blamed.

And this is the general perception the urban populace has of these people – as we found when we went to see Alberto in hospital – which is why, thirdly, the political aim is to numb the electorate's consciousness of how and why these people do things like inject heroin and cocaine in the city shadows. There are far more important things for the successful citizens to do, like go shopping or go out to a fancy bar to celebrate their supposed personal freedoms of choosing where to dine and how much to spend. So, when a summary of a drug raid appears on page 17 of the newspaper or flashes up on the television screen with the police or Civil Guard celebrating their drug confiscations, the citizen is reassured that none of this is in their neighbourhood, and that the authorities are doing a good job of controlling the 'problem people'.

Nevertheless, the uprooting of the drug market – and all its components like the *gitanos*, drug users and other informal players – from the centre of the city and its concentration in a contested space outside the capital creates major tensions in how to respond to it ... or perhaps not to respond to it. And this is why it won't change any time soon. Structurally orchestrated violence on vagrant populations like *gitanos* and drug users is about the spatial organisation of capital investment, which reflects the shifting fortunes of class struggle and the changing role of the city *within* global capitalism. As new projects of commercial glory are realised, urban marginalisation becomes intersected by class, gender, intergenerational and racial inequality, even when the very utopias that are constructed to replace the failed ones also flop (see Chapter 10). Therefore the spatial concentration of poverty makes for demonisation, surveillance and political neglect of the poorer classes, and renders them easy fodder for the criminal justice system and prison industrial complexes, ever stuck in cycles of prison, street homelessness and drug use.

Consented violence and its cultural norms

It should be no surprise that a kind of martial law governs the space of Valdemingómez, and that the respective authorities are fairly impotent in what they do and can do to reverse this situation. Consequently, the hyperghettos – ever spatially separate from our cosy city experience – fester in political neglect that allows for new cultural norms to be established and flourish. Years of poor social and housing policy and botched management of 'at-risk' populations, such as *gitanos*, immigrants and Madrid's urban poor, has resulted in a kind of social decay that has reached its terminal stage. Of course this is bolstered by the continual lack of strategic state intervention. In this absence there are only really law enforcement and harm reduction services, whose philosophies and agendas completely contravene each other. The best the police and Civil Guard can do are phases of intense patrolling, police checkpoints, raids and arrests between piecemeal responses from public services (such as ambulances). Remember that costs cannot drift too high in the management of city waste (see Chapter 3). This means that there are extended periods of neglect and abandon, and it is out of this that a form of 'consented violence' takes precedence: better to permit the zonal mutation of crime, drugs and violence in a political no man's land than to make the urban living experience more equal for hundreds of thousands of people who also run the risk of slipping into addiction as they take up ranks in the informal economy (see Chapter 6).

While the legal boundaries of the space remain contested, made worse by the muddle between three different councils and their ownership over responsibility for intervention, and the law enforcement collaborations are in crisis having been worn down by their own impotence to alter the situation, the result is that interactions in the area are left uncontrolled. Violence becomes perceived as a norm, something expected, seen by the authorities as a trade-off worth accepting seeing that it is taking place in an area where it doesn't draw complaints from the electorate or tarnish the precious city centre spaces. Consequently, crime and victimisation are seen as an inevitable part of the daily interfaces. Normalised, then, are *gitano* children playing in rubbish-and-syringe-infested streets; the desperation of a man instigating a neck injection to a crying prostitute under the cover of a tree while it rains down hard; and the fist fights between Juan and a new adversary to the area over a disagreement in a shared drug deal. Sitting in between all this, and literally looking on, are the harm reduction team whose remit is precisely the opposite – to help people get out of this. While their assistance and daily commitment to the cause is entirely exemplary as they develop relationships with these people, all they can do is look on as the *gitanos* batter their employees and the police continue to displace *gitano* families through raids. And all of this is far beyond the remit of the harm reduction team. Even if they were to play a major role in conflict resolution, they leave at 6pm each day, and until the next day at 10am there is nothing else.

This spatial restriction on cultural interactions also forces hierarchical relations to revolve around the maintenance of a particular set of symbolic interactions as a means of channelling the structural violence imposed on them. In the context of the *gitanos*, this does not make them socially excluded per se, as they demonstrate all the will to be socially included as consumers, only that they are set in ideological competition with each other rather than anyone else. This requires a hierarchical social ordering and a set of norms and codes that place others as economically, socially and culturally inferior to them. The first in line are the *machacas* whose function can be to do basically anything the *gitanos* desire. Indeed, such is their submission to undertake whatever that may be for a hit of cocaine and/or heroin that they become the objects of ridicule and humiliation. Giving a blow job to another *machaca* and having sex with him while being filmed become standard examples of this treatment, as does waiting outside all day and all night, in a permanent state of intoxication, in the wind and rain, to be woken up just to open a door and close it (see Chapter 6).

The '*machaca*' label encompasses someone who has lost all morals, a slave who is sitting out his own demise. However, these very same people reverse this interpretation by considering themselves to have work; someone who is working, they argue, is someone far more important than someone who is kicking around in the rubbish for money/drugs/used commodities to sell for a hit. No one wants to be the lowest of the low living among the low, so the figure of the *machaca* is the centrepiece in this *ideological ordering* as it regulates the spatial hierarchy and helps manage the identity power struggles that can be detrimental to perceptions of the self and assist in dependence denial.

However, at the very same time, this sets them in mutual competition with each other. The demands imposed on their characters mean that there is barely time to think about a 'way out' of their predicament because it is constantly set to 'ways of staying in'; this severely dents reciprocity and trust in social relationships, producing a form of meritocracy gone wrong (Briggs, 2016). 'Staying in' means doing so at any cost, frequently breaking the norms and codes of the moral economy that result in manipulation, victimisation and violence. In this respect, the norms and values displayed by these people reflect neoliberal ideologies of simply looking out for oneself rather than any communal resistance to their own exclusion. In the end, they get stuck in a kind of psycho-social cul-de-sac – in the spatial sense as well –with no real way to turn. The dead end lives on.

Abstinence doesn't make the heart grow fonder and nor does harm reduction: drug dependence in context

The conflict that is shared in both prevention campaigns and drug treatment philosophies in this context of our research is that *change* is required of broken people through the summoning of personal will and motivation to alter their own circumstances. So long as these perspectives prevail, few will continue to escape these situations. From initiation to cycles of habitual use to dependence, this work has shown that people's own conceptions of their drug addiction reflect dominant ideologies like Gateway Theory that rests on the idea that continual experimentation with drugs leads to the use of harder, more dangerous drugs. In essence, these people say that 'drugs have resulted in their destitution'. But this is what they are made to believe, so the structural mechanisms that have, to some degree, caused their situations remain hidden.

We show that the problem of dependence is far more complex and takes place over time in reciprocation with other social, structural and cultural elements. Initiation to drug use for most of this cohort came at a time when the country was quickly in transition from dictatorship to democracy, and from a producer to a consumer society. As neoliberal values started to poison the early form of democratic politics, so, too, did subjective identity politics start to reflect the acquisition of its ideologies such as 'live for today, think tomorrow'. A youth cohort, increasingly locked out of a diminishing industrial sector, who had lived in the city since birth or had congregated in the city for the precise reason of finding work, having been displaced by corrupt politics in their homelands, increasingly found it difficult to get a foot on the ladder of the labour market. Drug use therefore came about as these processes collided with the marketisation of drugs in Spain, which hit the urban working class hardest at a time when industry was rapidly downsizing.

Decisions to return to drug use, in more of a cyclical pattern, relate to problems in achieving ideologically constructed and culturally prescribed goals of success in education and the labour market and the allure of new informal relations made in deviant contexts such as that in Valdemingómez. Many of these people may place blame on the drugs for the tensions this causes with friends and family, the debt it creates, and the like, but it is less something external to their life-changing circumstances and more something internal to a shift in their subjective identities. Losses are balanced by heavier cycles of drug use. So, rather than what the drugs do to them, it is the investment they make in the drugs as a consequence of wider structural and social pressures that often catapults them into further problematic scenarios such as committing crime, being processed in the criminal justice system and the embracing of cultural contexts like the *poblados*, which facilitates a transition into dependency.

Thereafter, new neutralisation techniques are rationalised such as those related to the pull of the social space or, as we referred to in Chapters 5 and 8, *"el entorno me engancha"* (*"the environment gets me hooked"*). We are therefore describing an identity shift that is increasingly given rank through the use of drugs in a particular place where liberation on consumption increases the pull of the spatial context, hence the reference to the way Valdemingómez gets people *"hooked"*. What it actually is, is a way of neutralising an out-of-control drug use in a context of identity recalibration that is facilitated by the social acceptance/recognition they receive from others in a similar position (visiting/staying there).

These journeys to dependence are exacerbated by other processes of displacement from other areas of Madrid – people's drug dependencies, mental states and physical capacities also deteriorate because they have been moved out to an area where there is no infrastructure. Recall the words of Gamal, in Chapter 8, when he said, *"The more you take resources away from people, the worse they get"*. Of course we are talking about those who experienced this transition. Many disappeared along the way, and far more just died. This process accelerates dependence because mental and physical problems multiply in Valdemingómez, and consequently many quite quickly close the door on their own recovery. This is for three main reasons.

The first is because embedded feelings of fatalism reflect aspects of the death drive – the instinct to seek the state of quiescence that preceded birth. Instead, many are drawn to repeat painful and traumatic events/decisions/actions, and their compulsion to repeat them through the vehicle of drugs permanently binds their trauma to the psyche, hence its perpetual playback. There is a sense that there is no way out, and consequently, a reflexive tendency to only flirt with the dream of being drug-free, and recovery is resisted. Secondly, ways out hinge on an unfailing personal motivation to want to remain drug-free and commit to recovery at a time when self-esteem has been eroded to its core and is at its most fragile. Lastly, they inhabit a place that supports intrusive and manipulative social interactions, or, in the words of Adán, *"The pressure to take drugs comes from all sides"*. Even if they get past initial hurdles to engage with the harm reduction team, long waiting lists and a rocky pathway to recovery await them, which involves them conceding to the things that they have negated their whole lives, that they are responsible for their actions, not the drugs. It is for this reason that many people like Alberto fail in treatment and often fall quickly back into their former lifestyles.

While a few make it out, they are thereafter challenged by filling the empty subjective psychological space. Many fail because the alternatives on offer for them often leave them feeling more vacant than before, hence old habits and practices are revisited, as we saw with Luis in Chapter 5. These circumstances have little to do with an inherent 'self-motivation to return to drug use' or 'relapse' that Prochaska et al (1995) insinuate, because offering real alternatives to recovering drug addicts requires us to address the structural deficits in the economy that deliver to them, at best, extremely limited options. The vast majority of these people never get to own their own house, own a car, have a decent paying job, and thereafter they struggle in relationships, and the fact that this is inaccessible to them also assists in resetting the subjective preference to its default mode: harmful forms of intoxication. Better to have something in nothing than nothing in something.

With 'ways out' problematic, 'ways to stay in' are favoured, and a commitment to the social space is gradually made, along with the likely end result. Life is prolonged by a methadone prescription to numb their criminal capacity and confine them to the space by requiring them to turn up each morning to get the medication that temporarily alleviates the imminent pressure to generate more money or other ways of getting additional hits of cocaine and heroin. They are, as Roberto refers in Chapter 8, *"controlled consumers"*. In this respect, the *"accommodating"* nature of the harm reduction intervention abets in this 'personal surrender' to the space (see Chapter 7), and thereafter there await only slow steps towards the inevitable.

It is hard not to interpret this as being something quite deliberate, to be honest. Shove thousands of people out to the outskirts of the city, fail to provide for them, forget about them – only remembering them to criminalise their behaviour and produce propaganda about their activities in the media. On top of that, spend years in inconclusive negotiations over what to do, while spending money ring-fenced for interventions on their behalf, before underfunding a harm reduction team bus, paying the workers a crappy wage so their motivation wanes, and continue to strip away welfare resources like housing, social security and rehabilitation centres. Don't forget to offer the very same people substandard alternatives in the labour market, if they do get clean. To us it seems like a way of just sending unwanted people to a distant grave, to die quietly in piles of rubbish and waste: dead end lives. It is unsurprising, then, when people like Gema in Chapter 8 say things like, *"I am already dead."*

With fewer specialised resources, all this has consequences for the people who work within the intervention mechanisms for, given the density of the problem and lack of collective ability to make change, this results in a kind of 'professional impotence', the feeling that such is the scale of the problem that it produces feelings of resignation and, instead, cultivates attitudes that contribute to its cultural milieu – hence the police officers getting blow jobs from the prostitutes in Valdemingómez and the harm reduction worker taking a piss against his own bus. Such resignation can also sway them to instead start to conform to the dynamics of the area – hence the high levels of police corruption, for example. So, in some way, like the *gitanos* and drug users, they become part of the problem as well.

As public funds have dried up as a result of damaging corruption and fraudulent banking behaviours, so, too, has political interest in providing for these people – especially in zonal areas where they exhibit behaviour like taking drugs 24 hours a day, which ideologically underlines their own downfall and gives sufficient reason not to invest in helping them. Who has money to spend on people who throw away the chance to escape their own misery at a time when just eight people share as much wealth as 50% of the world's poor (see Oxfam, 2016)? Such is the concentrated nature of the drug market now, the constant flow of thousands of people every day to the area to buy drugs, the ever-flourishing networks of *gitanos*, the micro-scale corruption among the police, and the impotence of the harm reduction team, this makes for a moot point in terms of intervention: to the point, in fact, that everything seems to cancel each other out. And the people in the book seem to recognise this, which is why this is not really the conclusion.

Photo 34: A new arrival in Valdemingómez with his life's belongings

10

Epilogue

Introduction

In the time since our fieldwork was completed in November 2016, we are still reminded everyday about the people we met in Valdemingómez, not only because we often talk about them and reminisce about our fieldwork, but also because having researched what has been taking place here, we exposed ourselves to a brazen reality that is far from public consciousness and yet close to political inertia. This is especially the case when we walk around the glorious city centre paradise that is Madrid, knowing that only a few kilometres south, in a forgotten corner of the city, there exists an unimaginable poverty that has turned septic in its neglect. We got to know the people there, rather than judge them for their dishevelled appearances, brutal attitudes towards damaging drug use and absolute destitution. Although Rubén has now completed his Master's in Intelligence Studies and starts his preparation for the police exams, and Daniel moves on to conclude his research on the refugee crisis, high-class brothels and problematic tourist zones, perhaps, like our participants, we acknowledge that for a time Valdemingómez also had us hooked – the people's circumstances, their stories, and the sight of it all. And in doing so, we have unlocked a consciousness about how the world works that we cannot seal, for we are able to recognise where else similar destructive processes are taking place that ravage the lives of the most vulnerable in society. We see below the opulence and pizzazz of the commercial city centres, we see its oppressive undercurrents in action on a daily basis, in the city's shadows, where rampant inequality lurks and the conventional fractures.

Action plan for Valdemingómez

Towards the end of 2016, the various local councils (Rivas and Coslada) and regional government (Madrid) had started to 'gather information' and meet to discuss ways of improving living conditions in Valdemingómez. Already it seems various commissions have been established dedicated to urban planning, social integration, health, education and an integration plan for refugees and illegal immigrants. It seems there is some interest in 'including it in society' by 'putting down asphalt roads, lights, establishing a mail service, bus route, basic services, water and social controls'. Preference is to be given to those who were part of the census undertaken in 2011, and residents are to be offered the chance to own the land their house occupies. For those who don't 'qualify' for this, they will have the chance to be relocated to newly constructed housing along the stretch of the Cañada Real Galiana. The highly vulnerable residents in Valdemingómez, it seems, are to be relocated to second-hand housing dotted around Madrid and beyond. This was all promised by the Madrid regional president, Cristina Cifuentes, and it is estimated that this will take between 10 and 15 years to accomplish. But as we know, political promises are regularly broken.

Nowhere to stay, nowhere to go – in Norway

Daniel finishes a pizza with the Mayor of Hedmark – a province north of Oslo in Norway – and gathers his winter clothes to prepare himself for the cold. Outside it is a reasonable −20°, which feels warm compared to the −37°

they had experienced on the Swedish border a day or two earlier. Since there is food left over, Daniel asks to take it away. They walk out into the corner of what is mostly a park and pedestrian area that is empty, and where next to them is the glory of what looks to be a theatre. They walk up towards the tram that will take them to the outskirts where they are staying, and start to trudge up the icy Karl Johans Gate; all the shops are closed and each step they take shatters the cold silence of the night. Within about 100m, they see on the horizon a man lying in the middle of the pedestrian walkway wrapped in as much he can possibly find; it looks as if he was on his way somewhere, but was so cold he had to engage an emergency retreat to the frosty warmth of his sleeping bag on the snowy pathway. Next to him there is a little cup where sit a couple of kroner. They walk past his covered head and leave the rest of the pizza; the noise it makes as it is left by his side stirs him, and he says *"Tak"* (*"Thank you"*). They walk on, and after only a few seconds they hear horse's hooves: it is a policeman, tall on his steed. He starts to talk down to the figure in the cardboard and sheets. They don't hear the conversation, but suppose, after making periodic glances back, that he was swiftly asked to move somewhere else, as he very slowly and painfully picks up his things and shuffles on somewhere. This is perhaps untypical. Recent influxes of homeless Roma to the surrounding urban areas and, as a consequence, the main station – only just a few hundred metres further from where they walk – have resulted in stringent city laws against vagrant groups who appear criminal or do really offensive, evil things against society, like beg for money. Gone, now, also are the street prostitutes in the area, displaced from the dock area, which, over the last two years, has received massive investment and, as a consequence, has been gentrified.

From Russia – without love

Outside Lubyanka metro stop in Moscow, not 10 minutes walk from the wonder of Red Square, two men dressed in rags start to argue; their faces are chapped and their swollen hands are red raw from exposure to the cold. As one tries to land a punch on his comrade's face, he falls, and as he does, he lands on his hand. As he attempts to steady himself as his hand starts to bleed, the missed punch and fall seem only to motivate him more to restart the conflict. The other man, meanwhile, shouts abuse at him in Russian, with one hand holding his can of strong alcohol, and staggers in and out of passing citizens who seem invisible to them (and vice versa). The altercation then drifts into the wide Moscow roads where the traffic seems to have no mercy for those who stray from the curb. Still, the shouts and insults continue, which are mixed with pushes on the chest. However, within a minute or two, a *politsiya* (police) van steams onto the scene and the two men are quickly bundled into the back of the van and driven off, and the ugly scene disappears from public memory.

On a sunny day – in Aluche

We drive down the A5, eager to meet Roberto in another deprived part of the south of the city; it's been a month or two since we have seen him, as our time has been swallowed up with work and writing the book. Outside the weather is cold and breezy, and in the distance the snow has started to cover the Sierra in the background. Parking just off a roundabout, we walk down to a local bar where we have had several meetings with Roberto. Today is no different, for with a few minutes, a heavy-headed Roberto walks in, having just got up from recovering from a party the night before. *"I was in here last night drinking, we started early"*, he says, as he scratches his scruffy hair and leans over to order a lemon drink to quench his thirst.

He sits as we drink our coffees, and with the hum-drum of café blab, we start our conversation, talking first about people from Valdemingómez. It seems that not long ago, he bumped into Julia in the police station as she went to get a new identity card, and she looked, in his words, *"very pretty, her skin full and healthy"*, adding how she had *"recovered her smile"*. He tickled her young daughter before wishing her well. *"Unfortunately, the same can't be said for Juan, it seems, for he still remains in Valdemingómez, working for another gitano family in another fumadero, doing odd jobs, getting by and coming for breakfast, begging a cigarette"*, he says. It seems that Juan lasted only a day in treatment that the team had set up, given that he was to be a father, as Roberto reminds me how he is a *"very violent man"* who has been *"acting strange lately"*, perhaps because some time after the birth of his daughter, Julia wrote him a letter outlining how she didn't want to see him again, and how he couldn't be a father to their daughter.

Sadly Gema, who had been mostly hospitalised for a heart infection for the latter stages of our fieldwork, continued to deteriorate. After being discharged from hospital she remained on a waiting list to enter a treatment programme, but returned to Valdemingómez. *"There are long waiting times, then you have to do analysis, checks, scans afterwards, it's about a month-and-a-half after you are referred"*, says Roberto, as he looks below his wonky reading glasses and taps his fat fingers on his new phone to check his messages. Just off the *plaza*, Gema continues to live with Antonio in the *chabola*, only now such is the problem with her hand and its tendons that she can barely move it.

As we speculate where Alberto may be – the last we heard he had left the homeless hostel and was street drinking – we go outside so Roberto can smoke, and he lights up as the bright winter sun beams down. Roberto now sees Alberto from time to time in the *poblado*, but not every day. Similarly, Luis, who still comes infrequently in his *cunda*, he says, continues to appear and come to the harm reduction team desk. As he continues to talk about drug dealing returning to the *barrio*, pointing out a former Valdemingómez *gitano* family who deal within 50m of where we sit, we furiously write down notes. He lights up another cigarette and lets it burn in the wind as he praises the achievement of the harm reduction team having withdrawn over 200 people from the area in three years, yet how well they do in recovery he cannot say. Still, the *cundas* come, he says, as he starts to gesticulate before revisiting his criticism of the current treatment system:

> *Projects these days are funded on the basis of their economic value rather than social necessity. If you offer a drug service which costs €5 million a year and another company offers one for €4 million, they will take theirs over yours. It doesn't matter if the service is good or bad, it is cheaper, and as long as you don't pass what you ask for, they don't complain. The drug-free programmes [see Chapter 8] didn't have that. These days it comes down to money which the government plan to spend, and addiction to drugs is not high on their list of priorities. This means that with fewer funds, our service is affected. So we only have X amount of syringes, condoms, and can only dedicate X to wages. A drug education worker, like me, who works around high-risk people has less wages, which reduces his motivation, and this reduces the quality of intervention people offer because they are not economically valued for the good work they do. Now the priority is on cost saving rather than what the service is and what it can do to help people.*

Meanwhile, back in Valdemingómez ...

We follow the road down the A3 and take the familiar route to Valdemingómez, passing the main entrance and opting to go in the secondary entrance that comes directly into the *plaza*. As we are to see, this secondary entrance has less traffic as an asphalt road has been built that directly connects the side roads to the main *puntos de venta* (sales points). We turn into this entrance and the car struggles with the potholes and the mud from the recent rain. On our left as we follow the muddy/sandy road is a parked car on the right, in which a man leans over to attempt a heroin injection. Moving up the road – the car moving from side to side as we try to negotiate the potholes – the spire of the dilapadated church appears. As we reach the *plaza*, it seems as if it is business as usual. To our left, several tents sit as the light breeze barely moves them. In front of us there are a series of parked cars in which people are smoking heroin and cocaine, and to our right the rubbish blows around the intermittent efforts of some of the addicts to search for things of value among the commodities that other city folk have thrown away.

We park up and walk down, almost struggling to recognise some elements; there is a new wooden construction in the middle of the *plaza* and another large tent that sits intact. There is one next to them both that is in complete shreds and flaps around in the wind. We negotiate around needles and syringes on the floor, and wander over to the harm reduction team bus, where all the staff are busy handing out drug paraphernalia and breakfast. It is about 11.30 and they have already been there 90 minutes. We greet Marcos and Roberto, and to enable our conversation, man the food desk with them and help to distribute biscuits, chocolate milk and ham sandwiches to whoever asks.

We recognise very few, apart from Margarita, who still scavenges the rubbish tip for goods to sell. An Andalucian man with a bushy beard limps up to us and asks for a bowl of chocolate milk, and stuffs two packets of biscuits in his pockets. When the second doesn't manage to fit, he rams it in, which inadvertently splits the packet and some of the biscuits fall into the mud. Perhaps conscious this may be his only opportunity to eat today, he fishes them out of the mud and stuffs them into his pocket. There then appears a tall woman in a heavily stained white top who politely asks for breakfast before sitting down. Another thin woman in leggings and a tight vest gulps down the chocolate milk and hurries off; how it is she is not cold amazes us. There then appears Cristiano in a crude mix of clothes he has had on for the last year and those he has found in the rubbish dump.

Among a few others who we don't recognise, who come and go talking to themselves in the process, there is a new woman called Paula, in her mid-40s, who has only been in Valdemingómez for two months. She, like most, has lost everything to her dependence on heroin and cocaine. In her arms she has an extremely cute puppy that we don't know how she has come to acquire, but she clutches it as if it is the only thing that could possibly respect and love her, and that equally she, too, could respect and love; it licks her hands, and each time she holds it to her face she smiles, revealing the few teeth she has as the puppy goes into hyper-sniff mode with the occasional lick. As she approaches, she starts to shout at one of the men at breakfast, accusing him of robbing a bag of drugs in the house where she is staying, which, she says, looks as if she did it. Whether he did it or not, we will never know, but the man downplays it and continues to serve himself breakfast before driving off.

We are thereafter permitted some time to catch up with Roberto who has been incessantly handing out food and things since some of the staff had to leave to accompany some of the drug users to hospital appointments. It has been a difficult summer with a lot of conflicts and fights as the only water supply (the outdoor tap at the church) was broken and the harm reduction staff were threatened at times to provide water, even though they had scarce resources. We ask how Juan is, and Roberto says he barely sees him as he is working in the *fumaderos*. Although it seems he did write Julia a letter saying how he missed her, he has struggled to regain the motivation to engage with the services. With that, Roberto lights another cigarette and puts his arm round me, *"Que bien de verte, tronco!"* (*"How good to see you, mate!"*).

As a car pulls up next to the rubbish dump to load boxes of food that have expired into the back of the car, we see an argument develop. Paula, the woman with the puppy, stands in the middle of the *plaza* arguing with the man whom she had earlier insulted. He shouts at her from within his car before getting out, and starts insulting her, pointing at her, *"Puta ladrona!"* (*"Fucking robber!"*), he says. At this point, half of the people in the *plaza* start to look on at what is happening, as the shouts echo around the area. *"Vete fuera, vete donde sea, pero no en mi casa!"* (*"Go out, go out wherever, but not in my house!"*), *"Eres una ladrona"* (*"You are a robber!"*). Paula has little time to explain, and with only one hand to gesticulate − because the other holds the puppy − she tries to reason with him. However, the man slams his driver's door closed and opens the passenger one, reaches in for a polystyrene box and throws it out as hard and as far as he can. It almost happens in slow motion as the box lands in a large puddle, falling open and thereafter out into the mud and puddles tumble half of her clothes and belongings. As we look on, half of Valdemingómez then feels her humiliation as some of the harm reduction staff start to shake their heads and look down. We look on at Paula who looks lost in the middle of the *plaza*, wondering what to do now. She looks around at everyone looking down as we watch on, before she picks up the small bits of clothes, which drip as she shoves them into the box, and gently lays them in before dragging the box over the mud and puddle to the side of the *plaza*. All her belongings and life are in that box, and it's not even half full.

In search of Julia ...

Daniel looks confused at the road names as he stands at the bottom corner of Retiro Park. Thinking he is in the right place, he walks into a hospital before he is redirected to the Rehabilitation Clinic. Down the next street he sees it; it is a local unit that houses recovering drug addicts before they move on to supported housing. He rings the buzzer in anticipation that he may see Julia. As he enters, he has to wait in the reception area. Around him the patients walk slowly; as they have stability problems, many are accompanied by nurses. When Julia's nurse comes down, Daniel explains the situation. The nurse is eager for Julia to meet him, but Daniel has to wait for authorisation from her personal mentor who will first discuss it with her. The nurse leaves to get a piece of paper to note down his number. As damaged people in recovery walk around him standing in the reception area, drifting in and out of them are the medical staff dressed in brilliant white. When the nurse returns, Daniel asks if there have been many admissions from Valdemingómez. She says the number has dropped dramatically because there was a communication issue with the next-stage service. *"In any case, those that do come here don't last long. Many disappear. We had one young man who came, left, came back, we went to get him, he left and that was that"*, she says. He thanks her and leaves.

Homeless from your homeless home – in London

In the rush hour that is mixed with the flurry to do the Christmas shopping, people pour in and out of Charing Cross station. Up and down the Strand others also march, most of whom either have their mobile phone in their hand or to their ear, or are connected to earphones, locking them into their own personal worlds. The Christmas lights colour the dark clear night, and the bars and cafés are lined with post-work celebrations; among the chatter, people smoke, flirt and hold glasses of wine and beer in their hands.

Across from the cobbled road, Daniel notices a pile of clothes, bags and what looks to be general rubbish sitting on a carefully disassembled cardboard box. On closer inspection, it composes of a sleeping bag, rucksack, dog lead, Tesco bag full of clothes, an empty sandwich box and McDonalds fries and other miscellaneous goods. Its owner, however, is nowhere to be seen. It is only when Daniel starts to walk up, not far, that the possible owners appear. Around 10m away is a man begging, looking up intermittently from the warmth of his cover with a cup in his hand. But it can't be him, as in the doorway, behind him, are his belongings. Not far from him, another crouches in another doorway with a cardboard note asking for donations so he can eat.

Walking on, not even very far, perhaps 10–15m, a pair similar to these street folk argue; a man bellows down to a woman who sits under a sleeping bag, the interactions unobserved in the fast pace of the passers-by who have shopping to do, wine to drink and homes to go to. The man and woman both carry rucksacks, so it can't be their belongings. On the opposite side of the road, three of these people sit close to each other and swig alcohol from a brown paper bag; one seems to have fallen asleep over himself and his beer spills on the floor and puddles below him, as if he has urinated. As Daniel approaches, it turns out he is actually urinating. Under the seat, however, they have similar bags and items, so it seems they are not the owners. Set back from them, sitting on some steps of a grand building, are four others, at separate ends. As Daniel looks on, they watch the people who look and dress like him cruise past, as if they are following a tennis match. In the corner, they have made a small housing construction outside of which sit more bags. Can't be theirs. Some 10m further up, a man sets up a piece of cardboard on the pavement and starts to write as clearly and neatly as possible with a felt tip pen under the dim light, 'P l e a s e   H e l p'. He takes so much care that his tongue sticks out in concentration. He has to go over it a few times to try and underline the facts to the passers-by in the hope that it will therefore stand out and attract a donation. However, by his side, he has bags. Not his then. Beyond the black gates to the public toilets, locked in case these people go down there and perhaps go to sleep (god forbid), there is a community of about 10–15 who sit and stand around consoling each other and handing out what goods they have to share among themselves. They seem to have their homes with them. Not 20m further, on both sides of the road and between the grandeur of London's prime theatres and cinemas, more line the road with similar signs, with similar drawn faces, trying hard to make eye contact with someone who will sympathise with their situation. However, they all have their goods and bags. They have their own worlds.

A finely-dressed woman in a suit laughs as she talks on her iPhone.

A black man sits and gulps down a pint while he smokes a cigarette in just a few puffs.

Some young teenagers giggle and dance around each other as they meet up outside the metro station.

A woman storms down the road, her hands full with gifts purchased in designer shops.

Who, then, is the owner of that pile of clothes and bags? And how is it that everything they own sits on public display?

Forgotten cities: from Las Barranquillas to Valdecarros

Daniel gets out of the car as the wind whistles through the empty buildings of the failed urbanisation called Valdecarros, which sits in the same space as the former *poblado* Las Barranquillas, only a few kilometres north of Valdemingómez, divided by the M50 that circles Madrid. Las Barranquillas was dismantled in 2007 as new plans finally came to fruition after a 10-year delay to extend the city to the edge of the M50, supposedly to provide 48,000 new properties that would house 100,000 people. Yet, the construction of Valdecarros coincided with with the 2008 financial crisis, which probably partly explains why it is basically not even half-finished. Today, around 14,000 houses have been built, and around 35,000 people live there. Such was the investment made in this area that hundreds of millions of Euros were poured into constructing the biggest commercial shopping mall in Madrid, La Gavia, which took €290 million to build. Even the gardens next to it, designed by the world-famous Toyo Ito and also costing millions of Euros, were constructed on the site, as it was to form part of an Olympic bid, envisaged as the 'green vein' of the south of the city. Add to that the millions of Euros that were spent on the 2016 failed Olympic bid as well as failed bids previously, and most recently to host the 2020 Olympics. Today, however, the only green things about the barren half-finished park are the sporadically placed pint-sized trees that seem to have given up growing five years ago. Rubbish sits nestled in the patchy grass while the odd person who has been duped into buying property here hurries around, hiding from the cold wind.

There is no police station, a shortage of places in the local school and a medical centre running on scant resources. Almost all the residents complain at their overinflated mortgages and what they feel to be their political abandonment. Looking around, it feels like a ghost town. Many of the properties are empty – too expensive for working people. Banks rarely lend money now unless potential buyers have a deposit of at least 20% of the property's value, and even then there is massive discrimination towards low-paid and temporary workers, who do not qualify. Bizarrely it is actually too costly to tear the properties down, so there they sit, on this windy winter day, while the rubbish blows between them – like the 400,000 other empty properties in the capital, most becoming vacant as a consequence of families falling into debt and thereafter into homelessness. Here, in Valdecarros, around 70 properties have been squatted and 30 rented out to 'vulnerable people' – not that there is anything wrong with this, but it creates indignation among those who bought their properties, who have little sympathy for such people. More recently, some *gitano* families have started to move in where the residents claim they pay no rent and sell drugs – perhaps a consequence of periodic interventions in Valdemingómez. It is also common for there to be strewn syringes in the bushes and parks, and to see drug users going to and from the metro now that there are laws against *cundas*. Perhaps the area is literally returning to its roots – to Las Barranquillas.

Driving around, this whole area feels quite empty, even though in this part, with more residential constructions, the parks are overgrown and rubbish, sometimes whole bags full, blows across the roads. Daniel does a U-turn and heads south, passing the second-to-last metro stop, Las Suertes (The Lucks), towards the end of the line, Valdecarros. Approaching this area, it seems emptier compared to La Gavia. It is far less built-up and chequered with empty buildings, signs selling off houses and flats, and whole blocks of land for as little as €99,000. A few people are on the streets, but it feels strange, especially given the massive availability of car park spaces. The parks are more overgrown, stones overturned and weeds grow through the cycle paths. At the end of Avenida de la Gran

Via del Sureste, he turns right on to Avenida Verro Milano, and follows the empty road around. There is no shortage of places to park because there is no one around. When he gets to the middle of this semi-circular extension to the Gran Via, he parks up and gets out, looking back at the half-finished urbanisation that is dotted with the construction of the odd house. Grand projects are absent and plots of land are advertised for sale, from rusting signboards – a tell-tale sign of the failure of capital investment.

Daniel puts his rubbish in one of the many empty bins supposedly designed for people to be walking up and down and depositing their waste as they take a walk in the park. It feels like an urban dream-turned-nightmare – even the roads have started to crack in their neglect. He then walks up a stony path between young pine trees that were supposedly planted so that families and children could play among them. Further up, he sees an opening between the trees and strays from the path, stepping over the land – which, in 10 years, has not yet managed to grow grass – and peers out at the view over the M50, behind which sits the buzzing activity of Valdemingómez. In fact, it is possible to see the pathway that joins the two areas, and there are a few drug addicts walking up it.

He returns to the car, only to see a lonely jogger pass a drug addict. Driving around again, he stumbles on a lonesome block of flats outside which stand several *gitanos* next to five fridge-freezers; there they evaluate them as a white van pulls up and they start to load them in. Finding the road that leads to the pathway that connects Valdecarros with Valdemingómez, he follows it, passing more drug addicts, and further down the road there is a good view of the first entrance to Valdemingómez as more people stagger past him; on the side of the road there is rubbish, debris and burnt artefacts.

The more things change, the more they stay the same

At Valdemingómez's main entrance, the dust is kicked up from the lorries that pile in and out, so he opts to enter via the other entrance at the side, towards the church. Turning right, and over the dusty potholes, he parks up near to where Juan and Julia's tent used to sit. Instead, there now sit three others. The bus has parked in the far corner, perhaps to try and shelter itself from the wind, which is relentless. Even as he gets out of the car, the door is almost blown closed on him. He wanders over to Roberto, who gives him a big hug before filling up a hot chocolate for Sandra, who tries to drink it in a bowl. *"Are you a granddad yet?"*, he asks him, and Roberto replies, *"Tomorrow at the latest, it has to happen soon"*.

Roberto makes up a ham sandwich as one of the *machaca* volunteers reaches into the same box and pulls out some ham and gives it to Yolanda's large dog. Manuel, another worker, sits behind them on the steps, covered from head to toe to avoid breathing in the dust, while another worker stands away from the bus, looking out while getting some cover at the same time. Shortly after Margarita approaches, slowly wiping the dust from her eyes, and pulls aside one of the plastic breakfast chairs before dumping herself in it; her mouth is dry and she then comes over to get some water from Roberto.

A busy Adán then approaches, sweating as he navigates the potholes. He asks for some sandwiches and a hot chocolate, and looks impatient. He now has only one tooth that sits half-rotten in the middle of his mouth, and his hands are black. Raul arrives talking to himself and picking at scabs and scars on his face. It has been a month since Daniel has seen him, and he looks thin and weak. Raul then starts yelling at Adán for some reason. At first it is not clear, even when his blood-stained hands start to push him slightly. Naturally the whole team look on, wondering what exactly is going on, and it seems that Adán has stolen three of Raul's new sleeping bags that he had found in the local skip. Adán ambles off with breakfast in his hand as Raul shouts and gesticulates at him. *"Eres una mierda, vete a la mierda!"* (*"You are a shit, go to the shit!"*), he says, even though he, too, is living in the same 'shit'. When Adán then returns, perhaps also angry and ready to argue, Raul fronts up to him and tells him: *"Over my dead body you will take them. Never. Fuck you. You are a fuck.* [Looking around at everyone and the landscape] *these people are shit. Shit people. Shit. I have nothing, so how can you take nothing away from me and I be upset about it? Because, you bastard, I found them new and they are mine. Over my dead body you will have them,"* he shouts, as he returns to the table where he tips a whole packet of biscuits into his hot chocolate and scoffs them in his mouth. We all look on, wondering if he has finished. But he hasn't. He wanders over to Daniel and starts to gesticulate at him and shouts in his face while Daniel stands still, unflinching. *"It's about dignity, you know, people never ask me 'Raul, how are you, are you okay?' No one. No one cares or worries about me"*, he says, looking closely at Daniel, in the eyes. He kicks the stones and dust and returns to his sitting position and continues to wolf down his soggy biscuits. The harm reduction team just look at him; they seem used to these public monologues, not to mention the arguments.

Suddenly Roberto takes a call and disappears, only to return a minute later saying how he is a grandfather. We all hug him as he tells me he will go later this afternoon to see how the baby is. And with that, Roberto has to leave. It seems he has to return to get more food as they have run out earlier than expected. He shakes hands with Daniel and hugs him once again. Before he leaves, Daniel asks about Valdecarros, only to be interrupted by Roberto's colleague who lives there, *"Yes, you can walk, it is 20 minutes, but you need to take a pathway. I know, I live there and they go up and down there to the metro station. The area is run by gitano mafia who have claimed the empty houses and rent them out to people cheaply,"* he says, as his long beard blows in the wind.

Daniel walks back to his car and sits inside to take a few notes. Raul passes him, then soon after, Margarita trudges back somewhere. There is then a knock on his car window and outside stands a man, sweating in rags. Thinking Daniel is a *cundero*, he asks him *"Vas por Madrid?"* (*"Are you going to Madrid?"*), before Daniel says no. He trudges off. Then only a minute later, a young woman with spots and cuts on her head knocks on the other side. As he looks at her, she smiles at him, revealing a few teeth; she looks no older than about 25. He winds down the other window and she asks him if he wants a blow job for five Euros. He shakes his head. As he starts the car, he can see Raul reaching into what he supposes to be Adán's tent to take back the sleeping bags; as he takes them, he grumbles and talks to himself.

With that, Daniel reverses and starts to drive down the same track from which he had come, although now there is a police control waiting half-way down. Having nothing to hide, he sits and waits in the queue. With each stop, everyone is emptied out on to the road, and everyone is searched. Some 20 minutes later, as expected, they do the same to Daniel, asking him to stand outside the car while an inspection is done, one by one. Daniel is patted down and searched for drugs and weapons before being questioned. They first ask him if he takes drugs, and he concedes that it has not been for many years, before they suspiciously evaluate him and say, *"Well, you could be drinking and we have to make sure that people do not take substances and drive, which is why we are doing the control"*. It is understandable, and Daniel explains a little about his study as the police continue to circle the car, as if it were laden with drugs in secret compartments. Eventually, his story seems to satisfy them, and they ask him, *"Ves alguna solución a eso?"* (*"Do you see a solution to this?"*), before Daniel says

"No, no creo … no si solamente váis hacer redadas"(*"No, I don't think so, not if you are just going to do raids"*). *"Si, tienes razón"* (*"Yes, you are right"*), one says, and with that, he is waved on.

The next day …

Then there is a local newsflash. It seems that over 300 police stormed two *fumaderos*, arresting 29 *gitanos* in the process. Large amounts of heroin and cocaine have been seized and substantial evidence gathered against the families for laundering money. We contact a friend in the police from the area who tells us that many of the *cundas* were organised like taxis, and had communication links with the two families, in essence, to round up drug dependents from Madrid and bring them to the *fumaderos* to spend money. That's all the report seems to say.

…

A limp rain comes down in Madrid as Daniel once again buzzes the bell to enter the Rehabilitation Clinic. Inside, there is a mob of recovering addicts in the reception area looking bored. Daniel is told to wait in the comfy-chair area, where group addiction meetings are held. As he waits, he flicks through some of the activities the unit offers – page after page he turns, only to discover that almost all consist of visits to parks in Madrid. The nurse comes down who called him last week having given permission for him to speak to Julia. They walk up the stairs together, and on the first floor come into another reception area. As he stands with his bag full of spare baby accessories he was able to find lying about his house, he sees a smiling figure in the doorway pointing at him, and medical staff in white uniforms hang around. It is Julia. She looks slightly embarrassed as she wheels out her young daughter who is now five months old. Inside the pram he looks at this small human bundle with wonderful eyes; he strokes her face and smiles, before finally having the opportunity to embrace Julia properly. *"That's my little daughter, fantastic, isn't she?"*, says Julia, trying to hand-flap air to calm her red face and ensure the two pink hairclips have not allowed her hair to escape from their position.

Another nurse then wheels the baby off while Daniel is led by Julia through some double doors into the quarters where families sleep. It has a very clinical feel, the corridor reminding him of the lingering half-clean smell of some prison wings from his research in the UK. Daniel is shown into the first room where Julia and her daughter sleep. In the corner is a hospital bed with some pictures on the wall, there is a basic table on which sit some food and papers, and to his left is the cot, which is loaded with soft toys; on the corner of the bed a pink flower says 'Baby Girl'.

Photo 35: Safe haven

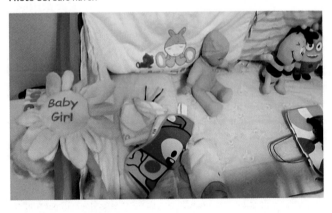

Julia then shows him into the adjacent room that she has as a sort of living area; to the right on the wall is a small TV, below it another table with some mandarins and pens on it, a baby chair where her daughter eats, and a battered sofa. They begin to talk. It is nothing short of a miracle that she is here, as it turns out. Soon after Daniel, Rubén and Inma came into the *fumadero*, she was whisked away by the Red Cross and given a place in an emergency Rehabilitation Unit. Her daughter was born in August 2016, and was healthy, with no side effects from Julia's drug taking. Her mum and family have since reunited around her, and there is a sense of hope for her future. The Red Cross give her €70 a month, and she is still waiting for her social assistance to come through, which could take another six months. This would allow her to claim €400 a month. For now, her accommodation and food are paid for and she attends rehab groups, where she has to *"own up to the past"*, as she describes it: *"My god, I had no idea what I was doing. I had 78 offences pending, robbing, stealing all sorts. It was all nullified when I entered treatment here, though,"* she says. Most days she gets up early, feeds her daughter, has breakfast, goes to the groups, takes a walk, and says she is grateful every day that she is able to enjoy time with her daughter.

When Juan comes up in the conversation, she seems clear that she wants nothing to do with him. Although he comes from time to time to the unit to see her, it is mostly to ask for money. *"He has not shown me that he can be her father,"* she says, reluctantly, *"it's not the same now."* It has been a few months since he last came, but she doubts that he will return, and if he does, it will be more *"words and promises, but no actions"*.

We get on to the subject of Valdemingómez, and she seems fully aware of the recent raids and operations on the *cundas*: *"it will continue anyway; if they close that poblado, they will open another one or it will go back to the barrio,"* she says. Daniel asks about other people she knows from the area, and it seems that most days she is approached in the street by offers to hook up for a *cunda*. The pressure is all around her. There have even been a few cases of people being thrown out of the rehab unit because they have taken drugs inside. *"Many relapse, almost all, more so now as they closed Ambite and that was the next stage for* almost everyone. Now people go straight to stage three and they aren't prepared so just relapse straight away. I think there is some problem with recruiting at Ambite which is why it had to close," she adds. In the unit, too, many have relapsed. Only recently a woman who also fell pregnant in Valdemingómez, who had been in recovery for a year, accepted the offer of a 'fiesta' from someone close to the clinic. Within a few days, it seems, she had relapsed completely and returned to Valdemingómez, even selling her baby to the *gitanos* as a means of supporting her addiction. Fortunately, somehow the authorities intervened when they realised she had left the clinic, and the baby was taken from the *gitanos* and put into care. To this day the woman remains somewhere in Valdemingómez.

When the nurse comes to get Julia, they have to wind down our conversation. Now the bag Daniel brought has been checked for drugs, they walk next door to look at the toys. Daniel reveals to Julia that her story, and that of others, has been documented and that she is central to the book that we now type out. *"Really? I want to read it, if only to understand how I was,"* she says, adding:

> I feel bad because I got angry with you, I remember, and you came into the fumadero. That's when I thought or started thinking to myself that I needed to do something. What was I doing? Two days later after you came that day, I was showering in the church, it was open and I had managed to get an appointment to wash when the Red Cross approached me because they had noticed I was pregnant, they said 'come with us' and I did. Just like that. I was seven months pregnant you know. You were the first people that made me think twice about things because I couldn't admit it to myself. I was in my own world, injecting heroin and cocaine, sleeping among rats, living among the rubbish.

Daniel embraces her and promises to return with some more toys soon. Outside it still spits with rain and the puddles on the road have formed larger ones. Daniel walks down towards the car park, seeing on the corner of the road a man begging for money; he sits unshaven, looking up at people while his little paper cup sits in front of his crossed legs. The man seems to have some idea that Daniel will give him a Euro because of the manner in which he walks towards him. *"Suerte amigo"* (*"Good luck friend"*), he says, knowing that he will need much more than luck. Suddenly all the messages start to come through on his telephone because there was no coverage in the unit. Several come from Roberto who is working today in Valdemingómez: *"It's quiet here today,"* one says. *"In the short term, they are disposing of the poblado,"* says another. *"The drug market is going back to San Blas, Caño Roto, Ensanche de Vallecas, I have noticed lots of activity there over the last three days since the mass raid on the gitano families,"* says one more. *"I want to know what strategy they [the government] have if they are going to tear down Valdemingómez"*, says the last. The rain falls on the phone screen and his fingers can't type the reply, although the answer seems clear: back we go to the *barrio*.

References

Aaron Ginzler, J., Cochran, B., Domenech-Rodriguez, M., Cauce, A. and Whitbeck, L. (2003) 'Sequential progression of substance use among homeless youth: An empirical investigation of the Gateway Theory', *Substance Use and Misuse*, vol 38, no 3, pp 725-58.

ACAIP (Agrupación de los Cuerpos de la Administración de Instituciones Penitenciarias) (2016) *Informe prisiones españolas enero 2016*, www.acaip.es/images/docs/ACAIP%20%20 INFORME%20PRISIONES%20ESPA%C3%91OLAS%20 %20ENERO%202016%20%20PRIMER%20RESUMEN. pdf

ACCEM and Fundación Secretariado Gitano (2010) *Informe diagnóstico sobre la Cañada Real Galiana*, Madrid: Fundación Secretariado Gitano.

Agar, M. (2003) 'The story of crack: Towards a theory of illicit drug trends', *Addiction, Research & Theory*, vol 11, no 1, pp 3-29.

Agencia Antidroga (1998) *Memoria Agencia Antidroga, 1997*, Madrid: Consejería de Salud y Servicios Sociales de la Comunidad de Madrid.

Agencia Antidroga (2004) *Memoria agencia antidroga, 2003*, Madrid: Consejería de Salud y Servicios Sociales de la Comunidad de Madrid.

Álvarez, M. (2016) 'La Policía Nacional detiene al segundo asesino del crimen de la Cañada Real y da carpetazo al caso', *ABC*, www.abc.es/espana/madrid/abci-policia-nacional-detiene-segundo-asesino-crimen-canada-real-y-carpetazo-caso-201602252307

Associació Lliure Prohibicionista (2004) 'Breve Historia del Consumo de Drogas en el Estado Español', Ekinzta Zuzena, www.nodo50.org/ekintza/IMG/article_PDF/BREVE-HISTORIA-DEL-CONSUMO-DE_a57.pdf

Atkinson, R., and Rodgers, T. (2015) 'Pleasure zones and murder boxes: Online pornography and violent video games as cultural zones of exception' in *British Journal of Criminology*, doi:10.1093/bjc/azv113.

Atkinson, R. (2015) 'Limited exposure: Social concealment, mobility and engagement with public space by the super-rich in London', *Environment and Planning*, vol 47, pp 1302-17.

Atkinson, R. and Flint, J. (2004) 'Fortress UK? Gated communities, the spatial revolt of the elites and time–space trajectories of segregation', *Housing Studies*, vol 19, no 6, pp 875-92.

Atkinson, R., Parker, S. and Regina Morales, E. (2016) 'Non-state space: The strategic ejection of dangerous and high maintenance urban space', *Territory, Politics, Governance*, www.tandfonline.com/doi/full/10.1080/21622671.2016.1220868

Augé, M. (2008) *Non-places: Introduction to an anthropology of supermodernity*, New York: Verso.

Auyero, J. and Kilanski, K, (2015) 'Managing in the midst of social disaster: Poor people's responses to urban violence', in J. Auyero, P. Bourgois and N. Scheper-Hughes (eds) *Violence at the urban margins*, New York: Oxford University Press, pp 189-212.

Baigorri, A. (2004) *Botellón: Un conflicto postmoderno*, vol 41, Barcelona: Icaria Editorial.

Bangieva, B. (2007) 'Italy with special law against Gypsies and travellers', http://international.ibox.bg/news

Barroso, J.F. (2014) '1.927 detenidos en la Cañada Real en los dos últimos años', *El País*, http://ccaa.elpais.com/ccaa/2014/05/30/madrid/1401454536_680059.html

Bauman, J. (1998) 'Demons of other people's fear: The plight of the Gypsies', *Thesis Eleven*, vol 54, August, pp 51-62.

Bauman, Z. (2003) *Wasted lives: Modernity and its outcasts*, London: Polity Press.

Bauman, Z. (2007) *Liquid times: Living in an age of uncertainty*, London: Polity Press.

Beck, U. and Beck-Gernsheim, E. (2002) *Individualisation*, London: Sage.

Belber, M. (2014) 'Distrito rico, distrito (más) pobre', *El Mundo*, 26 April, www.elmundo.es/madrid/2014/04/26/535bf7c522601d19778b4578.html

Birtchnell, T. and Caletrio, J. (eds) (2013) *Elite mobilities*, London: Routledge.

Bollas, C. (1997) *Cracking up: The work of unconscious experience*, Oxford: Hill and Wang.

Boróhorquez, L. (2016) 'Sexo, drogas y corrupción en la Policia Local de Palma', *El País*, 4 July, http://politica.elpais.com/politica/2016/07/03/actualidad/1467539442_889012.html

Boterman, W. and Musterd, S. (2016) 'Multiple dimensions of (spatial) fragmentation in metropolitan areas of Amsterdam, Rotterdam and The Hague', Paper presented at the Fracturing Societies Conference organised by the University of Sheffield, 20 July.

Bourgois, P. (1995) *In search of respect: Selling crack in El Barrio*, Cambridge: Cambridge University Press.

Bourgois, P. (2003) 'Crack and the political economy of social suffering', *Addiction, Research & Theory*, vol 11, no 1, pp 31-7.

Bourgois, P. (2015) 'Insecurity, the war on drugs and crimes of the state: Symbolic violence in the Americas', in J. Auyero, P. Bourgois and N. Scheper-Hughes (eds) *Violence at the urban margins*, New York: Oxford University Press, pp 305-23.

Bourgois, P. and Schonberg, J. (2009) *Righteous dopefiend*, San Francisco, CA: Berkeley University Press.

Bourgois, P., Lettiere, M. and Quesada, J. (1997) 'Social misery and the sanctions of substance abuse: Confronting HIV risk among homeless heroin addicts in San Francisco', *Social Problems*, vol 44, pp 155-73.

Briggs, D. (2010) 'Barriers to reintegration for los gitanos (gypsies) in La Coruña, Spain: Politics, the media and the Spanish community', *International Journal of Migration, Health and Social Care*, vol 9, no 1, pp 17-31.

Briggs, D. (2012a) *Crack cocaine users: High society and low life in south London*, London: Routledge.

Briggs, D. (2012b) *The English riots of 2011: A summer of discontent*, Hook: Waterside Press.

Briggs, D. (2016) 'Una lectura ligera acerca de historias oscuras del mundo del consumo: La obsolescencia programada en su contexto capitalista avanzado', in J. Soto (ed) *Aproximaciones jurídicas a la obsolescencia programada*, Bogotá: Universidad Externado de Colombia, pp 433-458.

Briggs, D. (2017) 'Los siete pecados del capitalismo académico y el crimen de la ciencia: Deconstruyendo la ideología de la "ciencia criminológica" en España', *Criminología y Justicia Refurbished*, vol 3, no 2, pp 1-27.

Briggs, D. and Dobre, D. (2014) *Culture and immigration in context: An ethnography with Romanian migrants in London*, London: Palgrave Macmillan.

Briggs, D. and Pérez Suárez, J.R. (2016) 'S3X_P0rn _ HOTGIRLZ69: Un acercamiento a la prostitución desde la marginalidad y el ciborg', *Criminología y Justicia*, no 6, pp 40-60.

Burbano Trimiño, F. (2013) 'Las migraciones internas durante el franquismo y sus efectos sociales: El caso de Barcelona', Unpublished PhD thesis.

Butcher, M. (2016) 'Cities of rage and mercy: Fracturing regimes of certainty in the global south and north', Paper presented at the Fracturing Societies Conference organised by the University of Sheffield, 20 July.

Callinicos, A. (2012) 'Contradictions of austerity', *Cambridge Journal of Economics*, vol 36, no 1, pp 65-77.

Campos, M.Á. (2015) *Operación Púnica: El sumario de la Púnica corrobora la financiación ilegal del Partido Popular*, Tribunales, Cadena SER.

Caravaca-Sánchez, F., Romero, M.F. and Luna, A. (2015) 'Prevalencia y predictores del consumo de sustancias psicoactivas entre varones en prisión', *Gaceta Sanitaria*, vol 29, no 5, pp 358-63.

Clemente, Y. (2015) 'Diferencias entre el norte y el sur de Madrid', *El País*, http://elpais.com/elpais/2015/10/14/media/1444838463_647499.html

Comunidad de Madrid (2009) *Planes especiales de inversión y actuación territorial*, Madrid: Comunidad de Madrid.

Comaroff, J. (2007) 'Beyond bare life: AIDS, bio-politics and the neoliberal order', *Public Culture*, vol 19, no 1, pp 197-219.

Cozzanet, F., Grieco, A., and Matthews, S. (1976) 'Gypsies and the problem of acculturation', *Diogenes*, vol 24, 68-92.

Cudworth, D. (2008) 'There's a little bit more than just delivering the stuff: Policy, pedagogy, and the education of Gypsy/traveller children', *Critical Social Policy*, vol 28, no 3, pp 361-77.

Davidson, M. and Ward, K. (2014) '"Picking up the pieces": Austerity urbanism, California and fiscal crisis', *Cambridge Journal of Regions, Economy and Society*, vol 7, no 1, pp 81-97.

Davis, M. (2006) *Planet of slums*, London: Verso.

DE (Departamento de Estadística) (2016) 'Paro registrado', Ayuntamiento de Madrid, www.madrid.es/portales/munimadrid/es/Inicio/El-Ayuntamiento/Estadistica/Areas-de-informacion-estadistica/Mercado-de-trabajo/Paro-registrado/Paro-registrado?vgnextfmt=default&vgnextoid=a9a2b350526e8310VgnVCM1000000b205a0aRCRD&vgnextchannel=f29e62a006986210VgnVCM2000000c205a0aRCRD

de Cauter, L. (2005) *The capsular civilization: On the city in the age of fear*, Amsterdam: NAi.

Delgado, B. (2008) 'Propuestas para un nuevo modelo urbano madrileño en clave de sostenibilidad: Del crecimiento a la rehabilitación', Congreso Nacional del Medio Ambiente.

EFE (2016) 'Rivas rechaza la propuesta de urbanizar y dar servicios a la Cañada Real', El País, 7 August, http://ccaa.elpais.com/ccaa/2016/08/07/madrid/1470584542_144648.html

Ellis, A. (2016) Men, masculinities and violence: An ethnographic study, London: Routledge.

Elteto, A. (2011) 'Immigrants in Spain: Their role in the economy and the effects of the crisis', Romanian Journal of European Affairs, vol 11, no 2, pp 66-81.

European Observatory of Drugs and Drug Addiction (2016) European report on drugs, Lisbon: EMDCCA.

FAD (Fundación de Ayuda contra la Drogadicción) (2014) Más de 25 años, más de 50 campañas, www.fad.es/

Gamella, J. (1999) 'Los gitanos andaluces. Una minoría étnica en una encrucijada histórica', Revista Demofilo, vol 30, pp 15-30.

Golub, A. and Johnson, B. (2002) 'The misuse of the "Gateway Theory" in US policy on drug abuse control: A secondary analysis of the muddled deduction', International Journal of Drug Policy, vol 13, pp 5-19.

Gómez Ciriano, E. (2011) 'Los derechos humanos y la responsabilidad de las administraciones en La Cañada Gallinero', Trabajo Social Hoy: Revista Editada por el Colegio de Trabajadores Sociales de Madrid, no 62, pp 7-27.

Gonzalez, E. (2008) Poverty and rural areas: Final report to the European Commission, Brussels: European Commission.

Goode, E. (1974) 'Marijuana use and the progression to dangerous drugs', in L. Miller (ed) Marijuana effects on human behavior, Burlington, VA: Elsevier Science, pp 303-38.

Gutíerrez Sánchez, J. (2015) 'The Romanian gypsy minors from "El Gallinero": Stages of development in a context of risk', Revista Electronica de Investigación y Docencia, 13 January, pp 27-44.

Hall, S. (2012) 'The solicitation of the trap: On transcendence and transcendental materialism in advanced societies', *Human Studies*, vol 35, no 3, pp 365-81.

Hall, S. and Winlow, S. (2005) 'Anti-nirvana: Crime, culture and instrumentalism in the age of insecurity', *Crime, Media, and Culture*, vol 1, pp 31-48.

Hume, M. and Wilding, P. (2015) '"Es que para ellos el deporte es para matar": Rethinking the scripts of violent men in El Savador and Brazil', in J. Auyero, P. Bourgois and N. Scheper-Hughes (eds) *Violence at the urban margins*, New York: Oxford University Press, 93-112.

IECD (Instituto de Estadística in Comunidad de Madrid) (2014) *Atlas de empleo de la comunidad de Madrid*, www.madrid.org/iestadis/fijas/estructu/economicas/ocupacion/atlas/01_empleo.html

Izquierdo, M., Jimeno, J. and Lacuesta, A. (2015) *Spain: From emigration to immigration*, Documentos de Trabajo 1503, Madrid: Banco de España.

Jalon, F. and Rivera, A. (2000) *Salud y comunidad gitana. Análisis de propuestas para la actuación*, Madrid: Asociación Secretariado General Gitano.

Kandel, D., Yamaguchi, K. and Chen, K. (1992) 'Stages of progression in drug involvement from adolescence to adulthood: Further evidence for the gateway theory', *Journal of Studies on Alcohol*, vol 53, no 5, pp 447-57.

Kane, R. and Yacoubian, G. (1999) 'Patterns of drug escalation among Philadelphia arrestees: an assessment of the Gateway Theory', *Journal of Drug Issues*, vol 29, no 1, pp 107-20.

Karandinos, G., Hart, L., Montero, C. and Bourgois, P. (2015) 'The moral economy of violence in US cities', in J. Auyero, P. Bourgois and N. Scheper-Hughes (eds) *Violence at the urban margins*, New York: Oxford University Press.

Kirk, D. and Matsuda, M. (2011) 'Legal cynicism, collective efficacy and the ecology of arrest', *Criminology*, vol 49, no 2, pp 443-72.

Lago Ávila, M. (2014) 'Another Madrid: The non-stop growth of shanty towns. Regional rehousing and social integrational policies 1997–2010', *Estudios Geográficos*, vol LXXV, no 276, pp 219-60.

Lanchester, J. (2016) 'Brexit blues', *London Review of Books*, www.lrb.co.uk/v38/n15/john-lanchester/brexit-blues?utm_source=newsletter&utm_medium=email&utm_campaign=3815&utm_content=ukrw_subsact&hq_e=el&hq_m=4353700&hq_l=9&hq_v=e59b4afdbc

Leal, J. and Sorando, D. (2016) 'Economic crisis, social change and segregation processes in Madrid', in T. Tammaru and M. Szymon Marcizcnak (eds) *Socio-economic segregation in European capital cities: East meets West*, London: Routledge, pp 214-38.

León, C., Araña, J. and de León, J. (2013) *Estudio de estimación del coste social de la corrupción*, Realizado por el Instituto Universitario de Turismo y Desarrollo Sostenible (TIDES), Universidad de Las Palmas de Gran Canaria, (2013) Centro de Investigaciones Sociológicas: Estudio nº 3021 del Centro de Investigaciones Sociológicas del mes de abril (2014) y Estudio nº 3114 del Centro de Investigaciones Sociológicas del mes de octubre (2015), www.cis.es/cis/opencm/ES/11_barometros/index.jsp

Luque, I. (2016) 'Paro crónico en el sur de Madrid', *El Mundo*, 2 October, www.elmundo.es/grafico/madrid/2016/10/02/57eeb3bb46163f4c148b4628.html

Mars, S., Bourgois, P., Karandinos, G., Montero, F. and Ciccarone, D. (2014) '"Every 'never' I said came true": Transition from opioid pills to heroin injecting', *International Journal of Drug Policy*, vol 25, pp 257-66.

Mars, S., Fessel, J.M., Bourgois, P., Montero, F., Karadninos, G. and Ciccarone, D. (2015) 'Heroin-related overdose: the unexplored influences of markets, marketing and source-types in the United States', *Social Science & Medicine*, vol 140, pp 44-53.

Martiarena, A. (2016) 'Madrid sigue vendiendo vivienda protegida a los "fondos buitre"', *La Vanguardia*, 12 September, www.lavanguardia.com/local/madrid/20160912/41159445352/madrid-sigue-vendiendo-vivienda-protegida-buitre.html

Martínez Ruiz, M. and Rubio Valladolid, G. (2002) *Manual de drogodependencias para enfermería*, Ediciones Díaz de Santos.

Mbomío Rubio, L. (2012) 'La cuidad invisible: Voces en la Cañada Real Galiana'. Unpublished report on a documentary, Antropodocus Productions.

Ministerio de Fomento (2010) *Análisis urbanístico de barrios vulnerables en España – 28049 Coslada*, Madrid: Gobierno de España.

Ministerio del Interior (2016) *Anuarios estadísticos del Ministerio del Interior*, www.interior.gob.es/web/archivos-y-documentacion/anuario-estadistico-de-2015

Mitchell, D. (1997) 'The annihilation of space by law: the roots and implications of anti-homeless laws in the United States', *Antipode*, vol 29, no 3, pp 303–35.

Mitchell, D. (2016) 'Mean streets: Capital circulation, class struggle and the fracturing city', Paper presented at the Fracturing Societies Conference organised by the University of Sheffield University, 19 July.

Muñoz, J. and Pérez Ávila, F. (2016) 'Policia Local bajo sospecha: 53 imputados desde 2010', *Diario de Sevilla*, 10 January, www.diariodesevilla.es/sevilla/Policia-Local-sospecha-imputados_0_988701189.html

Murray, S. (2006) 'Thanatopolitics: On the use of death or mobilizing political life', *Polygraph*, vol 18, pp 191-215.

Nightingale, C. (2012) *A global history of divided cities*, Chicago, IL: Chicago University Press.

Observatorio Metropolitano (2013) 'La decadencia de Madrid, ¿pero de cuál?', *PlayGround*, www.playgroundmag.net/articulos/columnas/decadencia-Madrid_5_1190330959.html

OEDT (Observatorio Español de la Drogas y las Toxicomanías) (2015) 'Consumo, percepciones y opiniones ante las drogas', in INFORME, *Alcohol, tabaco y drogas ilegales en España*, Madrid: Ministerio de Sanidad, Servicios Sociales e Igualdad, pp 19-120.

O'Malley, P. (2008) 'Experiments in risk and criminal justice', *Theoretical Criminology*, vol 12, no 4, pp 451-69.

Otero, J. (2014) 'Estalla la rama urbanística de Gürtel', *Tiempo*, vol 1645, pp 42-3.

Oxfam (2016) *An economy for the 1%: How privilege and power in the economy drive extreme inequality and how this can be stopped*, 210 Oxfam Briefing Paper, Oxford: Oxfam.

Peck, J. (2012) 'Austerity urbanism', *City*, vol 16, no 6, pp 626-55.

Pérez Infante, J.I. (2009) 'Crecimiento y características del empleo de los inmigrantes en España', *Revista del Ministerio de Trabajo e Inmigración*, vol 80, pp 237-53.

Petersen, A. (1997) 'The new morality: public health and personal conduct' in C. O'Farrell (ed), *Foucault: The legacy.* Kelvin Grove: Queensland University of Technology, pp 200–14.

Piketty, T. (2013) *Capital in the twenty-first century*, London: Harvard University Press.

Plan Regional sobre Drogas (1992) *Memoria*, Madrid: Consejería de Integración Social de la Comunidad de Madrid.

Poveda, D. and Marcos, T. (2005) 'The social organisation of a stone fight: Gitano children's interpretive reproduction of ethnic conflict', *Childhood*, vol 12, no 3, pp 327-49.

Prochaska, J.O., Norcross, J.C. and DiClemente, C.C. (1995) *Changing for good*, New York: Avon.

Quintero, G., Lilliott, E. and Willging, C. (2007) 'Substance abuse treatment provider views of "culture": Implications for behavioural health care in rural settings', *Qualitative Health Research*, vol 17, pp 1256-67.

Rae, A. (2011) 'Learning from the past? A review of approaches to spatial targeting in urban policy', *Planning Theory and Practice*, vol 12, no 3, pp 331-48.

Requeña, P.M. (2014) 'Pobreza y exclusión social en Madrid: Viejos temas y nuevas propuestas', *AIBR: Revista de Antropología Iberoamericana*, vol 9, no 2, pp 163-82.

Rimke, H. (2000) 'Governing citizens through self-help literature', *Cultural Studies*, vol 14, pp 61-78.

Rivas, P. (2014) 'El mapa de la desigualdad en Madrid', *Diagonal*, www.diagonalperiodico.net/global/24735-mapa-la-desigualdad-madrid.html

Rivera, A. (2016) 'Música, éxtasis y mucho más: Todo lo que no sabías sobre la Ruta del Bakalao', *El País*, 26 February, http://elpais.com/elpais/2016/02/26/tentaciones/1456488654_595072.html

Rodríguez Molina, J.M. (2007) 'Comparación de un programa libre de drogas y uno de mantenimiento con metadona en adictos a opiáceos', *Psychosocial Intervention*, vol 16, no 3, pp 361-73.

Rojas, G.J. (2014) *Evolución e impacto del riesgo de la pobreza y la exclusión en la Comunidad de Madrid*, Madrid: EAPN.

Sánchez Jiménez, J. (2001) 'La vida rural: La época de Franco (1939–1975)', in J. Jover Zamora (ed) *Sociedad, vida y cultura*, Madrid: ESPASA-CALPE, pp 102-298.

Sánchez Pardo, L. (2000) 'Evaluación de la efectividad de los programas de sustitutivos opiáceos', *Trastornos Adictivos*, vol 2, no 1, pp 56-72.

Sérvulo, J. (2016a) 'El número de multimillonarios crece un 8% en España con la recuperación', *El Páis*, 7 September, http://economia.elpais.com/economia/2016/09/06/actualidad/1473170787_748232.html

Sérvulo, J. (2016b) 'Un 26,8% de os españoles está en riesgo de pobreza y exclusión social', *El Páis*, 26 May, http://economia.elpais.com/economia/2016/05/24/actualidad/1464082093_364713.html

Singer, M. (2001) 'Toward a biocultural and political economic integration of alcohol, tobacco and drug studies in the coming century', *Social Science & Medicine*, vol 53, pp 199-213.

Sloterdijk, P. (2011) *Bubbles*, Boston, MA: The MIT Press.

Smith, O. (2012) 'Easy money: Cultural narcissism and the criminogenic markets of the night-time leisure economy', in S. Winlow and R. Atkinson (eds) *New directions in crime and deviancy*, London: Routledge, pp 145-59.

Soleares (2011) *Informe socio-ambiental sobre la Cañada Real Galiana: Sector 5*, Madrid: Asociación Colectivo Soleares.

Standing, G. (2011) *The precariat: The new dangerous class*, New York: Bloomsbury Academic.

Sway, M. (1984) 'Economic adaptability: The case of the gypsies', *Journal of Contemporary Ethnography*, vol 13, no 1, 83-98.

Tammaru, T., van Ham, M., Marcińczak, S. and Musterd, S. (eds) (2015) *Socio-economic segregation in European capital cities: East meets West*, vol 89, London: Routledge.

Telemadrid (2016) 'Desmantelado un punto de venta de droga en la Cañada Real con seis detenidos', www.telemadrid.es/noticias/madrid/noticia/desmantelado-un-punto-de-venta-de-droga-en-la-canada-real-con-seis-detenidos

Tomás, E., Pérez, J., Tixeira, M., Suarez, J. and Velasco, C. (2004) *Erradicación del chabolismo y integración social de los Gitanos en Avilés*, Avilés: University of Oviedo.

Vázquez, F.P. (2012) 'Sida y prisión las cárceles: Un lugar para la prevención', *Revista Española de Sanidad Penitenciaria*, vol 2, no 1, pp 5-6.

Villoria, M. and Jiménez, F. (2012) 'La corrupción en España (2004-2012): Datos, percepciones y efectos', *Reis*, vol 138, abril-junio, pp 109-34.

Wacquant, L. (2002) 'Scrutinizing the street: Poverty, morality, and the pitfalls of urban ethnography', *American Journal of Sociology*, vol 107, pp 1468-532.

Wacquant, L. (2008) *Urban outcasts: A comparative sociology of advanced marginality*, Cambridge: Polity Press.

Wacquant, L. (2009) *Punishing the poor: The neoliberal government of social insecurity*, Durham, NC: Duke University Press.

Wakeman, S. (2016) 'The moral economy of heroin in "Austerity" Britain', *Critical Criminology*, vol 24, pp 363-77.

Winlow, S. (2014) 'Trauma, guilt and the unconscious: Some theoretical notes on violent subjectivity', *The Sociological Review*, vol 62, pp 32-49.

Winlow, S. and Hall, S. (2013) *Rethinking social exclusion: The end of social?*, London: Sage.

Winlow, S., Hall, S., Treadwell, J. and Briggs, D. (2015) *Riots and political protest: Some notes on the post political present*, London: Routledge.

Wolf, E. (1982) *Europe's people without a history*, London: Allison and Busby.

Young, J. (1999) *The exclusive society: Social exclusion, crime and difference in late modernity*, London: Sage.

Young, J. (2007) *The vertigo of late modernity*, London: Sage.

Zubillaga, V., Llorens, M. and Souto, J. (2015) 'Chismoas and Alcahuetas: Being the mother of an empistolado within the everyday armed violence of a Caracas barrio', in J. Auyero, P. Bourgois and N. Scheper-Hughes (eds) *Violence at the urban margins*, New York: Oxford University Press, pp 162-179.

Index